Root and Roads Taken

Marlys Harper

ISBN :978-1-963502-70-1

Dedication

For my grandchildren:

Donovan, Jaylen, and Nathan.

"We delight in the beauty of the butterfly but rarely admit the changes it has gone through to achieve that beauty."

--Maya Angelou--

Table of Contents

Prologue

Unlocking the attic of my mind was like unleashing a sequestered memory trove that I had intentionally concealed for decades. The long-dormant memories surged into my conscious thoughts, each begging for attention and expression. I maneuvered through this deluge by creating empty chapters, like placeholders for these skeleton recollections. I would reincarnate them and reacquaint with them one chapter at a time.

Some memories surfaced readily, while others waited in the shadows, unwilling to disclose themselves. I embraced them all, even the ones tinged with humiliation or remorse. They were the threads that wove the fabric of my existence. Each memory, whether ordinary or deep, recounted history and conveyed lessons that changed my perception of myself and the world.

Reflecting on earlier choices, I welcomed the understanding that errors were not failures but stepping stones to progress. The road of self-discovery, defined by periods of vulnerability and perseverance, became a tale I felt obliged to pass on.

Reliving these experiences and allowing them to transform into words proved cathartic for me. I discovered a deeper appreciation for the twists and turns that characterize our human experience. The tales of my grandparents, parents, and ancestors reverberated in my own, prompting me to unravel the weave of my identity with honesty as a part of the continuum.

The rich tapestry of memories, storytelling, and contemplation helps us define who we are and reveal the beauty, imperfections, and complexity of life. Because of the common thread that connects all humanity, readers may find that my memories awaken some of their own latent memories.

Part One - Roots

Simian Start

The debut of their first child must have been disappointing for my parents. According to my father, Charles Errett Harper, who confided this to me when I was an adult, I looked like a stringy, wrinkled, yellow monkey when I was born. Weighing under six pounds, I narrowly escaped the incubator. Neither my appearance nor my furious constant wail boosted my charisma rating, and reinforcements had to be called in to care for me and my mother. My maternal grandmother came to live with us for a few weeks at a time, and I was taken to my grandparents' house when my parents needed a short reprieve.

My arrival, appearing more simian than human, only increased the tension between my parents that had brewed in the background during my nine-month gestation. Dad explained decades later that Mom had been adamant about the type of prenatal care she wanted, preferring a naturopathic provider. Skeptical, Dad wanted an MD behind the name of anyone providing care for his wife and offspring. Mom chose a naturopath, and Dad deferred.

My mother, Eleanor Marie Harper, formerly Gehrig, was teaching school when she became pregnant with me. At that time, pregnant women were not allowed to teach. However, she hid the contraband—me—until she was six months pregnant, then informed the principal that she would have to resign. I've wondered if she may have under-eaten during the first six months for the pregnancy to remain undetected longer. However, no one told me that.

As her pregnancy progressed, Mom developed toxemia[1]. As Dad told me this, his residual anger resonated in his voice. "The naturopath was ignorant, negligent, and inattentive" to my mother's symptoms.

---

[1] Toxemia, now called preeclampsia, is a complication of pregnancy characterized by high blood pressure and signs of damage to other organ systems, such as the liver or kidneys.

Her condition was allowed to progress, undiagnosed and untreated, until my birth. I was jaundiced and underweight because preeclampsia affects the arteries carrying blood to the placenta, resulting in an inadequate supply of blood, oxygen, and nutrients for the baby. Slow growth and low birth weight are not uncommon for the baby of a woman with preeclampsia.

Dad vowed that any future children would have prenatal and pediatric care provided by a medical doctor. Over the next eleven years, my four siblings were born without problems, except for a miscarriage Mom suffered when I was three.

Later in life, I carefully read my baby book, in which Mom painstakingly documented my early life. I learned that both of us were quite miserable for the first two months of my life outside the womb. Mom was unable to breastfeed me due to the treatment she was receiving to recover from toxemia, and Dad said I was given canned milk, which caused digestive problems and only added to my discomfort. Despite the early challenges, I must have evolved into a human-looking primate soon because my baby book does not include pictures from my simian stage. I debut in a bonnet, with little pouches under my eyes made more prominent as I smile broadly.

Compared to the norms of the time, my parents got a rather late start marrying and building their family. Dad was 35, and Mom was 31 when I was born. When Mom was in her eighties, she confessed to us that she feared she would be an old maid if she didn't accept Dad's marriage proposal, and she wanted children—six was her goal.

Although I don't know all the details of the timeline, World War II was an interrupter that influenced my father's decisions. He and some of his siblings worked for a while at a restaurant in Pasadena, California, owned by his oldest brother, after which he served four years in Germany during World War II.

Mom studied at three institutions of higher education until she found a learning environment that suited her perfectly. At Pepperdine

College (now Pepperdine University), she flourished, completed her Bachelor of Arts degree in 1940, and continued to receive her teaching credential.

From 1941 to 1942, her first teaching job was in Calipatria, Imperial County, California. She also drove the school bus in that economically depressed area with a population dominated by Hispanics, followed statistically by Blacks, and under 10% were white. She told me that some of her students came to school without shoes.

While teaching in Calipatria, she worked two-hour shifts as a spotter, "watching for planes," as one of the one million volunteer men and women who made up the US Army Ground Observer Corps. She said many teachers donated their time to this cause. Other teaching jobs followed, including teaching in Villa Park[2], California, until 1948, when she resigned due to her pregnancy with me.

Although she had spent time and money to achieve her goal of being a teacher and loved teaching, she gave up her profession to become a wife and mother. At that time, she must have thought the two roles were mutually exclusive. She would not use her teaching credential again or be employed until her third child was preparing to attend college. Then, she did substitute teaching to earn money for her third daughter's college tuition.

Mom met Dad's sister, Sue, at the church that they both attended. When Dad returned from Germany, he met Mom at that church. They began dating and were married in March of 1947. I was born in July of 1948. Mom chose my name, which she happened to read in a magazine. Without hearing the name's pronunciation, my parents placed the accent on the first syllable, and I started life with a unique name that had no stickiness in people's memories.

---

[2] An incorporated neighborhood in the City of Orange, California.

*****

Our first home was a small rental in rural Villa Park in Orange County, California. Dad was employed by Southern California Edison Company, an electric power utility, and started at the bottom of the corporate chain, climbing poles to resolve issues caused by weather and other damaging forces. I remember that he got called out at night for emergencies, and I did not like it when he had to leave. But Mom said I should be thankful because some little girls didn't even have a daddy, and she assured me he would be back when he finished fixing the problem.

I have a few vivid memories, more snapshots than videos, of my first four years in Villa Park. I loved to be outside with Dad as he worked building a brick outdoor cooking area and when he gardened. The lot was huge, bordered by towering eucalyptus trees. Down on my level, chickens scratched and scavenged. I don't know if they were ours, the owners, or the neighbors. Mom was inside with my new sister, Sherilyn, of whom I became protective in a big sister way.

In the tiny bedroom I shared with my sister, I was awakened one night by the sounds of choking and vomiting and the acrid, pungent odor. Her garbled cry made me think she was in trouble, and I yelled for Mom to come quickly. Of course, Mom told me her little tummy had to get rid of some of the milk she drank, cleaned up everything, and comforted me that my little sister would be fine.

I remember the reason for our move to another house was black mold on the living room ceiling. At four, I did not know another sibling was in the works and that our young family would need more space.

We were excited to move to our new home in La Habra, at the northern tip of Orange County. The tract of homes, which Dad jokingly called "cracker boxes," had invaded a large swath of orange groves, leaving most of the groves as sentinels surrounding the encroachment. In the backyard of each new home, a single orange tree was spared from the developer's bulldozer. After the interruption of the small tract, the groves continued undisturbed from the end of our block down to Central (later called La Habra Boulevard), the town's main street.

My maternal grandparents may have lent the money for a down payment on our first home at 550 N Lemon Street. It was a two-bedroom, one-bath, and den model, priced at $11,000. We moved in with a meager amount of furniture, but my parents were happy to be homeowners.

On the day we moved in, Sherilyn and I stood together on the cold parquet flooring at the sliding door, looking out. In the echoey emptiness of the living room, we watched splats of rain hit the patio cement. Exploring the backyard would have to wait.

Life on Lemon Street

Our young family clung precariously to the bottom rung of the middle class and was grateful. In their teens, both of my parents experienced the effects of the economic tourniquet, the Great Depression. Dad survived four years in the US Army in Germany during World War II while civilians at home lived through food and fuel rationing from 1942 to 1947 during the intrusion of War into their lives. So, in 1952, life was relatively good in our new house on Lemon Street.

Life in the 1950s and most of the 1960s was simple. Dad went to work, and Mom stayed home with us kids. We had one vehicle; I walked to kindergarten and every other grade through high school. We played barefoot up and down the sidewalk and in the surrounding orange groves until we heard the bell Dad rang, signaling us to get washed for dinner.

Mom sewed two-piece terrycloth "mud pie suits" for Sheri and me. There was a dripping faucet outside on one side of the house, which produced mud with the perfect viscosity for playing with our bowls and tea sets. We played without precautions about getting dirty until we were ready to come in. Then, we called for Mom to come and remove most of the mud and clothes before we could go inside.

By default, Dad became the primary cook for the family at some time before I could remember. It was logical for several reasons. First, anyone who knew him would tell you he loved all food-related endeavors and events. He had helped in various capacities in his older brother's restaurant and had been a cook in the Army. Mom would sometimes get exasperated about the large quantities he created, saying it was a habit acquired in the Army. Later, she told me that when they got married, she planned and wrote weekly menus. Dad would become impatient with her lack of experience and subpar interest in cooking, so Mom gladly let him take over that responsibility.

My sister Trisha was born soon after we moved to La Habra. She was petite, making her round blue eyes look even bigger. We nicknamed her Pee Wee. The addition of another child unbalanced the adult-child ratio, and our family was on its way to the large category. Mom was undaunted because she had two "Mommy's Little Helpers."

Like our mothers, without exception, all girls wore dresses to school. Because my favorite recess activity was the bars, I wore shorts under my dresses. I would hook one knee over the bar, place my hands on either side of the hooked leg, and spin. To avoid getting dizzy, I alternated going forward with backward spins. I liked it so much that I developed callouses behind my knees and on my hands.

In retrospect, Mom was far ahead of her time in terms of knowledge of nutrition. After school, we could eat all the fruits and vegetables we wanted but nothing else that may "spoil our dinner." On Halloween night, we could eat a few pieces of candy, but the remainder went into the candy drawer. Then, we could have a piece or two after dinner. No wonder it lasted almost until Christmas. I confess to the unauthorized use of the candy drawer, but the guilt after the transgression made me stop the practice. I feared I might be punished with a stomachache even if I ate only one piece and no human found out. Later, I learned that Dad would regularly buy a gigantic Hershey chocolate bar at Thrifty Drugstore for Mom. She stored her cache on the top shelf of the laundry cabinet and nibbled at it clandestinely.

We were all quite healthy due to Mom's influence and rules. If we were feeling ill, there was an edict about staying home from school. We had to be sick enough to stay in bed and be served our meals there. A bell on our nightstand could be used to summon her if we needed something. There was no TV to entertain or distract us from our discomfort. With good intentions, Mom would play 45 records for us on a kid-style turntable. If I was achy or had a headache, the zippy kid music reverberated annoyingly, and I would ask her to turn it off.

When I was in first grade, we began the day by all standing and reciting the pledge of allegiance with hands over our hearts. One day, I threw up right in the middle of the pledge. The teacher helped me to the nurse's office, where I was made comfortable, while the nurse called Mom, who had to ask a neighbor to take her to the school to bring me home. That morning, I probably thought my stomachache didn't merit a day in bed.

Today, my conservative siblings might jokingly say that the incident foreshadowed my future unpatriotic, left-leaning views. I would insist that I am patriotic but not nationalistic. I firmly believe I won the lottery when I happened to be born in the United States. Without that good fortune, I could have been born in any other country on the planet. However, you will not hear me say that the United States is the "greatest nation on earth." Greatness has myriad facets, requires constant maintenance, and is not guaranteed to last.

*****

Our one communication tool, the landline phone, was rudimentary. My parents decided we would have a party line phone, which meant that four households shared the same line, thus lowering the cost of the utility. In those days, if you had a party line, the proper phone etiquette meant completing your conversation briefly and leaving the line open for the other party liners. The fact that the other party liners could hear what you were saying if they picked up their receiver to make a call was also an incentive to be succinct. But there was a teenage girl who was blissfully ignorant of the etiquette as she talked at length with her boyfriend. We could listen in, but it didn't hold our attention long. If a party liner urgently needed to use the phone, they could interrupt, saying it was an "emergency."

Although televisions were becoming more affordable, at least the black and white sets, Mom firmly asserted that we would not own one. Instead of sitting passively in front of a TV screen, she preferred that we learn to love reading, letting books provide the stories to captivate our imaginations. She also wanted us to learn to sew, knit, and crochet.

We filled our time with all of the above and played outdoors after schoolwork was complete. A neighbor two houses down invited us to watch Zorro once a week with her children. Mom allowed us to do that, but we had to be in pajamas and slippers, ready to go to bed after the program. When I left home for college, we still did not have a television. Soon after that, Dad rebelled and bought a TV for the family.

Three years after Trisha's birth, my third sister, Denise, was born. She devised a much-improved version of crawling, which allowed her to carry a toy in her hands while scooting across the floor with one leg folded in front of her and one tucked back on one side. She covered an amazing distance in a short time. Our neighbor declared her the prettiest of the Harper girls.

*****

Our clothing came from various sources. Most of what we wore were lightly used hand-me-downs from cousins and friends' girls. Dad's older sister, Ruth, who lived in Phoenix, Arizona, once made matching church dresses for all of us. I'm not sure if there were three or four of us then, but they were frilly and in style. My youngest sister, Denise, said she got sick of the same dress coming down to her three times. An older friend of Mom's, whom we called Aunt Leta, made me a copy of a Lanz original. I felt special wearing the dress, made from dainty black and white print fabric with black piping, but I never quite understood or appreciated the fact that it was like a Lanz original.

Mom wore ordinary house dresses unless we were attending a church activity. The dress in current use hung on a hook on the back of the bathroom door. I don't remember ever going clothes shopping with her, and I am curious now about her sources for clothes. Dad's joke about Mom belonging to the NRA – Never Refuse Anything – might have explained where some of her clothes originated. My cousin, Kathy, once told me that Mom was pretty, but she didn't wear clothes or makeup to make herself look prettier. Dad said he bought her a beautiful red dress. (Red was his favorite color and the color of his midlife Mustang car.) He thought she looked stunning wearing it. I don't remember seeing it, but it may have been before I arrived on the scene.

Later, when we were in our teens and into adulthood, Mom asked us to give her any clothes we no longer wanted before we tossed or donated them. Using discretion to provide only the items we wanted to see her wear, we complied sometimes.

Although the family budget was tight, Dad thought it was important to keep current with clothing trends and would indulge in occasional purchases from a men's clothing store in Whittier. As he was promoted up the Edison ladder, he wore suits and ties to work and was aware of the impressions clothes could create.

*****

One time, when Grammie and Pops were visiting, Grammie was helping as Mom made lunches for those of us in school. Forever frugal, Mom was putting our sandwiches and other lunch components in cut-off bread bags and other bags she recycled and cut. At school, to avoid embarrassment, I covertly wrestled my food from the odd wrapping while it was inside the brown bag. It was no easy feat.

Grammie asked Mom why she didn't buy sandwich bags. Mom replied that they were too expensive. (She also had a two-squares limit on toilet paper; a mandate that proved unenforceable.)

"Well, you keep having kids!" Grammie replied, low but within my earshot.

It seemed we could always squeeze another little body around the U-shaped kitchen nook and table, with the youngest in a highchair on the open end of the table. But one bathroom for our clan was not working, especially with so many girls. It became clear that the family had outgrown the house. Buying a larger house proved unfeasible, so my parents developed an expansion plan: extend the front bedroom into the driveway and add a bath and closet near the front entry door of the house. The altered architecture would look a bit odd, but practicality won over aesthetics.

The contractor worked during the summer, hanging blankets to cover the temporarily exposed parts while we continued to use the original bedroom. When completed, we four girls had our dormitory, as Dad called it, another closet, and our bathroom.

Dad improved the appearance of the outside of the house by building a brick planter along the front, where the dormitory met the driveway, and he planted colorful annual flowers. The stucco exterior of our house was repainted a pale yellow, my favorite color.

If the outside alteration to our house was a little unusual, the dormitory inside was even more unique. Each girl had her own "property," the boundaries of which were formed with bookshelves, chests of drawers, and other utilitarian pieces of unmatched furniture. There was a twin bed, a trundle bed, and a full-sized bed, which was mine. The sewing table and sewing machine were near my property.

Each girl was tasked with keeping her property uncluttered, dusted, and vacuumed. Like our country's flag, articles of clothing were never supposed to touch the floor. Each of us had a specified section in the closets where hangers and hooks held the clothes. The hooks were for "started" play clothes that could be worn another day or two before going into the hamper.

As soon as Mom thought each of us girls was capable, she assigned other household chores. No wonder they kept having girls! Washing dishes, vacuuming, mopping, emptying trash, cleaning bathrooms, and hanging and taking down clothes from the clothesline were among the tasks.

Our house still did not have central heating and cooling after the remodel was complete. Each room had a wall heater, and the living room had a fireplace. The wall heater in our dormitory also served as my hair dryer. My long, fine hair dried quickly as I brushed it while standing in front of the heater. On hot summer nights, we opened the windows if there was a breeze. Mom had taught us to turn over our pillows periodically and to make cooling waves with our bed sheets.

*****

Mom was diligent about our immunizations, which we received at the Orange County Health Department in Santa Ana. There, the vaccines were free or cost very little. We may have carpooled with another mother.

One of the vaccines we received was protection from polio, which had robbed our family of Mom's sister, Aunt Margery, whom I was too young to remember. She died three days after contracting the disease, leaving my three very young cousins without a mother. My Uncle Carl was blessed to meet Ruth, who soon became my Aunt Ruth. Towering over Uncle Carl, she was the angel they all needed— efficient and organized yet loving. But there were critical murmurings from family and friends judging how quickly my uncle married Ruth after Aunt Margery's death. Uncle Carl made the right decision for his family, and Aunt Ruth proved to be an amazing stepmom and aunt.

We also became fully aware of the aftermath for polio survivors when we got to know the Sandersons. The family who owned the Sanderson Ford dealership in Glendale, Arizona, became like family to us. We met them through Dad's sister and family who lived in Phoenix. Kay Sanderson, who was my age, contracted polio when she was three years old and had to be in an iron lung for a while. It left her paralyzed from the waist down, and she used crutches and a wheelchair for mobility. Her mom, Laverne, would bring Kay and her older sister, Sue, to stay with us in California every year so Kay could be fitted with new braces and crutches as she grew. We all loved having them visit. Sue and Kay brought hand-me-down clothes and showed us how to apply their nail polish and makeup when we played "dress up." Dad was in his happiest state while cooking for all of us.

Laverne had a sense of humor and a way of telling stories, which made us all laugh most of the time. We would go to Knott's Berry Farm, Chinatown, and always to 31 Flavors for ice cream. When it was time to trade in our family car, we drove to Sanderson Ford in Arizona for a trade-in at a generous discount.

We had most of the childhood diseases for which a vaccine had not yet been developed, including chickenpox, mumps, and measles. Because there were so many of us, Mom would intentionally expose all of us by close contact to speed up the incubation and infection time. So, our misery overlapped, and I guess it loved company.

I had my tonsils taken out in a hospital during my kindergarten year after missing too many days from school. In those days, removing tonsils was fairly common, but my siblings still have theirs intact. I remember enjoying sherbet and ice cream, and a young boy shared the hospital room with me. His mother gave me a Christmas snow globe and was super nice to me.

Mom practiced all the prevention known at the time to keep us healthy. She bought daily vitamin capsules for us older kids and gave vitamins by droppers to the little ones. I tried very hard to get the little brown capsules to go down my throat with milk, juice, or water. They would always abscond to a haven in my mouth instead of going down the intended route. I came to believe, illogically, that my throat was too small to swallow a pill. I have to confess that the pills found their way into my bathrobe pocket, and I had to remember to flush them down the toilet. They could not reach the laundry hamper!

For an active family that grew to be seven members, we had a disproportionate number of trips to a doctor's office, and I can remember only one emergency room visit for us kids. Trisha was chasing Heiny, our neighbor's dachshund dog, who we were feeding while they were gone. When she caught up with the escapee, she tried to pick him up and carry him in her arms like a baby doll. Feeling quite insecure, Heiny bit Trisha's cheek, which required cleaning and stitches. Also, Trisha had to be treated for a pre-ulcer, and Mom had an untimely attack of appendicitis just after Dad had trimmed back his medical insurance coverage because we were all healthy.

Throughout my childhood, until I left for college, I remember going to a doctor's office only once. I didn't realize that a tiny boysenberry thorn had slipped under my right thumbnail while picking berries from our garden. It took a while to become infected and fester. Then, I became intensely aware of the problem. Mom got me in to see Dr. Aiken (an appropriate name for a doctor?), who had to lance my thumb due to the progression of the infection. I learned what it meant to feel throbbing pain.

Mom also took us to her dentist in Pasadena, who had been her dentist for eons. I'm not sure how we got to Pasadena, but I suspect we rode with Dad, who worked in Alhambra, which was in the vicinity. The fact that we traveled so far on a school day made me think the dentist gave her a special rate. I didn't have any cavities (until I was 21), but the dentist was concerned about the narrow cavern that was my upper palate and that my lower jaw was broader. He told Mom the disparity was caused by mouth-breathing while I slept and advised that she tape my mouth shut at bedtime. She did that for quite a while, to my chagrin. Of course, his solution was ineffective, and she finally stopped the procedure. *Now, dentists use a palatal expander to slowly broaden the palate for children while their bones and tissues are still pliable. In my 50s, the size disparity between my lower and upper jaws finally made thorough chewing impossible, necessitating jaw surgery.*

*****

Arriving home after school, we changed out of our school dresses and put on play clothes, which included pants and shorts. Pops, my maternal grandfather, made us two pairs of wooden stilts. Wisely, given the ongoing growth of our family, he made one set taller than the other and thoroughly smoothed the wood so we would not get splinters. At first, balancing was tricky. Trial and error taught us that we would have more control if we grabbed the sticks, putting our bent elbows in front of them. As soon as we were up with both feet in the wooden stirrups, we learned we had to quickly take a step and another and another. Otherwise, we would fall. After we mastered their use, we thought it was funny to watch the neighborhood children try them. We coached, and it took some practice, but they, too, became proficient.

Our front yard became a kid magnet. Dad cemented a hollow pole in the driveway, into which a tetherball pole fit. This was a big draw on Lemon Street. The player who managed to hit the ball connected to the rope so that it wrapped unimpeded completely around the pole won the game. While waiting for a turn at tetherball or to use the stilts, we could jump rope, play hopscotch on the sidewalk, or practice cartwheels and handstands on Dad's thick dichondra lawn. In the backyard, there was a swing set for the younger kids, and we had a ping-pong table on the back patio. Mom was a formidable player and merciless to challengers.

Mom practiced what she preached about exercise and being outdoors. She would use one of our bikes to ride downtown to pay utilities, making several stops to pay each and go to the bank. I learned this was unusual when, in fourth grade, Gary Lynch loudly asked his buddies if they happened to see Mrs. Harper riding her bike in town. They all snickered, and I ignored them, playing deaf.

Abruptly, at the end of the block was an orange grove. We played among the trees and smudge pots. Dad's only stipulation was not to climb the trees. One day, I found a tree with enticingly low branches, which I deemed harmless until I came crashing down, still holding part of a limb. A long, superficial scratch on my arm and a sibling's tattling story was evidence of my disobedience. I wasn't punished; my parents must have known I wouldn't try that again.

One day, a few years later, we noticed heavy equipment being amassed at the end of our street. It had never occurred to us children that additional clusters of tract houses would appear in our grove, or that Lemon Street would continue right through where we played and be lined with houses until it intersected the main street of town. When the ruthless bulldozers started pushing over perfectly healthy orange trees to clear the land for expansive development, I felt like crying. Our grove, where we had invented games and followed our imaginations, would disappear, replaced by more houses and pavement.

*****

Of all my years in elementary school, my fourth-grade year with Mrs. Lawson was my favorite. She was a widow who invested all her time and energy in us, her students. Although we had learned cursive writing in third grade, she knew we could improve our handwriting by practicing loops and circles on lined paper daily. Early California history was the curricular theme for the grade level. We studied the missions, went on a field trip to Mission San Gabriel, made tiny adobe bricks, and then formed our mission replicas. She arranged hands-on lessons to show us what it was like to be a pioneer, including churning butter, making soap, and square dancing.

One day, she invited our mothers (fathers were working) to taste some of the foods she had gotten from a deli in Los Angeles that sold exotic items the pioneers may have eaten: rattlesnake, which tasted like tuna, rabbit, fried grasshoppers, etc. When Mom arrived in the classroom, I said, "Close your eyes and open your mouth." She obeyed, and I popped a crispy, crunchy grasshopper in her mouth. She thought it wasn't bad until we kids told her what it was, but she was a good sport and swallowed it.

In October of my fifth-grade year, my parents planned a road trip with various stops on the way to and from Staunton, Illinois, where my Great Uncle Jack lived. As far as I remember, the trip lasted at least two weeks. My mother, who taught school before I was born, informed each of our teachers and requested classwork we could do along the way. I'm sure she must have named some of the stops and activities they planned for us while explaining why they had chosen October for the trip. There would be less traffic on the highways and fewer tourists at the sites, and we would get to experience harvest time in Illinois. I got the impression from Mom that the teachers were enthusiastic about our trip.

At least two of my siblings and I had assignments to busy us in the car and during other downtimes. It was understood that diligently doing our classwork was a condition for the privilege of taking a trip during school time. Denise was only three, so her distractions were nonacademic.

We six traveled in our white Ford station wagon (the "noodle wagon"), taking a southern route, probably Route 66, to Carlsbad Caverns first. I can still feel the underground damp coolness, where we learned about the rainbow-colored stalactites and stalagmites, the habits of resident bats, and the absolute darkness when the guide turned off the lanterns underground. We discovered a surreal subterranean world.

On our way to Staunton, we visited Springfield, Illinois, where we learned about the life and death of Abraham Lincoln. We saw various statues and the tomb where he and his family are buried. We made a total of at least three cross-country trips during my childhood. Some of the landmarks we visited were the Grand Canyon, Mount Rushmore, Yellowstone National Park, and The Grand Tetons.

Arriving in Staunton, even as a child, I was impressed by the charm of the small town where Grammie and her siblings had grown up. It was almost foreign to me compared to the towns where we lived in Southern California. A central plaza was surrounded by a neatly manicured park where residents could relax and converse. The gazebo in the center of the plaza served as a stage for live music in the evenings.

My parents wanted us to experience harvest time at one of my great uncle's farms. The Lander family leased the farm from Uncle

Jack, and the family lived in the old farmhouse. The Landers had two girls who instantly welcomed us, began showing us the animals, and unknowingly taught us farm life 101. The next day, we rode in the back of a combine harvester. The corn was mechanically separated from the stalks, sent up a chute, and shot into the truck bed where we rode. The whole process was amazing to us. In the early afternoon, Mrs. Landers prepared dinner for all of us and the men hired to help them during harvest. *It was a feast!* There were delicious, huge, homegrown sliced tomatoes and homemade pies. I got to stay overnight with my new friends and continue learning about their daily life, which fascinated me. We gathered eggs, fed the animals, and tried to milk a cow. When it was time to pack and resume our road trip, I was sad. Hungry for new experiences on my own, I said I wanted to stay and live there. My parents said maybe next trip. The Landers said we were always welcome.

When we returned to school, I took all my completed assignments to turn in to Miss Pelham, who said she did not agree with parents who take their children out of school during the school year, but she accepted them, and I settled back into normal school life. The trip was awesome!

*****

After all these decades, I still remember what I considered instances of injustice that happened in elementary school. My third-grade teacher was relatively new in the job and had been allotted a couple of particularly challenging boy students that year. One day, her numerous efforts to keep the boys engaged and quiet had failed miserably. We all heard her warn the whole class that we would skip recess if the learning atmosphere did not improve. Maybe the offenders did not believe she would follow through on her threat because the mayhem subsided briefly, only to return full force. When it was time for recess, she sternly announced that we would all spend the recess time at our desks in total silence. We could read, practice cursive writing, or do our homework, but it must be without a word or sound. I think a trip to the principal's office was promised to anyone who dared not comply. I was angry that a couple of students could cause us to miss recess. We all looked forward to the break when we could be active, use pent-up energy, and make noise. Why did my teacher, who was so smart, punish all of us, knowing very well which students had been disruptive? In retrospect, she was probably trying a strategy to get the rest of the class to turn their anger on the perpetrators. It didn't work.

Another incident, apart from being unjust, evidenced zero logic. In Mr. Zirkelbach's sixth-grade class, his emphasis was on the parts of speech and vocabulary. He gave daily assignments to diagram sentences, which became kind of fun, like a puzzle, and I liked the challenge. He also gave ten vocabulary words a week. We were to learn their definitions, memorize spellings, and use them all in a paragraph. One of the words this particular week was monochromatic. I cannot remember the others now, but they suggested a dour setting to me. I utilized all ten words to describe a hospital room with a patient in bad shape, mentally and physically. It was sad, but I used all the words.

A couple of days after turning in the assignment, my parents got a call requesting that they bring me and meet with the principal. They said I had plagiarized an assignment in Mr. Zirkelbach's class. What would an 11-year-old with braids and saddle oxfords know about plagiarism? After learning that plagiarism was copying or stealing someone else's writing, Mom and Dad asked me if I did that. I said no; I wrote it.

In the principal's office, we sat silently while he piously preached the evils of plagiarism, as if it were his responsibility to return me to the right track. He asked if I had done that. Again, I said no. I was admonished again never to plagiarize, and we left.

I think my parents believed me, but they would not confront the principal on my behalf. I wanted to ask the principal and my parents what the chances were of finding the ten vocabulary words Mr. Zirkelbach had assigned conveniently arranged in one paragraph for me to steal. But, in those times, at my age, a child did not question authority. Instead of realizing how completely implausible the accusation was, they saw the issue as one of my honesty or lack thereof. So, I learned early that life can be unfair, but those with authority were not subject to questioning. It was the Age of Acquiescence.

My parents believed that "Spare the rod; spoil the child" was the parenting principle most effective in preventing the raising of unruly offspring, but other measures were used first and more frequently. Discipline was meted out by such methods as having us stand silently facing a corner, thinking about the wrong we had committed against a sibling, while the minute-minder ticked away our sentence.

We had to watch our language, too. Of course, taking God's name in vain was never to be heard, and we were also forbidden to say, "Shut up." We, children, were all very aware of these restrictions, but sometimes emotions ramp up, and the cork flies out of the bottle.

Sheri and Mom would argue incessantly, neither willing to cede the last word. As it continued, decibels rose, and the rest of us got sick of it. Dad called it rhubarbing, as used in baseball jargon for a heated discussion. One afternoon, I was practicing what my friend Lynn had taught me on the piano, trying to concentrate and imitate her accomplished fingers. Mom and Sheri were reaching a fever-pitched point where I guess Mom lost control and was going to strap her with Dad's belt. Anticipating and hating the impending violence, I yelled, "Will you two dummies shut up?" I ended up lying next to Sheri on the bed, face down, with the backs of our legs vulnerable to the belt. Our legs burned and then became red and welted. Ashamed of the truth, I made up some story about my injured legs the next day at school, where dresses were required. In those days, we had never heard of Child Protective Services. Corporal punishment was normal at home and acceptable even in schools.

As I was growing up, I didn't realize the lack of physical affection my parents showed us or even between them. It was our normal, which, of course, is not to say they didn't love us; it was just not demonstrated by hugs and kisses. Dad would give Mom a perfunctory peck as he exited the front door for work. Later, even that token ritual disappeared. Ironically, however, we were taught to give a hug to our relatives as they arrived or left a reunion. Now, I realize that Grammie and Pops did not model the expression of physical affection either. We knew and felt they loved us, but the spontaneous display was not the family way. How can kids miss what they haven't known?

*****

Dad had a ritual we all witnessed but didn't understand. After dinner on Saturday nights, he would listen to Polka Party, sitting in his stuffed rocking chair to the left of the fireplace and next to the radio cabinet. The expression on his face was not easily read, but he seemed absent elsewhere. He would close his eyes, let his head rest backward, supported by the stuffing, and appear somnolent. As he relaxed, he entered a snoring, semi-conscious state, seemingly transported to another time and place. Could he have been traveling a road that had not been taken? When I was an adult, Dad mentioned a young German woman named Anna from whom he had learned some fundamental German. I didn't think it proper to ask him questions, but now I wish I had.

Another consequence of Dad's military service was his hearing loss, which increased as he got older. I'm ashamed to admit that we occasionally dared to mutter something purposely, but it was dangerous because Mom's hearing was just fine in those years. Much later, when Dad was in his seventies, the US Government finally recognized his disability and began sending him monthly checks. Dad considered himself wealthy when this unexpected good fortune was bestowed on him. True to his nature, his generosity to his children and grandchildren only increased.

*****

22

Four years after Denise was born, Dad finally got his boy, Charles Timothy, whom we called Timmy. Before his birth, Mom bought a huge bolt of light blue cotton flannel. We were going to make diapers. Although I had changed my sisters' diapers, babysat for infants, and folded multitudes of clean diapers, which I could have done in my sleep, I can't remember if they were pink or white. The first man-child in the family needed blue diapers.

Mom gave me the dimensions for cutting the large squares. The diapers were not sized for newborns. Size was determined by folding, and one size would last until successful potty training was achieved. I turned a small hem twice on all four sides, tucking the raw edge out of sight, pinned the hem in place at short intervals, and carefully removed each pin before the quick up-down needle could land on it and break. Two gigantic safety pins with cute pink or blue plastic closures held the diapers in place. They were fastened very carefully with one hand under the folds of cloth, protecting the baby's soft tummy. The pins were pointed outward to minimize danger, just in case the plastic closure broke, and they opened.

When Timmy was born, Dad said, *"Das ist alles"* (That's all! in German). I was eleven, so five offspring spanned as many years. My little brother was the first sibling to suck his thumb, and I was worried he would have buck teeth if he continued, so I sewed little mitts, which were held in place with ties around his tiny wrists to prevent the habit. Mom had to admit, "Boys are different!" I don't know if Mom, at her age, was just getting tired or if verbal commands were less effective for boys. When Timmy became mobile, Mom bought a harness for him. I remember her using it in crowded public places, like when we went to Disneyland with the Sandersons.

To us girls, our brother was a complete novelty. Of course, we had boy cousins who were older than us, and we went to school with boys, but now we have a resident baby boy. We would vie for the chance to choose his clothes (no hand-me-downs for him), dress him, and comb his hair. Mom had us, surrogate mothers, to help with his care. When we played "dress up," not wanting to leave him out, we dressed him in fancy girls' clothes and gave him a purse to carry. It all seemed normal and inclusive to us. There is even a photo as evidence, which will make my brother wince forever. At three, Timmy still had blonde curls until Dad took charge. Dad invited his barber friend to our house and filmed the shoring event in the backyard. Then, he looked like a handsome little boy. A few years later, Dad built him an almost luxurious fort in our orange tree, and Tim and his friends had their hideaway. I constantly patched his jeans with iron-on patches.

*****

Mom had learned from Grammie how to sprinkle, roll, wrap in plastic bags, and refrigerate any clothes that needed to be ironed. She taught me the intergenerational procedure. Dad's work shirts were a top priority, and I liked how they looked after applying a little spray starch. Some of my clothes needed to be ironed, too. I never minded ironing. It was a task I could perform well, and I was proud of the lineup of freshly ironed clothes. Dad noticed who had done the ironing, and I think he was grateful.

Dad briefly talked about the strike brewing among the union employees at Southern California Edison, his employer, who provided for our entire family income. It was the first I had heard the word union, but I began to realize what a strike meant and how it could affect our family. Striking was a matter of principle, a show of solidarity, and a luxury Dad could not afford. He went to work, as usual, endured the "Scab" slurs and various deprecations hurled at him from the picket line, and entered the building to be as valuable as possible to the employee-diminished utility company. Dad would laugh when he told people he couldn't strike because he "had a wealthy family to support." That was a sample of Dad's humor – sometimes a little higher on the tree and harder to get.

*****

When our neighbors, Ethyl and Leo Whitten, invited Ethyl's elderly bedridden father to live with them, they realized they could use more help with the housework. Ethyl and Mom arranged for me to work at their house on Saturdays for $.25 an hour. Entering their house, the distinct smell of bacon gravy and biscuits from breakfast hung trapped in the air. Although I could barely reach the clothesline in the backyard, I hung clothes, took them down, folded them, ironed, mopped floors, dusted, and vacuumed. The task that grossed me out was emptying the plastic-lined trash basket by her father's bed. He coughed up phlegm, and who knows what else? I tried hard not to see it as I gathered the plastic, knotted it, and deposited it in the big trash. Ethyl was nice enough, but it used to bug me each time she assigned a new task; she would say, "I'm going to let you mop the kitchen now" . . . and "I'll let you hang these clothes." The work was a drag, but I liked earning money.

We could earn an allowance from our parents, but the amount was not much of an incentive, considering the conditions for eligibility. We had to keep a ledger of income and expenses, an idea that I feel originated from Grammie. Furthermore, we were obligated to give an amount to the church and not omit any of our chores to qualify for the dole. I started a small ledger, being a compliant child, but soon decided it wasn't worth the effort. I know Grammie's intentions were for our financial education, but I decided to earn my own money.

I started babysitting for pay in the neighborhood when I was eleven. Sometimes, Sheri, who was then nine, would come with me. We took care of babies and toddlers. I guess their mothers trusted us because they saw how much we helped with our younger siblings, and Mom was just a couple of houses away if we had a problem. One neighbor admonished me not to tell her mother how old I was when her mother visited. We liked earning and having our own money. I used mine for the fabric to learn to sew and for other projects.

A neighbor girl and I got interested in tropical fish. At first, while I saved money for an aquarium, I had only a bowl with very prolific guppies. Eventually, I had my tank with a pump and decorative rocks. With an increase in earnings, I could buy the more exotic types of fish: angel fish, black mollies, and betas. There was even an industrious platypus that cleaned the glass aquarium walls meticulously. The guppies were promoted to the upscale environment, too. I didn't expect illness, bullying, and an occasional incidence of cannibalism from this kaleidoscope of inhabitants, but the fish community became a microcosm of the world outside of the aquarium glass. The black mollies were prone to ick, the symptoms of which were white dots on their sleek black bodies. They would shimmy near the surface and meet their waterloo a few days later. I never caught the bullying perpetrators of the betas, whose tails and brilliant flowing fins bore the scars of harassment, but I learned they required solitude and had to be separated into a bowl of their own. Cannibalism occurred when other fish would eat the live-born guppies unless they were smart enough to dart and hide until they were too big to eat. The platypus, oblivious to this violent community, just continued his never-ending task of cleaning the aquarium glass.

Across the street and one house up lived Alice Hempstead and her young son, Jackie. To my knowledge, Alice was the only single parent in our neighborhood. Appearance-wise, on a scale of one to ten, feminine to masculine, she fell hard on a seven. Her occupation was taxi driver, so she had a volatile schedule and needed help with Jackie's care. I remember joking that I could just picture Alice with a cigar in one hand and gripping the steering wheel with the other. My mother did not see the humor in the image I had invoked and told me I should not repeat it.

Jackie was an under-disciplined only child who specialized in wanting and receiving negative attention. He was also an accomplished manipulator. It's an understatement to say he was high maintenance for us during his waking hours. Sheri and I took turns at the only unpleasant job in the neighborhood. Mom felt sorry for Alice, and we felt we had no choice but to take care of Jackie.

For a while, we were paid after each job when Alice came home, as was customary. Then, she sometimes apologized and told us she couldn't pay right then. Next time, she would make up for it. We let Mom know when this started and continued to take care of Jackie. I don't know if Mom said something to her or if Alice approached Mom. The result of the conference was that they agreed that Alice would buy new shoes for both of us at George Allen, an upscale shoe store where she had a credit card.

Again, without a choice in the matter, we went with Alice to George Allen Shoes. There were only expensive leather shoes in adult styles that kids were not wearing. We wore Keds, oxfords, and slip-ons for church. As we continued to look around the store, Alice made suggestions, holding up one shoe after another. I remember feeling trapped. Not even one looked like a kid's shoe, and I was being forced to spend my hard-earned nonexistent money on something I didn't want. The sales lady came to measure our feet, find the right size, and close the deal. We both chose awful loafer-type shoes. We thanked Alice because we were taught to be grateful, and she brought us home. I don't think I wore those shoes once, not even to church. I resented that Mom was complicit in the rip-off. After that, both Sheri and I would already have plans or jobs when Alice asked us to watch Jackie. I wasn't going to let her or Mom force me into a situation like that again.

Apart from that one troublesome incident, we enjoyed our tight-knit neighborhood, where there was interaction and mutual support. There were other children to play with, and the adults were protective of all of us. The lady directly across the street was musically talented and took on the challenge of preparing us for caroling at Christmastime. We practiced under her patient guidance for a few weeks, then had fun going from house to house, singing, and being invited in for hot chocolate and cookies by some neighbors.

We always walked to and from school unless it rained. Knowing that Dad took our only vehicle to work, a neighbor at the end of the street gave us a standing offer to come down to ride with her children on rainy days.

*****

After work, Dad often used a pressure cooker to prepare dinner quickly for his hungry offspring. When I was old enough, I prepped some items before he arrived. When Sheri, Trisha, and I were capable, we each got to plan a dinner during the week and prepare it. Dad would take us to the grocery store and buy whatever we needed for the meal. The hands-on experience was fun; Dad was there if we wanted assistance. If ever anyone complained about the menu, Dad would say, "It's a long time 'til breakfast."

There were occasional nights when Dad would stay at work for an evening demonstration. On those nights, Mom would serve us a fish dinner or liver and onions because Dad didn't like seafood, much less liver.

One night, Dad came home with incredible information. He had performed the minor miracle of perfectly cooking a whole potato in ten minutes. He was demonstrating a commercial microwave in front of an audience of restauranteurs. I'm sure those night presentations were the most enjoyable aspect of his job.

On weekends, Dad had time to cook more labor-intensive meals, which I think was his favorite hobby, followed by gardening. Around 6:00 am Saturday mornings, he would open the dormitory door, switch on the glaring florescent overhead lights, and announce that breakfast was ready for us: pancakes, French toast, waffles, biscuits, eggs, or grits, accompanied by bacon, sausage or gravy. He would say, "C'mon, you gonna sleep all day? Daylight's burning."

He was famous among family and friends for his pies, especially apple pie. But it seemed he could make just about anything. We were all surprised when the ornamental banana tree he planted in the backyard produced miniature bananas. He made a banana cream pie with them. The La Habra Star newspaper sent a reporter to document and taste the rarity, after which Dad's picture and a short write-up appeared in the small-town paper. Dad also planted a peach tree, which matured and became prolific. We loved eating the juicy peaches from the tree, over ice cream, or in the cobblers Dad made.

Quite often, Dad's sisters Sue and Marge would bring their children, our cousins, and husbands to our house for a get-together. Dad got up at dawn to start baking pies and prepping enormous quantities of everyone's favorites. Aunt Sue was a plump, hilarious lady. She would tell our cousins Greg and Randy to "pretend you have manners." If the boys got a little out of order, she jokingly threatened to fall on them. While the adults chatted, we kids would practice a "show" to be presented to the adults after dinner. Ronny, Auntie Marge's son, who was a little older than us, was the director, but we all contributed ideas. We used a couple of blankets for a curtain and took our entertaining seriously, having several dress rehearsals. We had so much fun when Dad's family visited.

*****

The neighborhood grapevine was fully functional when Ethyl and Leo, next door to us, decided to sell their house due to a job transfer. The Bybees, across the street from Ethyl and Leo, let my parents know of their concerns about the buyer of the Whittens' house. They had gotten word that the buyers were "Spanish." Anyone who spoke Spanish was labeled that, regardless of their nationality or even the continent of their origin. The Bybees wanted the rest of the neighborhood to be warned of the impending devaluation of our homes, even though they were powerless to prevent it.

At the time, La Habra had a substantial Hispanic population, but they mainly lived in their cluster on the other side of town. Of course, the children from both sections of town attended the same schools, so we did not understand or share the adults' concerns, which soon proved completely unfounded.

Dad thought it was humorous to call Hispanics "beaners[3]," which made me feel uncomfortable when he said it. But I don't remember that any animus accompanied his stereotypical slur. Our family certainly ate various types of beans. Also, Dad liked to stop by Nacho's, a tiny Mexican store, to bring home hot, freshly made tortillas. My parents didn't seem too worried about our soon-to-be neighbors.

Soon after we moved to Lemon Street, Dad started a family tradition. Dad, who loved to cook and bake, initiated the welcoming gesture of taking a decorated, homemade, from-scratch cake to new neighbors. Being the eldest child had its advantages. I got to help Dad make and ice the cake. He never used a cake mix. Instead, he told me how meticulous measuring, sifting the special cake flour, and buttering and lining the cake pans would bring the best results. Cakes were rather delicate to make. As he taught the best practices, he would say, "Lemme show you a little trick." I helped make butter frosting and then divide it into separate bowls, which I would color with food coloring. I learned that yellow and blue coloring drops made green; blue and red made purple, and red and yellow made orange. Then, we created a rudimentary design for the cake top.

Delivery of the cake would be on Sunday when we still had our church clothes on. Imagine being new in the neighborhood and watching from a window as two adults, one with a cake, followed by three stair-stepped sisters (and later another sister and toddler boy), came up your driveway toward your front door. It was always fun to deliver the surprise.

When the Ponces moved in next door, we surprised them with our cake tradition, as we always had when a new family joined our neighborhood. We learned that Al Ponce was the head groundskeeper for all city parks and city buildings in La Habra. Ironically, his wife

---

[3] A racial slur for Hispanics, especially Mexicans, for beans as being a staple ingredient in Mexican cuisine.

Dora took painstaking care of the landscaping at home and became a great friend to Dad as they shared stories while holding a hose and watering the pampered flowers along the divider where the two driveways met. Over the years, Al and Dora embarked on several remodeling projects to update their home and add value. Their home became the showcase on Lemon Street. They had two sons, Al Jr. and Ronnie, who were polite but slightly shy around so many girls. The Ponces were always friendly to us. On Christmas Eve, Dora brought us homemade tamales to introduce us to their tradition.

Some years later, Dad was gardening in the front yard while Al Jr. was working on his car in their garage. Dad glanced into the open garage and saw him lying on the garage floor. He jumped the low divider between the driveways and ran to pull him out of the garage and onto the cool, lush grass. He regained consciousness soon after, and Dad was always credited with saving his life.

*****

Mom modeled a love of reading, and I credit her for encouraging us to read. She would be lying on the couch reading when we arrived home from school. We knew she hadn't been there all day because the clothes were washed, and I guess she needed a little "me time." Later in life, Mom told us she thought she "was addicted to reading." Denise confirmed it was true, saying she even read her junk mail.

At Washington School, where I attended kindergarten through eighth grade, I got hooked early by reading several series of books, like Nancy Drew and *Little House on the Prairie*, from the school library. In sixth grade, I read *Grapes of Wrath* by John Steinbeck. When I finished that book, he instantly became my favorite author, and I read nearly all his books, including *East of Eden*, *Of Mice and Men*, *The Winter of Our Discontent*, *Cannery Row*, *The Pearl*, and others.

The school librarian, Mrs. Phelps, must have noticed that I frequented the library. When I was in eighth grade, she unofficially mentored me when I was preparing for high school. Her individualized attention was welcome; She made me think I might be smart. I believed her when she told me more than once that I must take Latin. She said it would be the foundation for higher learning and various careers. So, that is how I found myself in Miss Varnum's Latin class as a freshman in high school.

Grandparent Nurture

My maternal grandparents, Arthur Gustav Gehrig (1887-1970) and Julia Etta Smith (1888-1976), played a positive and supportive role in my life, especially during childhood. According to my baby book, in which Mom detailed my life until I entered kindergarten, the first few months were not much fun for anyone around me. When Mom and I were both trying to overcome the effects of preeclampsia, Pops brought Grammie for a couple of extended stays to Villa Park to help.

After a couple of months, I had become a happy, normal baby and traveled to reunions with both maternal and paternal families, could go to church, went camping with my parents, and ate at restaurants. I also spent time alone with Grammie and Pops at their house. My baby book says I cried when I had to go home.

One very early memory was when Grammie and Pops went with Mom, Dad, and me (I'm not sure if Sheri was there) to stay in a mountain cabin for the weekend in winter after it had snowed. Pops woke me in the night, bundled me in a blanket, and put me on his shoulders to go outside to check the temperature. It was 15 degrees. Even at their home in Pasadena, Pops kept records of temperatures, rainfall, and probably more. He was an engineer, and all scientific topics interested him.

Grammie showed me pictures of Pops when he worked on the construction of the Panama Canal. He was attending the University of Illinois, working on his degree in engineering, and working in construction for ABC Company. This company called him to go to Panama to work on the canal. A 500-foot-wide artificial waterway was dug to connect the Pacific Ocean and the Caribbean Sea.

He wrote postcards and letters every week to his mother and Grammie. When he came back to Staunton to date Grammie seriously, she told me she would watch for him to come down the street from her second-story bedroom window. At the first sight of him, she began pinching her cheeks and biting her lips to create a healthy pink color. They were married soon after he came back from Panama. Pops' proposal included a request that they honeymoon in Panama. She accepted, and they lived in Panama for a while until the Panama Canal was finished. I remember she said they had a maid who did everything for them: washing, cooking, and cleaning. She admitted there was little to do there and would have preferred to be active. She mentioned the pickaninnies, whom she thought were precious and loved holding them. I had never heard the word, so she explained they were little black babies. I wish she had told me more about her experiences.

To me, Grammie was a paradoxical lady. She was trim and wore fitted, belted dresses and laced shoes with chunky heels always. Her hair was white for as long as I could remember, and she had it permed and trimmed regularly at Penny's salon. A tin of mints was always in her pocket or purse because she wanted to be sure her breath was pleasant despite her false teeth. She kept her fingernails filed and coated with clear polish. Every time I visited her, she would give me manicures, which made me feel like a lady.

Her appearance was always maintained, even though she performed every household task, including cooking, canning, cleaning, washing, and gardening. She was always clean, although she must have bathed before I got up or after I went to bed. She took pride in the beauty of the ample front and back yards, where she spent hours pruning and pampering trees, plants, and flowers.

The washing machine, a large washing tub topped with a tall wringer, was in the enclosed back porch area. After the clothes swished and jostled in the tub and were rinsed, she fed the clean, sopping-wet clothes and linens through the wringer's double rollers. They exited like pancakes, drier and flat. We would shake them, put them in a basket, and take them to the backyard, where lines were stretched taut. I helped her hang them with clothes pins from a cloth bag tied around her waist. The clothes dried quickly outside in the breeze.

We gathered the dry, fresh-smelling clothes and took them inside for sorting and folding. I had never known anybody else who ironed sheets, but it seemed Grammie ironed and starched everything. All items to be ironed were sprinkled with water from a special container with holes in the top, rolled tightly, placed in plastic bags, and refrigerated until a designated ironing day.

I liked to help her and had specific tasks. When she was cleaning, the baseboards were at the perfect level for me to dust. Outside, I could grab the avocados from the picker and place them in a basket. As I grew, I could contribute by gathering plant trimmings, raking leaves, and carrying trash to the incinerator in the far backyard.

My baby book says that I spent 12 days when I was six, helping Grammie can peaches. My job was peeling off the fuzzy skins after a quick dunking in boiling water. Canning was an all-day, sometimes multi-day process. Placing the Ball jars and lids in a huge pot with water brought to a boil, she explained that the jars must be meticulously sterilized so that no germs could grow while the canned fruits and vegetables stood in orderly rows in the pantry. I listened for the pop to ensure they were properly sealed because Grammie's ears missed some noises. During the winter, we sometimes ate the peaches on ice cream for lunch.

Grammie never learned to drive. I didn't know if it was her preference or Pops'. So, we went on the bus to downtown Pasadena, just she and I, and it was always a fun day. One time, she was looking for new kitchen curtains. We went from store to store to find the right size, color, and style. She finally found what she liked, but said they were too expensive. When I tried to convince her to buy them anyway, she said every dime she could save would be for us when she was gone. It made me sad to hear her say that. I wished she would have bought them.

Before California had laws to reduce harmful emissions, my eyes watered and became irritated by the smog in the city. Grammie held my hand out on the street because my watering eyes made everything blurry.

Lunch was the highlight of the trip when we went downtown. We both loved ice cream! We sat at the counter at Woolworth's, and each of us ordered a sundae or a banana split. We each had our own, and there was no sharing. What a treat!

*****

Another stop was Penny's Beauty Salon to get Grammie's hair trimmed, permed, and styled. Mom had never taken me to a beauty salon, so I was fascinated by all that went on there. Women chatted with women they didn't even know, contributing to the upbeat atmosphere. The perms, curlers, pin curls, and distinctive odors were all new and exciting.

Mom cut our bangs. We thought she cut them very short so they would stay out of our eyes for a long time. We begged her not to give us "Chinese bangs," but she didn't heed our pleas. The rest of my hair was long and fine, without curl or body. When I was at Grammie's, she tried admirably to make it look presentable. Curling it with rags (fabric strips twisted with my hair) was attempted, but after all her effort, my hair returned quickly to its fine, limp state. She tried to braid it, as Mom did, but she was not adept and became frustrated.

Grammie noticed how much I enjoyed the beauty salon when I went with her. Without being manipulative, she said she could make an appointment for me for my next visit if I wanted to get my hair cut. In the meantime, I could think about it. I was excited and told her that I wanted to make an appointment. It was quite a while before my next visit, but Grammie remembered and called Mom to see if I still wanted a beauty appointment. Yes, please, was my immediate answer.

At her house, the night before the appointment, I could hardly get to sleep due to anticipation. I could picture myself in one of the special chairs that went up and down where the ladies sat to have their hair done. And I was only eight.

We rode the bus and arrived at Penny's just as I had visualized. The beautician treated me like an adult while consulting with Grammie, too. We all decided my hair would behave the best cut just at my chin. I could clip the sides back with colorful barrettes. My hair was washed in another special chair with a sink attached. Then, the cutting began. Grammie asked the beautician if we could take the silky straight strands of cut-off hair with us. I was proud of my grown-up experience and thanked Grammie for arranging and paying for my new style.

When we got home, I brushed my hair in front of the bathroom mirror on tiptoes and suddenly realized my loss. There would be no more ponytails, buns, or braids for hot summer days. There was a different me in the mirror whom I was having difficulty accepting. I was fighting tears but did not want Grammie to know. Under the bed would be a good place to gain control. The full-sized bed was very low, but I managed to wriggle under it. It was dark and scary. Suddenly, I felt wispy dust bunnies that had escaped Grammie's perfectionism, and I wriggled quickly in reverse. As I backed out into the light and safety, Grammie found me. I confessed that I wasn't sure I liked my new style. She was understanding, telling me she had noticed how fast my hair grew. I could let it grow, and in no time, it would be long again. It was a lesson about seemingly bad decisions that were not as final as I imagined. With time, they could be reversed, accepted, or both.

*****

Baseball was Grammie's passion! Over the years, she had learned all the rules, even the obscure ones. The Dodgers were her team, and she made it a point to know about their personal lives – if they were married, how many kids they had, etc. Granted, player trading was not so frequent in those times, but she kept up with her team. They were almost inducted into the family. If she couldn't sit and watch a game on TV, she had her transistor radio firmly pressed against her ear. It was not a time to interrupt her. Our family once took Grammie to Dodger Stadium to see a game. Even though our seats were a bit high up from the field, we all enjoyed the excitement of being at the field, but Grammie was ecstatic.

She had a prodigy parakeet, Pretty Boy, who talked when water was running in the kitchen sink. She may have trained him while washing dishes. He made her proud when he consistently performed for her and guests. He could say his name, whistle, say "play ball," "Strike three," and "You're out!" He had his wings clipped to prevent his escape, but he enjoyed a privileged life otherwise. He was even trusted to have time out of his cage.

One day, something went wrong, and he tried to fly into a wall. His sky-blue body fell to the floor, but he was still alive. Grammie called the vet, put Pretty Boy gently in his cage, and we hurried to the bus stop with the cage. Grammie's chunky heels hit the pavement in staccato steps while I ran beside her. We were lucky to board a bus immediately when we reached the bus stop, but by the time we finally got to the vet, it was too late to save him... if that was even possible. The vet thought he may have suffered a sudden massive failure in his tiny blue body that made him fly into the wall. We took him back to bury him in the far backyard.

*****

I spent hours playing with Grammie's doll collection. Dolls used to be made with soft fabric bodies topped with angelic ceramic heads, intricately painted. She trusted me to be very careful with the antique dolls, especially with their fragile heads.

Grammie provided colorful fabric remnants, scissors, buttons, ribbons, needles, and thread so I could make clothes for the dolls. Creativity surged as I sat on the floor, surrounded by endless possibilities for making fancy clothes. She taught me how to sew with the thinnest of needles ("no railroad ties," she would say), use a thimble, and mend socks by inserting a wooden form into the sock, then making long stitches in one direction across the hole and weaving through those in the opposite direction, over and over. She introduced me to sewing, which became a favorite and practical pastime as I got older.

*****

Sometimes, Grammie coordinated with Aunt Ruth Shaner to have my cousin Kathy, who was one year older, visit with me. We were never bored. We spent most of the time outside and were old enough to be safe up and down the sidewalk. Both of us brought our roller skates. They were the type that could be lengthened and shortened with a key, and they had metal pieces on both sides of the toe that wrapped up around the sides of our shoes. They were perfect for growing kids and multiple-kid use. I was so envious of Kathy because she had learned to make her skates glide, first on one skate and then on the other. It looked so easy, but I could only plunk one skate on the sidewalk after the other. For me, it was just belabored walking. Kathy tried to teach me, but it wasn't something I could learn. I kept trying for days while Kathy glided far ahead. Suddenly, I had my *eureka* moment. I could glide, too! We could skate up and down the block, always within Grammie's view if she came out. When we got sweaty in the summer heat, we came up to the inviting coolness of the house's wrap-around covered front porch. The cement refreshed our legs while we played jacks in the shade.

One time, Grammie gave us lots of blankets and clothespins to make a tent on the clotheslines in the backyard. It was quite impressive, containing dividers for rooms and even a roof. We asked if we could sleep in our new creation that night. Grammie said we could. So, at bedtime, we took a flashlight, pillows, and more blankets to our tent. I don't think we went to sleep before we heard noises that our imaginations exaggerated to the level of danger, resulting in a quick retreat inside the house.

Grammie was emphatic about manners, etiquette, and grammar. We were taught to say, "Yes, please," and "No, thank you," without exception. If we were telling what happened to others and ourselves, we must list ourselves last. If we said we were "done," she would act surprised and ask if we were cooking in the oven like Hansel and Gretel.

Before marrying Pops, Grammie went to St Louis on her own to attend business school, where she learned grammar, shorthand, and accounting. According to Mom, Grammie was a star pupil in Staunton, and training for a profession was quite progressive for a young woman at that time.

With that knowledge, I wondered why she worked in a drugstore in Staunton when she finished her studies. I find it ironic that a young, courageous woman, driven to educate herself, would become so dependent after marriage. She became economically dependent and did not even learn to drive a vehicle.

Could it be that social and/or family mores of the early 1900s did not allow single women to live independently? Could that be the reason she returned home to live with her parents? Staunton was a rural town surrounded by agriculture, but it was a step up from the farms where her parents had started, and Pops had been born. Maybe there were no jobs in Staunton that would utilize her skills. If my conjecture about mores is true, a young woman would be severely limited by where her parents lived, even if she was ambitious and intelligent enough to have continued her education. Professional opportunities and the availability of young men to marry would be diminished.

*****

One of her platitudes recited more than once was "Pretty is as pretty does." Her other rules concerned eating and conversing civilly. We learned to serve our food by being mindful that we had to eat all that we served and belonged to "The Clean Plate Society." Another rule we all knew, including our parents, was that there was no discussion of religion or politics in her house.

I remember only one time Kathy and I managed to arrive at the brink of trouble. We were at the dinner table with Pops and Grammie when one of us started to giggle about something that had happened that day. Revisualizing the hilarious scene caused increasing, unstoppable laughter. Grammie sternly reminded us that dinnertime was not the time for our laughter. The harder we tried to stifle ourselves, the stronger the outburst would erupt. Grammie warned us we would be dismissed from dinner if it happened again, and we did not doubt that she would follow through. With great difficulty, we diverted our thoughts and enjoyed the tasty meal.

Whether I was visiting Grammie and Pops alone or with Kathy, there would be one fun evening activity per visit. The one I chose repeatedly was night swimming at the plunge after Pops came home from work and we finished dinner. The warm air, the smell of chlorinated water, and the lights along the pool's edge made for an entirely different atmosphere from daytime swimming. There was a high board to jump from, but it took a few seasons to muster substantial courage for that. Relaxed from the activity, I slept so well after swimming. I was too sleepy for Grammie to read to me, as she always did at bedtime. My favorite books were *Brer Rabbit*, *Heidi*, and Robert Louis Stevenson's poems.

*****

A neighbor, Mrs. Haftner, sometimes invited her granddaughters, who were a little older than me, to visit when I did. Mrs. Haftner's cat had kittens a couple of months before I visited when I was nine. We spent hours gently holding them and were entertained by their antics. I fell in love with a calico kitten and wanted to take her home.

Grammie explained the responsibility of pet ownership to me in detail. The kitten would need a litter box until she was old enough to be outside unsupervised, and I would have to keep it clean so it would not smell. I would always feed her before I ate and wash her food and water bowls daily. She said she thought I was old enough to care for a pet if I committed to it. I was so excited that Grammie thought I could handle it. Now, she had to get my parents' approval. They consented, although I don't think cats were Dad's favorite pets.

The kitten was almost mine. I chose the name Beatrice because I had read it in a book, and we could call her Bea for short. A few days later, when Dad came to pick me up, we put her in a box with a comfy receiving blanket. Dad patiently tolerated her high-pitched, desperate cries all the way home, though I tried to comfort her with gentle petting. When we finally got home, I set up all of her necessities and was excited to begin my responsibilities laid out in detail by Grammie.

Bea turned out to be a good indoor-outdoor pet, but she became a kitten factory. One day, Dad and I were in the garage putting the sleeping bags back up on a hanging shelf after a camping trip. As I was coming back down the ladder, instead of the garage floor, I was horrified to feel the squish of soft tissue. I froze and wouldn't look down. But almost immediately, I heard a smack. Dad's quick reflexes had stopped the suffering, and he headed to the backyard with the kitten in the shovel.

We found homes for all of the kittens, but now I'm not proud of my family's failure to spay her. Beatrice must have had at least nine lives but finally met her demise quickly in the street at the advanced age of 14.

*****

During the week, Pops was already gone to work before I got up. But the smell of his Colgate toothpaste lingered in the spotlessly clean bathroom. Grammie laid out his clothes for work the night before, always choosing a tasteful but conservative combination for the suit, shirt, and tie. I never saw Pops in short sleeves, much less short pants. When it was hot, he pushed the long sleeves up and secured them with rubber bands after work. Mom says he took her hiking occasionally, but I still imagine he wore long pants and long-sleeved shirts.

On the weekends, Grammie taught me to whisper in the morning until we heard Pops was awake. All my life, they slept in separate bedrooms at opposite ends of the house, with the guest room where I slept in between. I just assumed they could have their own rooms because there weren't as many people in their house as ours.

Pops was handsome, although mostly bald, with darker skin than Grammie's and dark brown eyes. Grammie's eyes were steel blue, and both their daughters had blue eyes, so Pops must have had a recessive blue gene for that to happen. He kept himself in good shape, working in construction when he was younger, horseback riding, and playing tennis. "Eat before you are hungry; sleep before you are tired" was his mantra. He broke his first bone at age 75 while ice skating.

He invariably deferred to Grammie for permission in matters concerning the grandchildren, telling us, "We'll have to ask the boss." It was his opinion that kids should be able to eat all the candy they wanted once a year, but both Grammie and Mom vetoed that leniency.

Pops embodied many of the stereotypes about engineers. He was orderly, methodical, and fascinated by all scientific phenomena while preferring to delegate decisions about food and fashion to Grammie.

What I know about Pop's career is that he taught Engineering at Pasadena City College, worked at both Lockheed and Hycon, and retired three times. He showed us an impressive, framed aerial view of Pasadena, which had been given to him at one of the retirements. The photograph might have been a forerunner of the processes now used for Google Maps.

In retirement, Pops started on the laborious project of leafing out the Gehrig-Leutwiler Family Tree. In those days, he had to write numerous letters to relatives and possible kin in the United States and Europe. Waiting for responses by mail required patience, but he finally had it compiled and printed for all interested. He sent a copy to all the grandchildren. It covered 176 years (1788-1964) and included a total of 482 persons from Europe and the United States.

Every Sunday, Pops went to the Baptist Church alone. This seemed out of the norm because our family attended church several times a week. Grammie was hard of hearing and wore an aid or two, so I assumed maybe she couldn't hear well enough to benefit from the service. However, her rule about not talking about religion might suggest another reason.

When Mom was 91, at my 60th birthday celebration, she told me many things I didn't know about her and her parents. I tried to make notes intermittently while attending to my hosting duties. She said both Pops and Grammie were born in Illinois in Macoupin County. Grammie had four siblings, and she was next to last in birth order. Her family moved from the farm to the town of Staunton, where Grammie was born.

Pops was the last of nine children in a family who stayed on a farm near New Douglas. His mother, Elizabeth Leutwiler Gehrig, was 43 when he was born. His father, John Gehrig, donated part of their land for a one-room schoolhouse and paid the teacher's salary. Pops left home after finishing high school and found employment as a surveyor with the American Bridge Company. He was involved in the construction of the Free Bridge over the Mississippi River, known by that name because there was no toll originally. Later, tolls were added for auto traffic, and the bridge was renamed for Douglas MacArthur. It took Pops 13 years to graduate from the University of Illinois because he could take courses only between jobs.

One of these jobs, also through ABC, was the opportunity to work on the construction of the Panama Canal. In 1904, when the revolution in Panama installed a new administration, the United States took advantage of the circumstances to ratify an agreement to build a canal that would connect the Atlantic and Pacific Oceans. One of the Man-

Made Wonders of the World, the Canal was a 500-foot-wide (further widened in 2007) artificial watercourse that transports huge ships from one ocean and drops them gently into another.

Building the canal was a daring endeavor that the French gave up in 1889 after nine years of engineering problems and a loss of approximately 20,000 lives. Facing the same challenges the French encountered in the mountainous jungle, the US had only the advantage of superior engineering. Like the French, US workers succumbed to the perils of rolling boulders, yellow fever, malaria (which Pops contracted, too), and poisonous snakes. One account of the construction period (1904-1914) stated that dead bodies were transported by train daily. Another account mentioned that a manufacturer of prosthetic limbs contracted with the project managers.

The construction faced additional challenges due to the region's annual rainfall of 105 inches. Upon its completion in 1914 by the US, the project had claimed 25,000 lives.

When Pops returned to Panama with Grammie for their honeymoon, he was offered and accepted a promotion to Paymaster, which entailed processing payroll for all the employees who worked on the canal until it was completed. He had the honor of being on the first ship to go through the locks of the canal.

President Theodore Roosevelt brokered the agreement with the Panamanian Government, and the canal became his legacy project. He visited the construction site in 1906 and did hands-on inspections. He may have also been on the first ship to pass through the locks.

When my grandparents returned to Illinois, Pops built a small house in Champagne, near the University of Illinois. Mom was born there while Pops was finishing his master's in civil engineering. At completion, he was offered a fellowship to teach at the University of Nebraska in Lincoln. Two years after Mom's birth, her sister Margery was born in Lincoln.

Pops traveled alone by train to look for work in San Francisco and Los Angeles before moving his family. In Los Angeles, he was offered a job as a surveyor for C.P. Day Company, which made sidewalks. He bought a home on 5th Avenue and told Grammie to pack up and bring the young girls on the train to Los Angeles. "You don't need a heater here, and nobody has basements," was his description of the West Coast to Grammie.

The train trip took three days, during which Margery (9 months) had diarrhea. The kitchen chef gave Grammie boiled rice water to calm Margery's ailment.

They lived in Los Angeles for only one year because C. P. Day relocated to Pasadena. They moved to the suburb of Lamanda Park and were there for a year until Pop's Grandma Miller gave them a huge loan to buy a house in Pasadena on Wilson Avenue. It was in this house that most of my memories related to what I have mentioned above.

C. P. Day relocated again, but Pops left the company and went back to using his construction skills. He was kept busy building houses, brick commercial buildings, and apartments as Lake Avenue was booming after the trolley was installed and put into use. Grammie was unhappy with the volatile nature of construction and urged him to get a "regular job."

When the depression came in 1929, Mom was 13 years old. The construction industry is often the first to feel the harbinger of an economic downturn. It became difficult for Pops to support his family while paying back the loan from his grandmother for their house. Mom had to get glasses, and other expenses made frugality imperative. Grandma Miller was both understanding and lenient, letting Pops slide on the debt. When she died, it was in her will that the debt be forgiven. Pops applied for a teaching job at Pasadena City College, was awarded the position, and their economic outlook improved somewhat.

Until talking with Mom when she was 91, I didn't know Grammie's health was delicate. Mom said she had a rare disease. It caused her to suffer from "fierce" migraines, and it may have caused her early hearing loss and the premature need for false teeth. When Mom was about four years old and Margery was two, Grammie was hospitalized for a "problem with her knee." Mom and Margery were sent to different caretakers. Mom said Grammie "could never walk very far." I think she meant Grammie did not accompany Pops and the girls when they hiked and backpacked because I never noticed that she had any problem walking all over Pasadena. However, Mom said Grammie became more of a homebody.

Mom rated her parents' marriage as fair to poor. Pops wanted to be active, travel, and "absorb knowledge," as Mom described him. Grammie could not physically do many things Pops liked, but they both enjoyed nature.

According to Mom, they had separate friends. I was shocked to hear Pops had an affair with a lady at the Baptist Church. I don't know when this happened or how either of my grandparents dealt with it. Could that have caused them to sleep in separate rooms? Until Mom related this to me, after both Grammie and Pops had died, the affair had been securely locked away. Mom said Grammie "bore an awful lot silently."

Learning about Grammie's secret burden, I had to add a third consecutive generation (to my knowledge) of strong women in our family who chose to stay in unhappy marriages and/or with unfaithful spouses. I suspect economic dependence weighed heavily in their decisions.

I wished I didn't know Grammie's secret, but knowing helped me create empathy for her, even after her death. The capacity for empathy sometimes lies dormant until age and experience catch up and awaken the feeling. I realized we have no idea about the invisible burdens people courageously carry.

Mom filled in some of the unknowns that had surrounded her sister's death for many decades. Margery was taken to Los Angeles Hospital when she suddenly had trouble swallowing, but no one thought it was more serious than the flu. She was diagnosed immediately with polio, put in an iron lung, and lasted only a couple of days, dying at age 31. Her mother-in-law came to their house in Arcadia to take care of their three young children, Lynn (5), Kathy (3), and Daryl (5 months).

When Mom and Sheri would argue fiercely, and Mom would sometimes take away her curlers or makeup and make her pay money to get them back, Dad reminded Mom of something we did not understand at the time. Later, he told us that Grammie and her daughter Margery were at odds or not on good terms when Margery died of polio suddenly. When I asked Mom about Grammie's estrangement from Margery at the time of her death, she said she was unaware of it.

She went on to tell me Margery attended the University of California, Berkley, and then worked in Public Health in San Francisco. Although Mom wasn't sure where her sister met Carl, they were married in Hawaii, where Carl, an Air Force Lieutenant, was stationed. They came back just before their first child, Lynn was born, and they lived with Grammie and Pops. Later, they moved to their own home in Arcadia, California.

When we were at Pepperdine, Kathy told me that all pictures of their mother were put away when Uncle Carl married Aunt Ruth. According to Kathy, who carried resentment for years, her questions about their mother went unanswered. I suppose the withholding of knowledge of their mother was intended to protect and more quickly install their stepmother, Ruth.

Both my maternal grandparents died of a stroke. I went to see Pops in the hospital after a massive stroke from which he never recovered. My siblings and I, who saw him in that unconscious condition, regretted carrying that last image with us because he was always full of life and good humor. He died at age 82. Mom said Grammie survived her stroke for a while but was unable to speak or write. She succumbed at age 87.

*****

Unfortunately, I have very few memories of my paternal grandparents: Arthur Errett Harper (1880-1958) and Pearl Mann Harper (1880-1950). Pearl died when I was a toddler, and Arthur died when I was ten.

Grandpa Harper was a minister and exchanged pulpits occasionally with R. N. Hogan, a black minister. At these events, my whole family and some of my aunts, uncles, and cousins attended tent meetings at a black church in the Los Angeles area. I liked the outside atmosphere of the tent meetings and loved the singing. The service was happy and lively. The congregants were animated, singing and clapping.

I can remember only once that Grandpa Harper came to our house. It was after Pearl died and Grandpa had married Georgia. My baby book says they came to stay a few days with us in October 1953. I overheard my parents say that Georgia had cancer. At age five, I had no idea what that was. I remember asking Mom if we should wash her dishes and glass separately like we did when we were sick. I asked her if cancer was "catching," and she said we couldn't get it from her or her dishes. Georgia didn't seem to be suffering any symptoms, so I decided I would rather have cancer than the stomach flu.

Five years later, Grandpa Harper died. We were on the way to the funeral in our 1950 white sedan Ford when the car came to a noisy, sudden stop. It was the transmission, a major problem. Someone stopped to help us and went to call one of my uncles to pick us up so we would not miss the service.

We entered the darkened room of the mortuary, where the family members sat together. My aunts and uncles, who were always joking and happy, were crying loudly, and it all seemed like a bad dream to me. The casket was outside of the dark room where we were at the front of the main room. I was with Dad in the line of people waiting to file by the casket where Grandpa's body was on display. When we reached the casket, he held me up to see. I was repulsed at the sight of the corpse. Dad wanted me to touch his body, which he said would feel cold. I would not do it and wriggled out of his arms. When my feet touched the ground, I backed away from the casket. After that experience, I refused to attend funerals for decades.

Even as a young adult, it seemed incongruous to me that so much attention was given to a body whose spirit had already flown. The religious teachings about death support the "dust to dust" ending of the body. It was no longer needed, which is akin to a butterfly not needing its cocoon after emerging from it. I prefer the current "Celebrations of Life," during which people share their stories, often humorous, about the deceased, and they support the grieving family.

*****

When Dad was in his seventies, he started to talk more openly to me about his family history. He was born in St. Mary's, West Virginia, where his father was an evangelist and instrumental in growing a congregation of the Church of Christ. His father supplemented the family income by working in construction when he was not doing church work.

Dad was the fifth child out of seven born to his parents. He had three older brothers, an older sister, and two younger sisters. I got the impression that Dad was not close to his father, who became an itinerant preacher. He wasn't at home very often or for very long. Sometimes, he moved the entire family to locations across the country. His mother tried to feed seven children with a very sparse income, supplemented by what she and the children could earn. Dad recalled the frequent scarcity of food when his father was absent, saying that sometimes they had only flour and some bacon or lard. His mother would make biscuits and cover them with gravy.

She was a strong woman who struggled in her role as a mother and wife because of a lack of support from her husband. There could be no escape in those days, especially for an evangelist's wife. She must have resigned herself to the trap which had closed in around her. Divorce was an unthinkable option in their church and would have cut her off from her support system, the church members. Her husband returned only long enough to plant the seed of another mouth to feed, then left for an unpredictable length of time. Although I don't remember her because she died when I was two, I feel intense empathy for her, as I do for my maternal grandmother. Her die was cast, and I added her to the other resilient women in the three consecutive generations who chose to stay married despite their plight.

What prevented these women from acting on their behalf and by extension, their children's? Was it economic dependence, social and religious mores, or the few extra-familial roles considered appropriate for women? Had women's collective independence not yet evolved to the stage to allow it? Was a decision, once made, no longer pliable, despite the circumstances? I can only speculate why they remained stuck in their status quo.

Dad's father moved the family from West Virginia to Colorado Springs, Colorado, and then to California in 1921. In California, they lived in Riverside, Pasadena, and Pomona. The Depression years must have exacerbated their economic situation. I am missing most of the details about their lives in those cities, except that my uncle Paul became an evangelist, like his father, and owned a restaurant where the younger siblings worked for a while. Uncle Ken, the third son, learned printing skills and operated a printing press in Riverside. Later in life, Dad moved to Riverside and became very close with Ken and his wife, Gracie.

While researching recently to fill in some of the knowledge gaps about my father, I came across data from the 1940 census. My father lived with his mother and two younger sisters at that time. Although my grandfather was alive, Dad was listed as Head of Household in that census. That small fact fomented more mystery for me concerning my grandfather and may be part of the explanation for my father's lack of affection for his father. It may have given Dad even more desire to be the best father he possibly could.

La Habra High School

After spending eight years at Washington School, I again found myself at the bottom, subject to the mild harassment that upperclassmen (yes, male) felt was their duty to dispense. Between classes, they would line the raised sides of the wide central corridor, making clever comments to entertain and impress their buddies.

I heard one comment a few times: "Hey, your knees are dirty." The strict dress code stated that our dresses must touch the ground when we kneeled. Any administrator or teacher could ask us to go down on our knees if they doubted our skirts complied. So, I guess the sideline critiquers suggested my skirt was too short, and/or they were noticing my legs. Feigned oblivion was my usual response. I wasn't quick-thinking enough to whip back a witty reply.

One big difference in high school was our daily Physical Education period. We all bought at least two sets of the required blue shorts and snapped up white blouses. It was our responsibility to come to class with a clean, or at least clean-looking, uniform. Dressing out at the beginning of the period, hurrying in from the field, showering, and changing back into school clothes was a new experience, requiring organization and speed. I did not want to walk in late to my next class.

We played a new sport every quarter. Besides common sports like softball, basketball, track, and tennis, we were also introduced to field hockey, tumbling, folk dance, modern dance, and swimming.

When swimming was my sport for the quarter, it was winter. I tried special chamois head wraps that promised to keep my hair dry, supplemented with plastic bags under the mandatory swim cap. Nothing worked. We had to wear the school's gym-issued one-piece single-ply swimsuits, which included no enhancements or support (remember, it was cold). *Lovely*! The guys were in football practice on the other side of the chain link fence surrounding the pool. It was all quite humiliating. I stayed in the water as much as possible and then found my way to the middle of a clump of girls as we speeded for the locker room as soon as the period ended.

In my freshman year, following Mrs. Phelps' advice, I was initiated into foreign language study. Miss Varnum must be admired if only for her courage to attempt to teach a "dead language" to high schoolers. She was slight, had perfectly coifed white hair, and dressed impeccably. The declinations of Latin, which required the suffixes of nouns to change according to how they were used in a sentence, were so confusing. Reading about the Gaelic Wars was less than riveting, too. When we asked her a question about why the grammar was so difficult, she frequently insisted she wasn't around during the Gaelic Wars, but we weren't sure.

She made the class fun with an annual Toga Party. We wore homemade togas, lounged on cushions on the gym floor, and fed each other grapes and other tidbits. Even Miss Varnum wore a toga. I received a B grade in the first semester, but in the second semester, I got the hang of it and got As the rest of the two years offered.

The required frosh classes were English, Algebra I, and World History. I took Typing I, but I could never get a better grade than a B. If my accuracy improved, it would be at the cost of my speed and vice versa.

During my sophomore year, luck dealt me a sequence of classes with Speech following PE, which happened to be swimming for the first quarter. Our Speech teacher, a former Miss California, was aware of the effect her mere presence had on males. The fact that some years had passed since her reign did not deter the boys from vying to be the teacher's pet. She basked in their attention, creating a novel educational atmosphere.

I hated to be the focus of attention when I had to deliver my speech. Standing at the podium, with uncontrollably shaking knees, long, straight, wet hair, trying to read quivering notecards was torture.

I got through the class with a B, was grateful, and vowed never to take another Speech class. My other sophomore year courses were Geometry, Speech, Homemaking, Driver Education, and Health Ed, along with English, Latin, and PE.

I'm not sure why, but I didn't get into the social scene much. Daily, I tried hard for academic excellence while at school and then walked straight home to do homework. In those days, high schoolers did not use backpacks. I walked the mile to and from school, with my shoulders pulled forward by arms encircling the stack of textbooks and a binder needed for that night's homework. Then, I carried them back to school the next morning, where they were deposited in my locker until class time. After school, creative projects, like sewing my clothes or making homemade gifts, had to wait until the completion of schoolwork and chores. Work before play had been ingrained early and reinforced regularly. Besides, the hope for creative time incentivized me to finish my schoolwork.

I had not grown up with football and didn't understand it, so I had little desire to attend the games, except a Homecoming game or two. My parents had taught us that dancing was sinful, so going to dances was out of the question. Mom urged me to join the Girls Athletic Association, which practiced and competed after school, but it wasn't for me.

The social hierarchy became visible early, and I wasn't motivated to climb. "Soshes" included the most popular students, athletic stars, and a few others who somehow managed to climb to the heights by association with bonafide soshes. I had gone to school with many of the students since elementary school because La Habra was a small town with two schools: Washington School (first through eighth grade) and La Habra High School. But in high school, different circles were created. A new social order, almost caste-like, was forming around me, and I chose to remain oblivious. It just didn't interest me.

La Habra had begun to grow, and by the time I got to high school, another elementary school had been built, where some of my younger siblings attended, and another high school was in the planning stages.

I had a few trusted girlfriends. Kathy Hawes was a friend from church whom I had known for years. Her father, a doctor, and her lovely mother invited me to their home for sleepovers when we were younger and one time to vacation in Newport Beach, California. Kathy's mother carefully monitored her time in the sun and water, calling her back under the huge umbrella frequently to protect her inherited flawless skin. In retrospect, I should have heeded the warning as well, but I loved the sun and salt water. We became close friends in our younger years, although I don't remember Kathy ever visiting my house. We were still friends in high school but distanced into different circles.

Maggie Karr was my closest friend in high school. I think our friendship started in my sophomore year and lasted until we graduated and left for college. I felt very much at home with her family. There were six children, and Maggie was in the middle of the birth order. Her parents were unpretentious, friendly, and down-to-earth, not at all bothered by another kid or two joining them. Like their parents, Maggie and her siblings were outgoing and self-confident, ignoring the unspoken social rules of high school society. I liked being around Maggie; as if through osmosis, she made me feel confident.

I remember going to Doheny Beach with the Karrs. It was a unique, less frequented beach along the southern coast, just North of San Clemente. In those days, we could find sand dollars and colorful shells. Maggie and I each created collages arrayed on dark corkboards with the natural objects we collected and won awards for them at an Art Show at school.

While I was at LHHS, I knew Maggie's older brother, Dave, who was two years older than me. I admired that both he and Maggie could float among the social circles without recognizing any boundaries. He gave me a delicate opal necklace for Christmas and invited me to Disneyland for the New Year's Eve Party. I was allowed to go with him because my parents knew Maggie well and liked Dave. He was a cheerful, easygoing guy who was fun to be around. When he graduated, I don't know if he enlisted or was drafted into the army. If he enlisted, it was because he would have been drafted anyway to go to Vietnam like many of the guys had been after graduation from high school. I wrote to him and sent cookies when he was in the Army, but he did not respond. That fact puzzled and hurt Dad because he knew and liked Dave and knew I liked him.

The Vietnam War overshadowed most of my high school years and beyond. By age 18, every male had to register for the draft. There were some exceptions, including being accepted and enrolled in an institution of higher education, but even if a waiver was granted, it had no permanence. At one time, there was a lottery that determined who would be drafted; for many male students, post-graduation plans seemed futile due to the uncertainty of draft status.

The public became aware of the conditions endured by US servicemen. Apart from encountering guerrilla warfare in miserable jungle environs, our troops were not even provided the most basic hygiene products. Donations were requested, and drop-off sites were announced. I talked to hotel management persons in our area to request that they save remnants of soap from guest rooms, and I made regular collection trips for leftover items to be sent to Vietnam.

At my 20-year high school reunion, there was a memorial area set aside honoring our classmates who had lost their lives during military service. Who knows how many additional classmates suffered physical and mental wounds and/or became addicted while in Vietnam? It was difficult to accept that friends we had sat next to in classes, watched on the football field, and voted for as student government candidates were detoured from personal plans and met their demise in the jungles of Vietnam. Of course, it is the nature of war to snuff out young lives, robbing families, communities, and countries of their potential.

Probably the most memorable event of my sophomore year was walking in the main corridor between classes and hearing the announcement on the loudspeaker that President Kennedy had been shot. We students stared at each other incredulously, hoping that he would survive, but soon found out that he did not.

In my junior year, I took beginning Spanish. It was exciting to be learning the native language of some of my classmates. The grammar was less complicated than Latin and much more enjoyable to learn. Our teacher, Mr. Johnson, was not a native Spanish speaker, but he sounded as if he were. He kept us alert, pointing at individual students for quick answers, making it evident to the whole class who had or hadn't done the homework. There was an important and well-enforced rule in his classes: No English is to be spoken. On the corner of his desk was a jar, partially filled with nickels, one for each English word spoken. At the end of the year, the nickels financed a party. I felt motivated to learn Spanish under Mr. Johnson's mentoring and continued the following year for Spanish II. As a Junior, my other classes were English, US History, Biology, and Clothing (tailoring) I and II.

I discovered it was more economical to buy fabric and sew my clothes, which I could assure would fit. In the fabric store, I would first peruse huge books of patterns for one I might want to sew. Then, I looked for the pattern number and my size in the long drawers containing patterns in stock. Many times, I didn't find one for exactly what I imagined, so I bought one that I could adapt to my artsy style. I changed necklines and sleeves and added piping, buttons, and beads. The choice of fabrics was amazing! I began visualizing the finished garment and grew excited to begin the project. I became fully immersed in the creative flow, which sometimes lasted into the early morning hours, especially if I wanted to wear the outfit to school the next day. Now, I'm surprised my parents allowed me to sew in the dormitory at night while my sisters slept. I used only a tiny lamp directed at the stitching, and I don't think the intermittent hum of the sewing machine kept anyone awake. At school, I was shocked to be awarded "Best Dressed" one month. I never knew who the judges were, but I guess they noticed my outfits were unique. However, they didn't notice that they were few and methodically rotated.

Toward the end of my high school years, two-piece bathing suits came into vogue. As expected, clothing that exposed previously covered square inches of skin was considered *risqué* by some. A two-piece swimsuit was exactly what a long-torsoed young girl needed, freeing me from the constant up-down tugs on the suit fabric. I found a sewing pattern I thought would work. The shorts were fitted to the waist and covered the bum. The top was like a bra but became swimwear when made of tropical fabric. Also, sewing a two-piece made alteration easier. Later, beach shops adopted the lucrative idea of selling the pieces individually. Genius! But expensive. It was progressive in the comfort department, and the danger of indecency was nil for me because spillable tissue did not exist.

*****

Now, in 2024, a previously unearthed memory was forced to the surface after a revelation from my youngest sister, Denise. During my junior year, Mom suddenly left us to stay at her friend's house in another town. My memory didn't record any goodbyes to us kids.

I think Dad may have informed us that she wanted to get away, but he didn't provide any further information. Maybe he was embarrassed and didn't want five offspring mouths to give their version of what was going on at home to everyone. The less we knew, the less others would know. Keep it under the radar.

After a few days, I borrowed the car in the afternoon to go to where Dad knew she was staying. He must have given me verbal directions, which I had written down. I was a new driver; it was rural horse country, and I got myself hopelessly lost on the winding roads. Cell phones and GPS did not exist then. I kept wandering until I decided to give up and find my way home before it got too late.

Suddenly, a road listed in the directions appeared, and I finally found my way to the house I had never seen before. I think Mom was outside, and I didn't know where the owners were. I don't remember a hug, which would have been uncharacteristic anyway. She may have shown me around the property. My visit was surreal and uncomfortable, which added to my sense that something was seriously wrong. I was afraid to ask questions because I didn't want the answers. I must have felt the death of her dreams hanging in the somber, silent air, and I had to leave. I wanted to find my way home, cook dinner with Dad, be with my siblings, and search for normalcy. I vowed not to become a dependent woman, stay in an unhappy marriage, or have so many children.

Recently, when I was talking with Denise, she mentioned a letter she found in Mom's things after her death. It was a mystery to Denise, who was nine at the time Mom left. She must have blocked the scary memory. However, it was a puzzle piece that fit with my repressed memory of going to visit her.

In her exemplary schoolteacher cursive, Mom penned poignant words in a goodbye note to her five children, ages 16, 14, 12, 9, and 5. She called herself a miserable failure as a wife and mother, although she said she had tried her best "to make ours a loving Christian family." She would miss us, but "you can probably do a better job of having a happy home without me." At the bottom of the letter, in a different colored ink and written in shaky handwriting, was, "4/13/65 I left & went to Marion's in So Pasadena."

I'm almost sure I drove to a different friend's house in Villa Park because, at 16, I would not have driven to South Pasadena, which is much farther away, near Los Angeles. There is so much that will remain unknown, but the year coincides with my memory.

Reflecting now, I can only conjecture about what had brought Mom's self-esteem to the level of starvation. Had she undernourished it all her life, comparing herself with her younger sister who had graduated from the University of California, Berkley, married an Air Force Lieutenant, and started a family before Mom had? Did she feel sidelined because Dad was much more gregarious and a great cook? Did she feel non-essential because we older girls had been trained to cook and take on many household chores? Did she get married only to spare herself from being an old maid, as she later told us? Was it too difficult to play her role as a loving Christian wife?

All I remember is that Mom reappeared at our house, and life continued, status quo from my perspective, without an explanation. We wouldn't know how close their marriage came to the brink until after both my parents had died and Denise found Mom's letter. I would leave for college the following year and had plenty of other priorities to focus on.

After this revelation, Denise and I asked ourselves questions that monopolized our minds for days. Why did she keep the undelivered note? In her advanced age, evidenced by her shaky handwriting at the bottom of the note, she had a chance to rip it up, and none of us would have known about her desperation at that time. Did she want someone to find it? Did she call Grammie for advice while she was away from us, and was Grammie able to calm her and restore her patience? Did she find peace and regain her reason in her solitude? Did she leave more than once, going to different locations?

Around the same years, she exhibited some bizarre behavior a few times. One of us discovered her in the closed garage, in the station wagon, with the doors locked, the interior light on, and she was reading magazines. I felt a twinge of guilt, wondering if it was one of us or a subconscious team effort that pushed her to withdraw so completely. The guilt evaporated when the story spread among us kids, and it became humorous. She also slept some nights in the treehouse Dad and Tim constructed.

Since she married Dad, she forfeited her profession, suddenly became her parents' only child, and gave birth to five children, the last at the age of 42. Doing the math, she may have been on the threshold or in the throes of menopause. I overheard Laverne Sanderson tell Dad when she recognized Mom's symptoms, that there were pills that would help her. She would not have taken them; she took only vitamins and herbs.

*****

I worked my first paid job, besides housework for Ethyl Whitten and babysitting, during Christmas break when I was 16 and could get a work permit. Builders Emporium hired me to work in the Toy Department but made it clear that it would be only for the holidays. Learning the inventory of the huge variety of toys was challenging, but it was fun to help excited shoppers find just the right gifts. I felt mature having a real job, complete with dinner breaks and, of course, paychecks.

I was starting my junior year when Sheri entered LHHS as a freshman. Although we were socially distinct, we were both excited to be at high school together. Sheri had many friends and quickly climbed the social ladder, becoming a Homecoming princess during one of her years. Her friends were always pleasant to me, but we did not overlap in our social circles.

At school and home, Sheri was more daring and rebellious than me regarding the rules. At school, for example, she was discovered by the vice principal while having breakfast with her friends during class time at a nearby restaurant. A less significant sign of noncompliance, but worthy of mention for its sheer ingenuity, was winding wide elastic around her bare feet to simulate sandals, which were permitted while going barefoot was not.

Debbie Clouda, probably her best friend, invited Sheri to spend weekends in Palm Springs at her parents' condo there. Our parents did not give her permission. So, Debbie and Sheri would collude to make it happen anyway. At the agreed time, Sheri would be ready with a few clothes to run out the front door, jump in Debbie's little red compact car, and speed away. Our parents did not know her parents or have their phone number, which was the reason for not permitting her to go with Debbie for the weekend. Sheri returned safely on Sundays, and I don't remember what or if any punishment was meted out.

My parents seemed unprepared for outright defiance. Grounding would not work because the misdemeanor was sneaking away and could be successfully repeated. For other infractions, like unfinished or sloppily executed chores, Mom confiscated Sher's curlers, makeup, and other daily necessities. An arbitrary monetary retribution was required for their return. Making her pay from hard-earned babysitting money seemed irrelevant to the infraction but may have proved a deterrent.

We, siblings, remember with embarrassment when Dad dashed from our house in his boxers to meet and chase away a guy who came looking for Sheri one night. She had always been his favorite and had become the most rebellious. I had not paved the way or accustomed my parents to disobedience. By the time my three younger siblings hit high school, they attended the new Sonora High, and I had left home. There probably were subsequent rebellions, major and minor; I just wasn't around to witness them.

The most rebellious thing I remember doing while living at home was writing my parents a letter, critiquing their disciplinary action, with which I did not agree. It was carefully written, complete with examples from US history, to bolster my argument. I don't remember the issue that got me so riled, but neither of my parents ever mentioned my letter placed under one of their pillows. I guess my grievance was not up for discussion. Oh, and I don't deny running from the house to jump on the motorcycle of a friend I met at Pepperdine. But that was when I was older after I came home from Pepperdine.

*****

By this time, although my parents carefully kept up the veneer of marriage, we felt the effects of the Cold War. They didn't yell or argue, that I remember, but just lived separately under the same roof. Sarcastic, barely audible remarks were mumbled more frequently. Mom refused to attend the Edison Christmas Party with Dad. She did not accept the Evening in Paris perfume Dad gave her for Christmas. Maintaining a unified effort concerning our discipline required collaboration. The discipline was eroding along with the collaboration.

However, an exception to that laxity of discipline created a lasting memory for Sheri and me. I was a senior, and Sheri was a sophomore. A friend from church and his friend invited Sheri and me to the Junior-Senior Prom. We would all go together. This would be my first and last chance to attend the Prom in high school, and I did not want to miss the experience. Some of Sheri's friends also had the good fortune to be invited by older classmen.

Before asking our parents for permission, we planned all the details to make them feel comfortable consenting. We would both sew our formal, floor-length dresses, buy our elbow-length gloves, and pay to have our hair styled professionally. We would not ask them to pay for anything. Also, our parents knew the parents of the boy who asked Sheri for many years because they attended the Whittier Church of Christ. We thought we had covered all the possible contentious points.

But incredibly, their sticking point was that we would dance. I guess I should have foreseen that impediment because I was not supposed to square dance in elementary school (Mom pinned a note on my dress stating as much) and was given an unquestionable "no" when I wanted to learn ballet. Dad was a deacon in the church where dancing was considered sinful and was the doorway to petting and sex. These were their worn-out words, words the church had preached to us for years, antiquated words we did not believe.

Sheri and I had allied over the years when necessary and were not so easily deterred. She used her well-honed debating skills that she practiced regularly with Mom, and I interjected repeatedly, trying to deflate the parental arguments. As the hours passed midnight while the younger siblings slept, we tried to convince them that the event was an undeniable rite of passage from which we would return unscathed. Yet, they were still denying us the experience! Exhausted, we began crying out of sheer frustration that we had parents who would not accept our logical arguments and instead stubbornly stuck to their incredibly weird beliefs.

They must have silently signaled surrender to each other because they finally relented, with conditions including a non-negotiable curfew and a promise not to dance. So, Sheri and I went to the fabric store to choose patterns and fancy fabrics worthy of prom dresses. We bought long white gloves and started sewing, working around school schedules, doing homework, and doing housework. Most importantly, we could accept our invitations.

The evening of the event was a series of novel experiences for me. Our dates brought corsages for our wrists, and they wore coordinating lapel buds. I didn't know my date very well, so the canned conversation was punctuated by uncomfortable silences. The formal dancing was stiff and stressful as I tried not to call attention to my complete ignorance of anything close to dancing. Of course, some students had been in cotillion classes since they were young. I just wanted to be invisible and avoid unforgivable *faux pas*.

As expected, our parents' fears proved completely baseless in the well-chaperoned, bland atmosphere. We attended The Prom, with pictures as proof, complied with the mandated curfew, and could say we chalked up the experience.

*****

In my history, civics, and economics classes, term papers were required. We were supposed to choose a controversial topic, research it, and present the contrasting views.

My parents believed it was worth the drive to take me to the John Birch Library in Buena Park, although I had no idea why. Now I know the John Birch Society was the most prominent right-wing political fringe group at that time. Some of the group's issues were withdrawing the US from the United Nations, exposing "Communists," and wanting to prevent all US-Soviet cooperation.

It was my first term paper. Believing I was demonstrating excellence in academia, I spent hours in the library until a parent picked me up. I was intent on getting the order, arguments, and footnotes right. When the teacher returned my paper, it was a morale-deflating experience. She noted that it would have been all right to include sources from the John Birch Library if I wanted to, but those views had to be balanced with more objective sources. After investing so much effort, I was not satisfied with my grade, and I told my parents not to bother taking me to that library again. Without a thought, I had consented to my parents' choice of library. It was a lesson in critical thinking, which I should have already mastered.

I improved my term paper grades by conducting actual research, but I can't say the dread of the process diminished. It was a multi-step exercise in drudgery. When the last one of about eight was due in my senior year, I decided not to write one. I maintained my usual discipline in other coursework, mostly immune from "senioritis," but I could not rally any desire to complete one more drudgery paper. The efficacy of the learning tool had peaked and plummeted for me. I steeled myself for the consequences.

Discreetly the teacher privately reminded me that he had not received my paper as the deadline neared. I told him I would not be writing the last one, that too many term papers were required, and that I could find zero enthusiasm for producing another one. I think he was kind of shocked but did not try to persuade me to complete the assignment.

I had been on course to graduate with the California Scholarship Federation (CSF) medallion around my neck and had attended the Top One Hundred Banquet that honored the cream of our senior class of 666 students. Yet, I could not discipline myself even to begin the uninspiring labor of the last term paper. As it turned out, the skipped term paper somehow did not affect my Civics grade, and I ended the quarter with straight As. I was pleasantly surprised to learn on graduation night that I still made CSF when a CSF medallion was slipped over my head.

*****

When my seasonal job ended at Builders Emporium, I applied at Knott's Berry Farm for weekends and holiday work. They hired me at the Chicken dinner restaurant to bus tables and assist the waitresses. Mrs. Knott required the restaurant staff to wear calico dresses, ruffled aprons, hairnets, and bright red lipstick. I sewed simple dresses with the old-west look and aprons to match, braided my long hair down my back, and covered it with the finest netting I could find. Lipstick was a problem. I smiled a lot and always had lipstick on my teeth when I tried to comply with that rule. I kept lipstick in my apron pocket when I wasn't compliant.

Mrs. Knott sat on a high stool, surveying her domain, at the end of the lengthy, narrow river of hot oil where the chicken traveled at just the perfect speed and temperature to its destination and then on to the customers' tables. Once, she called me to her stool so she could verify my braid was covered. Another time, she caught me without lipstick, and I quickly applied the screaming red stuff to my lips. She was quality assurance personified! Maybe she thought, as owner, she could never show a friendly or grateful demeanor. I wondered if she even had those qualities. There were rumors she had been sighted at the Pussy Cat Theatre. Who knows?

As in all my previous jobs, I followed my intuition, endeavoring to please the one who paid me. In addition to my hourly wage of $1.60, the waitresses in the section to which I was assigned paid the bussers an arbitrary tip at the end of the shift. I quickly learned which ones would compensate me well for the extras I did. It was a silent agreement that an efficient team raises customer satisfaction, which should translate to more generous customer tips, and we could turn more tables. Occasionally, customers would "stiff" us, meaning they would tip nothing. Although it was maddening, it wasn't often.

Knott's Berry Farm Chicken Dinner Restaurant was continually busy and had a perpetual line of hungry people outside the building. There was a half-serious mandate from the waitresses: If a customer puts his fork down, take the plate. Head 'em up; move 'em out. I had nightmares in which I was serving an extended family who sat at a length of innumerable tables slid together to accommodate them, and there were multiple highchairs interspersed. The babies strew colorful food in all directions, and it had to be cleaned up as if the disaster had never happened before the next group of diners inherited the tables. But the money was good for restaurant work, so I persevered. After graduating high school and being promoted to a waitress, it would finance two years at an expensive private college.

As my senior year wrapped up, I was characteristically oblivious to the speculation about whom my classmates would vote as Most Likely to Succeed, Most Talented, Best Personality, Friendliest, Biggest Flirts, Funniest, Most Spirited, Most Athletic, and Most Attractive. I don't even remember voting if I did. So, I was surprised when someone on the Highlander Yearbook staff approached me to schedule the picture for Quietist Girl with Quietist Guy. I tried to deny the designation; I could name others more deserving of the descriptor, but declining was not an option. Pictures were to be taken by or on classic cars on a specific date. A certifiably silent guy and I were posed on the hood of an old station wagon, instead of a woody Model T, T-bird, or even a VW which were some of the cool cars used. It was humiliating, and the photo evidenced our pain as we sat, victims of excess and uncool recognition! We focused our heads in opposite directions and prayed for deliverance. In my yearbook, Maggie wrote, "It isn't true. You aren't quiet at all."

By the time graduation was approaching, I had been accepted to Pepperdine University and was ready for the next phase of my education. Dorm life, living with girls other than my siblings, sounded exciting! And I was overdue for a little more independence.

Religious Inculcation

Our family life revolved around religion from the start. Mom and Dad met at a Church of Christ, a denomination similar to Baptist, although members believed their church was distinct from all others and acknowledged no kinship to Baptist churches. Many members believed it was the only source of truth. I think my family qualified for that group.

My baby book says I went with my parents to church after my first couple of rough months. Dad's family members were all active members of the Church of Christ, except my uncles, Ken and Harry, two of Dad's older brothers who 'saw the light' and separated from the constrictions of their upbringing. My paternal grandfather was an evangelist, and Uncle Paul, Dad's eldest brother, followed in the same vocation.

My first memories of church were in La Habra, where we lived close enough to walk the few blocks to church. Sometimes, a preacher from Texas or another Bible-belt state would be brought West to enlighten us. That was the first time I remember hearing a thick Southern accent, which sounded strange. Occasionally, there would be a missionary couple who came to show slides of their ministry in another country and solicit donations. Mom was susceptible to these presentations. Later, Dad told me he gave his paycheck to her, and she dispersed it, being extraordinarily generous to missions. Many Sundays, she had us skip breakfast (not an individual choice), explaining that she would send a dollar for every skipped meal to missionaries. In retrospect, Dad regretted giving her that financial freedom, never expecting her to divert so much of his wages away from our family, in addition to the regular weekly contribution to the church.

The two Sunday services were just the start of the week's religious activities. On Tuesday nights, after homework and dinner, we visited different families' houses for Bible study and dessert. Participating families rotated hosting in their homes. Then, it was back to church on Wednesday evenings for mid-week services.

The La Habra church may have proved slightly too conservative, even for my parents. I remember sermons, whether delivered by the local preacher or an imported one, I don't remember. Topics were the evils of women wearing pants (not to mention shorts) and the evils of dancing and going to see movies. I remember one about insurance: purchasers demonstrated their lack of faith in God to keep them from all harm. The Churches of Christ did not have instrumental music and fiercely defended that stance by interpreting scripture narrowly and literally.

After a few years, my parents decided to try the Church of Christ in Whittier, a neighboring town. The congregation there had many more members than in La Habra, and I was happy there were lots of children of all ages. The Whittier church was farther away, so we attended the two services on Sunday, but we may have dropped the mid-week meeting.

On Sunday morning, various age-appropriate Bible classes were followed by a sermon that all ages attended. Our family often sat in the balcony section, where my younger siblings would disrupt fewer worshippers until they learned to be silent.

Of course, we always wore dresses, which were a bit fancier than our school dresses. We had poofy petticoats, sometimes more than one, to make the skirts stand out more. I constructed a homemade hoop skirt out of straightened coat hangers and fabric, but sitting down was a maneuver that required *finesse* to avoid a Marilyn Monroe show. Sunday was the day we could wear slip-on shoes, and on Easter, we could even paint our fingernails. Early Sunday, Dad polished the younger kids' white, high-top shoes, putting them on newspapers to dry in time for church, while the rest of us rotated through showers in our only bathroom. The younger kids took baths Saturday night to

71

simplify the Sunday morning preparations. We older ones helped Mom with the younger ones, dressing and styling their hair.

Meanwhile, Dad began to assemble the Sunday dinner, knowing we would all be hungry when we got home from church. A chicken or a roast with vegetables was often seasoned and put in the oven for baking low and slow. Returning from church, walking into the house, and inhaling the delicious aromas made us change clothes quickly and wash to eat. After the big meal, the younger children napped while the rest of us read or did quiet activities until it was time to redress and return to church.

Occasionally, on Sunday afternoons, the whole family went to Rancho Los Amigos Los Angeles County Hospital to visit some of the patients who did not have family in the area. I remember one, Nettie Pugh, a diminutive, elderly patient who was bedridden. She didn't talk or hear much, but her smile communicated. We tried to brighten the patients' day by singing songs, mostly hymns. Once, we brought a couple of Beatrice's kittens for patients to hold and pet.

Sunday evenings, Dad drove us all back for the night service. When we got home, we had a light supper – maybe soup, grilled cheese sandwiches, avocado on toast, or root beer floats, which were a special treat because we did not usually drink carbonated drinks.

Before anyone began eating at mealtime, someone in our family said the prayer, thanking God for the food we were about to eat, thanking Him for our health, and voicing any other pertinent requests. Dad asked for volunteers to say the prayer, or he made an assignment. Everyone had a turn, and it became a perfunctory expression. Even the youngest at the table soon learned that prayer was the prerequisite to picking up a utensil and enjoying the meal.

In the mornings, one of us read a short devotional message in addition to the prayer. It usually came from a pocket-sized book that had brief writings based on a Bible verse for each day. Comments about the writing were rare because we had limited time to eat a light breakfast, get ready for school, and leave in time to walk to school. The devotional was more a ritual than a time to ponder.

If my parents heard of Church of Christ events in the greater Los Angeles area via Dad's family or Pepperdine College, they would take us to them even if they were held on weeknights and we had to go to school the next morning. We were instructed to finish our homework and rest to prepare for being out late on a school night. The younger kids had mandatory naps.

One time, we went to a church-sponsored Youth Meeting where Pat Boone gave the message. The event was also a book promotion and signing event for him. We waited in line until it was our turn to buy his book and have it personally signed. Pat Boone was a pop, country, and gospel singer in the 1950s and early 1960s who also appeared in over a dozen Hollywood films. Dad felt a kinship with him because he also had many daughters.

We also attended Bible Encampments at Camp Tanda in Big Bear, California, every summer. I think the greater Los Angeles Churches of Christ may have managed to buy Tanda. In any case, a Board was created to run it, and the camp principles seemed identical to those at church. Apart from the summer camps our family attended, with designated weeks for Family Camp and Youth Camp, church youth groups could reserve weekends for winter snow camp. These events helped maintain a year-round revenue stream (or trickle?) for Camp Tanda.

Our family participated in ongoing fundraising schemes for camp coffers: Rummage sales and newspaper collection come to mind. We collected newspapers from our neighbors in a wagon. The collection was ironic because our family did not subscribe to a newspaper, but that was not the end of our labor. One of our chores involved prepping the newspapers for recycling and sale. We opened each newspaper in its middle and stacked the full sheets flat, carefully keeping corners and edges straight until they reached a height of four inches, then rolled and tied them into a large, heavy roll. We did the stacking, and Dad tied the rolls. These were sold by the pound, and the money was donated to Camp Tanda.

My parents were involved with the survival of the camp, seemingly at the core group level. One year, Dad was President of the Board. One of his duties was to open the camp on weekends for winter groups, and he cooked for everyone. It didn't get much better for Dad, even if it involved lots of time, driving, and work. Many times, he would take me with him for the weekend. Maybe Sheri came, too, when she was old enough. It was fun to get used to snow and cold and have some time away from the entire clan. On Sunday, after the campers left, we closed and secured the camp, assuring it would be ready for the next group.

When we were in our teens, Sheri and I stayed as counselors for Kids Camp following Family Camp in the summer after our parents and younger siblings went home. We enjoyed camp traditions, learned to teach arts and crafts, adhered strictly to camp rules, developed responsibility, and experienced more independence than we had ever known.

There, I met my first boyfriend, who was also a counselor and happened to be a year younger than me. Any signs of interest must be clandestine, and they were probably demonstrated most by my racing heart and difficulty sleeping. Camp rules dictated no handholding unless a stick was between the hands. One of the last activities of the week was riding the Snow Summit ski lift, an activity that kept girls wondering all week if a boy would invite them. He asked me, and we rode the ski lift side by side. On Saturday, we went home, and I never saw him again.

Religion was inextricably woven into our lives from birth. My parents cultivated friendships with people at church, and we naturally did the same. Of course, we developed friendships at school, as well. I never understood my parents' reasoning when they would not allow me to visit my Jewish and Catholic friends' churches when they invited me. However, my parents said I should invite them to come with us. I told my friends that my parents would not allow me to attend their churches, but I did not invite them to come with me. It seemed so blatantly hypocritical!

One Mother's Day Sunday will always stick in my memory. I was 15, and most of my church friends had already been baptized. I knew I was overdue, but routinely, with only a modicum of guilt, I passed up the weekly invite during the special hymn. The rest of the week, no thoughts of baptism entered my mind. I could have elected to be baptized at Camp Tanda in the unheated pool, which I considered but never found the courage to do.

My problem was that public attention was extremely uncomfortable. I would have to "come forward" by tripping over the people in our row, finally reaching the aisle, and then walking with all eyes on me to the front where the minister was standing. If I chose to be baptized, the day would have to be planned, strategically sitting on the isle to reach the front before the verses of the song ran out, or it would be even worse to finish the walk alone in silence.

On this Mother's Day Sunday, I sat beside Dad in the middle of a pew mid-church. They were singing the invitation song, *"Just as I am."* The service would soon be over. My stomach was growling because we didn't usually have breakfast on Sundays. My mind wandered to the roast Dad had put in the oven early that morning. I teased my hunger by summoning the aroma of juices from the marbled meat, releasing around and saturating potatoes, carrots, and onion wedges.

Suddenly, Dad's elbow was in my ribs as he leaned over, his English Leather cologne overpowering my enjoyment of the smell of the roast.

He whispered loudly, "Why don't you be baptized today? Mom would be happy."

Like a marionette, my legs straightened, and my feet moved involuntarily, hurriedly brushing churchgoers' knees, stumbling over purses and diaper bags to the aisle, where I turned left to make the long trek toward the front of the church. The multitude of eyes from both sides of the aisle affixed themselves to me, and I wanted to evaporate and become invisible. When I reached the front bench and stood in front of the preacher, a few lady members swarmed me, and I felt unwelcome arms around my shoulders and waist as I answered the preacher's question.

"Yes, I wanted to give my life to Christ and be baptized."

The baptismal pool sat high, framed and inset in the wall behind the pulpits and huge pots of tall salmon-colored gladiolas. What remains of the memory is mercifully numbed. I remember undressing and putting on something like a hospital gown and a shower cap, walking up a few steps, then down into the water where the minister – in high boots, I assume – was waiting. With one hand at the back of my neck and the other smothering my nose and mouth with a cotton cloth, he dunked me backward, making sure to submerge me completely. Then, he brought me up, shower cap askew, to be viewed by the whole congregation.

Did God require a personal commitment to be so painfully public? I dried myself, dressed, combed my long, wet hair with the communal comb, and attempted to prepare myself for the dreaded onslaught of members who would congratulate me.

My parents and the congregants wore smiles, although their lunch plans were delayed by what they thought was my decision, and some were desperately trying to hold their cigarette addiction at bay. I hoped I looked happy too. I was just glad the ordeal had ended. That expectation was behind me.

Recently, my sister Denise told me she, too, waited for a spiritual urge to be baptized, which she was told would be unmistakable. It never manifested. Yet, until her death, Mom felt it necessary to remind her repeatedly that she was unbaptized. Again, I question why personal spirituality must be verified by public demonstration.

*****

Just as religious services brought my parents together, I think it may have been the life-encompassing church activities with friends and family that kept them together for 32 years. Other than their religious beliefs, there seemed to be a lack of commonality in interests because their personalities were almost opposites.

Dad was gregarious, loved cooking and social events, and found humor in abundance, a quality that probably made the rough times more bearable for him. Mom was introverted, for whom reading was a passion, although time to indulge it was a luxury. She enjoyed being alone (yet she said she wanted six children!) and was a little slower to "get" humor.

During my childhood, I never saw either of my parents or my grandparents drink anything alcoholic. Mom said alcohol had never touched her lips. We had no doubts that was true; she wouldn't even drink coffee. I hope Dad enjoyed some beer while in Germany. But, nestled among the cache of "on-sale" canned vegetables on shelves in the garage, a bottle of "cooking wine" was reportedly seen after I left for college. Much later, when we were all adults, Dad would have a glass of wine with us. No one drank too much, and we were happy that he joined us.

Both our parents unquestionably valued family as a sacred institution. They endured many years of marital cold war before either could consider divorce. When other parents divorced, my parents used the term "broken home" for that family. The children of the terminated marriage were "from a broken home," as if that act by their parents produced a stigma, predicting emotional distress and limited success.

Years later, after Grammie's death, Mom received the combined inheritance from her and Pops, who had predeceased Grammie. Mom finally had financial independence and told some of us kids about her intention to divorce Dad. We were unsurprised and unanimously agreed that they should have separated years earlier. Mom said she wanted to wait until we were all old enough to be on our own. We refuted her defense, citing the dangers of modeling an unloving, dysfunctional marriage to us for many years.

She was not seeking our blessing at that point; she merely stated her plans that would soon become a reality. We learned that communication between my parents – sparse and superficial for years – must have degenerated to non-existent. Dad had to find out about Mom's plans for the rest of their lives when he answered the doorbell and was served divorce papers.

He was devastated, completely caught off-guard. He told me later that he thought they might travel after we were out of the house. Maybe denial protected him from the unthinkable and closed his eyes to the reality of what their relationship had become.

I believe both of our parents tried to reach the limits of their capabilities, aided by their spirituality, to be an honorable family and raise honest, God-fearing children. If we were sheltered and our experiences curtailed, that was done with the best intentions so that we would be immune to most of the sins that could afflict us.

Expectations

For my parents, attendance at Pepperdine College represented an insurance policy that Christian professors would enlighten their eldest daughter, that she would associate with fine Christian students, one of whom she would almost certainly marry. Pepperdine was a private school my mother attended, and we children were raised with the idea that we would also attend. Mom had taken us to Pepperdine's annual religious lectureship, which took place one week each summer. We stayed in the dorms, ate in the dining hall, and attended Bible classes. It was a lot like a church camp but held on a college campus.

Pepperdine College, founded by a Christian businessman named George Pepperdine in 1937, was in South-Central Los Angeles, surrounded by an economically depressed, undesirable neighborhood when I attended. However, college was expensive, and kids from families who could afford it attended. The new campus in Malibu, CA, was not opened until 1972.

When I graduated high school in 1966, and it was time for me to go to college, the decision had already been made for me. I didn't even consider other colleges or universities. My upbringing had afforded me limited latitude for thought or action; I had not spread my wings and had made few decisions or mistakes. I usually took the path of least resistance, compliance. Almost inconceivably, my coursework and a major were not discussed, nor was how I might utilize my college education after graduation.

I received a $300 per trimester scholarship – tuition was $35 per unit in 1966 – and an opportunity for work-study. I accepted work in the library, hand lettering labels on refurbished books, reshelving, etc. The relabeling was quasi-creative, and I liked it. These financial aid concessions helped, but I had to pay for the room, board, books, and other expenses. Of course, I took a full load of academic units. I worked non-stop at Knott's Berry Farm during the third trimester when I was not in school. Then, I had to hand over all my earnings to begin another year, bracing for an increase in cost each year.

On Pepperdine's campus, some rules were considered prudish and overreaching, even then. Women could not wear pants except on Saturdays before noon. We had to be checked into the dorms by 10:30 p.m. every night. (I don't remember if the men's dorms had that rule.) If a female student accepted a date with a male student, he would have to come to the Women's Dorm to pick her up. An announcement, "Man in the Lobby," would be piped to the female student's room. Going to "chapel" on Thursdays was mandatory for all students, and roll was taken.

In my first year, I was assigned to the older dorms where I stayed with my family during lectureships when I was younger. Two dorm rooms had a bathroom between them and were shared by four students. My assigned roommate was nice enough, but she had a boyfriend and was hardly in the room except at night. Her absence allowed me to practice my Spanish lessons aloud, trying to gain speed and an improved accent. It might have helped. At least I never got caught talking to myself in Spanish.

My cousin, Kathy, was a year ahead of me at Pepperdine and had the privilege of living in the new dorms, which were suites. There were four double-occupancy rooms configured around a large bathroom and a sitting area. I spent much of my time in her suite. I especially liked her roommate, Linda, and got to know all of her suitemates, becoming almost one of them.

Linda was a diminutive, barely over five feet sociology major who loved gymnastics and was blind. When she was born, forceps were used to facilitate a difficult delivery. The forceps damaged both eyes, causing total blindness from birth. I'm not aware of the circumstances, but her mother decided to institutionalize Linda at Perkins School for the Blind in Watertown, Massachusetts. She experienced a complete, well-rounded education there, living and studying with students with visual impairments. She was taught to read and write Braille and was also proficient in using a typewriter. Life skills like cooking, physical education, including gymnastics, and how to dress aesthetically were also taught. With the assistance of sighted instructors, she memorized the colors of her clothing items and which pieces could be paired. She was taught to distinguish individual voice qualities to identify people. Perkins provided not only instructions but became her family all her life until she was accepted into Pepperdine.

When I met her, Linda had completed one year at Pepperdine and had integrated well. Textbooks on tape or in Braille were sometimes available. The Braille books were enormous, spreading across her tanned, muscular thighs. She read with her head up and looked straight ahead while both agile hands skimmed across the oversized pages. If the assigned textbooks could not be found on tape or in Braille, the State of California would pay a reader a nominal amount per hour to read her textbooks aloud to her. Among other subjects, I read Statistics and Logic textbooks to her, vowing never to take those courses.

She had a white cane that stayed in the back of her closet; she preferred to memorize the routes to her classes each trimester. Lightly touching the back of her hand to one of our arms, she walked beside us and learned an unfamiliar route. It took her only a couple of times to mentally program it, including stairs.

There are ample stories about Linda, but I will choose just a couple to describe her personality. She was mischievous, with frequent evidence of a well-developed sense of humor. In the central bathroom of our suite, she sometimes stood on one toilet seat to "look" over into the adjacent stall when it was occupied. Even though she couldn't see, it was disconcerting. She could hear better than an animal, so we could never sneak up on her without her calling us out.

One day, we planned a little irresistible revenge. She was showering in one of the enclosed areas, which included a bench in the dry part just inside the door, where she had methodically placed a

81

towel and her clothing. With the shower water on, her hearing was dulled. When she turned the water off, she touched only a fairly large palm frond we had strategically substituted for her things.

We all talked about various students, especially male students, whom we found interesting around campus. Linda mentioned a guy with increasing frequency, who was kind to her and had a good sense of humor. As we heard more about him, it sounded like there might be a mutual spark to be fanned. One day, she recognized his voice as we passed and introduced him to us. He seemed to fit her description, and we could see how she would be attracted. We silently asked ourselves: Does Linda know he's black? We didn't mention that fact, and I internalized the lesson.

The suitemates were an eclectic group of young women who accepted each other and learned from the diversity of the group. There was May, a Chinese student from Hong Kong. Her refinement and intelligence were at the high end of any range, but she related to us all admirably, sometimes shocking us with explicit humorous tidbits. She was to graduate that year, and her parents had planned a huge wedding for her. We were all invited and made to feel welcome.

Rozalyn (Roz), a Jewish girl, became very close with Kathy, Linda, and me during my first year. Linda had pierced ears and earrings from when she was quite young; Kathy, Roz, and I had always wanted to pierce our ears but knew our parents would say no. Now, we could make that jewelry decision for ourselves. We bought small gold stud earrings, following individual tastes, and went back to the dorm to pierce each others' lobes. Our tools were a strong sewing needle, alcohol, a cork, and ice for numbing. We had more difficulty with the thicker lobes, but mine were small and thin. One of my holes was not dead center, but no one has seemed to notice in the past 56 years. We nursed our punctures with daily alcohol, Vaseline, and numerous earring rotations. All was well, and we notched a little more independence.

Roz had a Jewish boyfriend named Murray, who had a friend named Sergio (Serge) Ortiz, who was originally from Nicaragua. Both Murray and Serge were excellent photographers. Serge showed an interest in Kathy, and they agreed to go out with Roz and Murray. Kathy and Serge's relationship was flirty, witty, and teasing, never seeming too serious. Kathy had also learned some Spanish in high school, and we bantered some with Serge. We became a tight tangle of friends.

Martha was an outgoing, easy-to-know, Black suitemate. Everyone in the suite was included in whatever mundane activity any of us was doing. On sunny days, some of us put on swimsuits to go up to the penthouse roof to work on our tans while we studied. Martha always declined, saying she disliked being in the sun. Now, considering my long history of skin cancer, I should have stayed in the dorm with Martha.

Susie had a double-occupancy room to herself. I don't remember if an explanation was given. She seemed to prefer solitude but occasionally joined in activities and conversations with the rest of us. She was obese, with the body type of Mama Cass. There were two more suitemates, whom I can't remember in detail.

*****

With the backdrop of Pepperdine rules, it is difficult to explain how I found myself in Baja California, one weekend in the company of some students in my Design class. I've always wondered if someone dared one of the guys to invite me and why I dared to accept. There was one girl on the trip who had a hard time even being civil to me and three guys. I realized on the way down that marijuana was a huge part of their lives, obscuring everything else. They were not an articulate group, and I felt like the complete outsider that I was. When we arrived at a deserted beach, they fanned out individually across the sand and near the water, each in a private world. I had no interest in trying their stuff. It was a long couple of days for me. There were no bathrooms or even porta potties. I don't remember what we had to eat,

83

but it wasn't much. The guy who invited me tried to share my sleeping bag but was fiercely denied.

The trip was a nightmare, start to finish, culminating with a problem at the US border upon reentry. The border guards, who must have felt sure they could find an illegal stash, motioned the car off to the side for detailed inspection. We got out of the car, watched, and waited while they tore up the inside flooring. Then, they looked at every nook of the old vehicle. The encroaching twilight brought me multiple fears. I felt sick with self-incrimination. If they found something, would I be implicated by association? Even if they couldn't find anything and finally released us, could we make it back to Pepperdine before 10:30 p.m.? My parents would be alerted if I were found missing from the dorm at 10:30.

The border guards finally gave up the search. I never knew if there was any stash left or where they might have hidden it. I was just praying to make it back to school on time and promising all kinds of penance. I did make it to the dorm before 10:30, and the story was left untold until now. Lessons learned!

Although the Pepperdine cafeteria offered edible food, we rarely ate three meals a day there. Kathy, Linda, and I walked to Ralph's grocery store a few blocks from campus to buy snacks like crackers, peanut butter, and fruit to supplement. As we walked, we were taunted by black girls sitting on their porches yelling, "Hey Whitey!" repeatedly. I had never encountered that kind of mockery, but we were on their turf. We soon learned they were harmless and ignored them.

*****

At the end of my first two trimesters, Kathy and I were accepted to work as waitresses at Knott's Berry Farm Chicken Dinner Restaurant, where I started as a busgirl in high school and worked the summer before entering Pepperdine. My Uncle Carl, Kathy's father, towed the family's 18-foot trailer to an RV park near Knott's Berry Farm, and his mother, Grandma Shaner, lent us her "Green Hornet" bulbous car for transportation. Whatever model it was, the lines and uncool color made it almost cute. We were grateful to have wheels to get to work.

The RV Park was adequate for our needs. It had a central bathroom, a shower facility, and a laundromat, which was essential because the trailer had only a small toilet room, a full-sized bed, a compact kitchen, and a dining table with facing seats. Our shower bags stayed packed and ready to take to the bathhouse daily. We had to pay our space rent, which included water and electricity, and order and pay for propane before it ran out.

We settled in, bought food, and cooked sometimes. We even added a pet, a small rabbit that we named Mayo. Because we were still minors and completely uninitiated by alcohol, Kathy approached one of the waitresses at Knott's to see if she would buy a bottle for us. She was happy to do us a favor.

We decided a batch of beef stew sounded good, and we started to experiment with our bottle as we cooked, mixing it with Diet Coke. The booze may have been bourbon. I had some but didn't like the taste much. Kathy liked it better than I did and served herself repeatedly. That night, she became very sick and stuck close to the trailer toilet. Not being able to tolerate the sounds and sights of vomiting, I told her I would be in the bathhouse. It became a joke, full of truth about me and sickness involving upchuck: If you need me, I'll be in the bathhouse.

Kathy also furthered my education by introducing me to cigarettes. I don't think she smoked much, but she had bought a pack to teach me. Her family attended church and would be considered conservative, but she had somehow acquired much more worldliness than I had. We were at the beach, where I tried my first cigarette. After a few inhalations, I felt uncomfortably lightheaded and feared that it might progress to nausea. I decided smoking wasn't for me.

Now, we were waitresses who worked as a team, probably the youngest. We had bussers to help us, and we tried to be fair and generous with them. We had to declare our tips on a form and sign it monthly. The first time we did this, we were around a table with other waitresses filling out their declarations. Unprepared for this requirement, Kathy and I were trying to remember what we had approximately received each day to come up with an average. One of the older waitresses quickly and firmly straightened us out. No! We should never report the real amount, just a small percentage. We learned we would be taxed on whatever we reported. So, we told them the approximate actual amount, and they instructed us concerning the amount to report to be in the same ballpark with all of them. We worked straight through from April to August. Most of our earnings were to pay tuition and all the other Pepperdine expenses.

Serge came to visit our trailer periodically. A few weeks before we were to start back to classes, Serge had an idea. His proposal was a well-deserved break for the three of us before classes resumed. He had good friends in Mazatlán, México, where he would stay, and Kathy and I would stay at a nearby motel. The friend's family was excited we were coming and wanted us to have all our meals with them.

Kathy and I each told our families about our planned adventure, with the omission of the fact that Serge would accompany us. We would take the bus from downtown Los Angeles to Mazatlán. We joked that we would carry our umbrellas for protection. Neither family voiced concern nor tried to dissuade us. I think the perception of danger was different then. Female high school grads took trips to Europe, traveling on Eurail and staying in hostels. My sister, Trish, went with her friend Karen Fink to Europe. The world must have been less dangerous then, or we perceived it so.

Our trip to Mazatlán took more than 24 hours. The bus made numerous stops for us to stretch and buy food, return in a few minutes, sit in our seats, and count down the hours to arrival. Fortunately, the bus had a restroom. We tried to sleep but could only doze between the stops and passengers brushing by us.

Finally, we arrived! Serge's friends met us, helped us check into the hotel, and said they expected us back to eat with them soon. The simple meals mostly consisted of various kinds of seafood, deliciously prepared. We swam and sunned, walked into town, and walked on the wharf during the daytime. In the evenings, we went back to the beach, where friends gathered with guitars to play, sing, and drink beer. With each interaction, our ability to use the Spanish we had learned improved.

I think it was on the last day of our stay that Kathy started feeling the repercussions of a change of food and drink, commonly called Moctezuma's Revenge. Then, Serge followed with the same symptoms. For some reason, I continued to feel fine. They could not eat much on the long bus ride back to Los Angeles. I remember they asked for some warm tortillas a couple of times when I got off at the stops *en route*. But, overall, the trip was just what we needed after working hard and before beginning classes again.

Much later, I found out what happened with Serge after he graduated from Pepperdine. He was hired by the Los Angeles Times as a photojournalist. On assignment in Vietnam, he was wounded in the leg and could no longer perform his duties. Another casualty of war, and it was noncombat.

*****

About this time, when I was to start my sophomore year, Kathy suddenly decided to leave Pepperdine after two years to attend a less expensive college closer to her family's home. Although I would miss her, I completely understood how attending Pepperdine created a financial burden that increasingly got heavier. I applied to take her place in the suite and be Linda's roommate. It was granted!

While enrolled at Pepperdine, I took classes that interested me: Spanish, Design, General Psychology, and Volleyball, for example. I completed the required English and History courses for the first two years and aced the required religion classes, having spent a disproportionate amount of my waking hours in church and religious activities until this time in my life. My Grade Point Average was excellent, but I did not have a plan.

I had attended Pepperdine for almost two years when I became discontented due to my lack of goals. My concerns about the cost of my education might have been lessened if I had clear goals and a passion to pursue them. However, I had no idea how to transform my interests and talents into goals. Because I was self-supporting and struggling to pay for my education, I felt free to change my circumstances. Although I still did not have a plan for alternative progress, the seed of discontent was sprouting.

(Decades later, Trish's youngest son was accepted to Pepperdine, but he and his parents declined the offer. To my knowledge, no one else except Sher's youngest son wanted to attend Pepperdine. He was accepted, and Mom paid his full tuition to attend in 1997.)

VISTA

On a bulletin board at Pepperdine, I saw a flyer wanting recruits for Volunteers in Service to America (VISTA), now a part of AmeriCorps. It was initiated in 1965 and was advertised as a domestic version of the Peace Corps. The organization aimed to fight poverty by collaborating with community and non-profit organizations, as well as government agencies, to generate private sector commitment and resources. Believing it would be rewarding and give me purpose, I filled out the application and decided to leave Pepperdine at the end of the school year.

I was accepted and given instructions and flight information, which was to be paid for by the US government. It didn't take long after arriving at the University of Oklahoma in Norman to realize I was way over my head! We were subjected to psychological tests, some involving physical challenges, like rappelling from a second-story height with ropes. Others involved drawing on butcher paper. There was talk of inciting workers to organize to form unions. It all seemed very political, and I was lost. I had imagined teaching sewing or nutrition in rural communities.

In Norman, one morning after breakfast, we were put on a bus without the chance to return to our rooms for clothes, toiletries, or even money. The bus took us to a rough area of Norman, where we were told to disembark and that we would be picked up in three days at the same spot. We were to introduce ourselves and get to know the community.

Another girl from California and I teamed up to survive the three days. We were both in shock, trying to process the predicament we had gotten ourselves into. We already knew we would quit when we returned to campus; if we survived, we would go home. VISTA was not for us; we were not good candidates. I had not taken any money with me when I left my room for breakfast, but my new friend had a little with her. Of course, I would pay her for my expenses in purgatory when we got back to the university. Meanwhile, we had to find a place to stay and eat on a minimal budget. We walked to find a motel while being whistled at and enduring various solicitous comments.

"Hey, I'll pay you 100 dollars," a black man offered me. I guess we were mistaken for prostitutes because I don't remember seeing other young white girls.

The room we could barely afford had a single light bulb in the middle of the ceiling and was sparsely furnished with a bed and a small bathroom. That night, we kept our clothes on, lay on the bed, and did not sleep. The lock on the door was not to be trusted. Outside our room, there was a lot of activity and noise all night, making it impossible to sleep and raising our alertness to a high level.

The next day, we found a YMCA and explained our plight. They let us stay there for very little or no charge. Those three days were the lowest time I had ever experienced. We stayed inside the YMCA. I don't remember what or if we ate. I spent my time writing on a piece of paper we found in the room to connect with something within me that would help me get through this hell. And to think, I volunteered for it!

Finally, it was time to meet the bus. The first thing I did back at the university was to ask to speak with the administrator of the program. I had no concern for anyone's opinion of me. I just wanted to return to my normal life, which would require a new beginning because I had already quit Pepperdine.

The administrator was understanding, did not try to dissuade me, and scheduled my flight for the next day. I asked if I could call my parents to ask them to pick me up at the airport. On the phone in the administrator's office, I couldn't give my parents the reasons for my overwhelming dissolution but said I would explain when they picked me up. They were shocked!

"What are we going to tell everyone?" Mom asked. That was not what I needed to hear. I disappointed her again, and now she would have to explain it to those who asked.

I was trying to deal with my discouragement and self-doubts. I thought joining VISTA would be a step toward finding purpose and usefulness. Chasing that goal had only made it more elusive. What others may think about my failure did not cross my radar.

"Tell them it wasn't for me."

Marie Calendar's Pie Shop #3

After returning from VISTA, I found work at Marie Calendar's #3, which meant that it was only the third MC shop in existence at that time. It was only a few blocks from my family's house in La Habra, where I returned to live. My sister Sheri was attending Whittier College, a small private school, at her own expense, and she also worked at Marie Calendar's.

Sheri and I decided it was time to leave the nest and rent an apartment. Although we slept in sleeping bags at first, we felt lucky to qualify for brand-new, affordable housing. Slowly, we received some furnishings from friends and family and began to feel the freedom and responsibility of being on our own.

Later, Trisha, Denise, and my future sister-in-law, Lisa, also worked at Marie Calendar's. Yes, we were Calendar Girls, we would joke. There were other waitresses, of course, and two guys who worked with the owners making pies in the large area at the back of the building. We were a tight group who got to know each other well and enjoyed our work.

Marie Calendar's served only pies at the time I started working there. The franchise was owned by two partners, Jack and Jay, who knew how to satisfy the corporates, run a tight ship, and be fair and friendly to their employees. Exhortations, probably not original, included "Time to lean; Time to clean" and "Busy hands are happy hands." The shop was spotless.

At any time, Janie could show up. She was the corporate's itinerant quality control inspector. Along with checking everything concerning the recipes, pies, and the cleanliness of the shop, she took note of the employees' attire and hygiene. We were individually inspected. She noted if our ruffled aprons had been starched and ironed, tied with perky bows in the back, our fingernails were short and clean, and we wore hair restraints. She was the enforcer-in-chief.

At night, after the last customers left, we cleaned the entire front area, scrubbing the lacey white wrought-iron tables and chairs with ammonia solution and mopping the floor. While we sanitized the front, the guys were equally diligent in the back. I can still hear the Led Zepplin songs the guys blasted while we cleaned. All cut pies were up for grabs for employees to take home if we brought back the pie tins. Probably to his detriment, my slightly paunchy Dad, who was a great cook and baker himself, was very interested in the leftovers we brought home.

In the fresh strawberry and peach season, waitresses rotated to the back to wash, stem, and arrange the fruit in the single pie shells the guys made. I developed an original assembly method for the strawberry pies. The small berries went in the middle, while the large, most beautiful berries formed a rim near the crust. Then, I made a volcano shape using the best medium, and finally, small berries were built up to a peak. One large dipper of glaze was deftly swirled over the fruit so that it reached the edge of the crust and stopped.

The fresh peaches were dunked in hot water briefly so the skin could be removed. I sliced them, leaving them together in halves like seashells. Then, I splayed them slightly, arranged them decoratively in a swirl in the pie shells, and applied their peach glaze.

I upped my assembly speed with repetition, knowing I must produce the same quantity in about the same amount of time as other employees who did not arrange the berries. The pies were placed on tall racks with many shelves until they were needed for the front of the store. Jack and Jay, co-owners, let me work in the back as much as I wanted because of my pies' pleasing appearance and uniformity. I enjoyed it, even though my hands became stained and wrinkled, and there were no tips earned in the back. The fresh fruit pies were always a big seller.

There were strictly enforced procedures concerning the handling of money. Three cash register drawers, stacked in the large register, were used simultaneously; each waitress had her own. At the start of a shift, after punching the time clock, we collected a register drawer from the bookkeeper or one of the owners. We counted the bills and coins to ensure the $100 bank was correct. At the end of the shift, we first counted a $100 bank back into the drawer. We arranged our customer tickets in numerical order, totaled them, and placed them with the cash from the day's sales and a form we signed that itemized the cash. This procedure assured the owners we had counted and submitted the revenue. These went into a zipped bank bag that we gave to the bookkeeper.

One day, we were told that Peggy, the bookkeeper, reported a loss of revenue to the owners. Of course, the employees were implicated. Because of the strict protocols, we could not imagine how any money could be missing. The owners did not know who might be pilfering, but we all felt the loss of trust we had enjoyed with the owners. There was a cloud over the shop as we worked our shifts, still trying to be friendly and efficient with the customers.

One day, a man came to the shop and asked to see the owner. The owner ushered him into the small office and closed the door. After a while, the man left the shop quickly through the front door. The owner told us employees that Peggy would not be coming back to work. Her husband had come to inform them that she had a problem and had been taking the shop's money. He apologized to the owner, possibly made arrangements for amends, and asked him to express to us how sorry he was that we were blamed.

When we related the story to Dad, he told us he could empathize with us. When he was young, while helping in his brother's restaurant, he and his younger sisters were accused of taking money from the register. The truth finally surfaced that it had been his brother's wife who had been dipping.

Soon, the shop was remodeled to serve hamburgers in addition to the pies. Usually, the guys would cook, but we were all cross-trained utility employees who could cook to the exact specs. The shop became even more popular, and we had more "regular" customers.

A few years later, the owner partners opened an additional, full-service Marie Calendar's restaurant in Whittier. I was always welcome to work at either shop during my time off from my primary job. I worked sporadically in various capacities and enjoyed it.

Immersion

Since leaving Pepperdine, I searched for a college or university where I could continue my education while working. I would first have to earn enough money for a car, but I wanted to make an informed decision about my education this time.

An advertisement caught my attention as I researched California State University in Fullerton. The university was offering a six-week summer Spanish program in Guatemala City. Participating students would live with a host family for six weeks while attending two classes daily at the public university, San Carlos de Guatemala. One class was to improve Spanish conversational skills, while the other was to learn Guatemalan and Central American history. Both classes were taught exclusively in Spanish.

I was very excited about this potential experience! It would be a novel challenge for me to spend the summer living with a family in a Spanish-speaking country. The cost was all-inclusive - airfare, room, board, and tuition. It was a special, reasonable price for students.

Dad could tell I wanted to participate. I was surprised and grateful when he offered to pay the program cost for me. He felt terrible that he could not contribute to the costs of my higher education while I was at Pepperdine because I was the first of five children. When I graduated high school, my mother did not work outside our home. Later, after I left Pepperdine, she began to do substitute teaching to save money for Trish's college education, but Sheri and I did not receive financial aid for college from our parents. Later, I learned that Trisha paid for half of her education, and Mom subsidized half.

So, I registered to spend the summer in Guatemala. I was apprehensive to tell Jack and Jay that I would like six weeks off from my job, but they supported my educational adventure and assured me my job would be there when I returned.

When I arrived at La Aurora International Airport in Guatemala City, a lady with a sign with my name on it met me. She warmly introduced herself as Sara Barrios, who would be my hostess for the six-week stay. I appreciated that Sara talked clearly and slower than usual in Spanish. We grabbed my bags from the claim area and headed for her car.

I knew she could switch to English if I looked perplexed, but I was determined to acquire the full benefit of this wonderful opportunity, so I tried my best to listen and converse. She told me she and her husband, Manuel, had two girls who lived with her in the city so they could attend school. Manuel was the Port Director in Champerico, Retalhuleu, which is approximately three hours' driving distance from the city. She said we would go visit the port sometime during my stay.

The Barrios' home ran parallel to one of the main streets in what seemed to be mid-city and was a short walk from the university where I would attend classes. When we arrived, I learned that two other guests in the program would also be staying with Sara and her girls.

Both ladies were older than me: one was from Kansas, and the other was a nurse from California who wanted to learn Spanish to be more useful to her *fiancé*, who was also in the medical field. The student from Kansas who had very little training in Spanish found the classes and the entire experience too challenging, despite Sara's efforts to help. She stuck it out for a week or two, then returned to Kansas. The nurse was enthusiastic and motivated to learn. We both laughed at our mistakes, and Sara was experienced in correcting us kindly. We were not her first guests; she did her part to augment the family income while introducing her girls to people from other cultures.

The older girl was in high school and quite involved in her studies and social life. However, the younger girl, who was eight or nine years old and eager to learn English, spent time with me, asking and answering my questions. For me, it was the ideal stress-free way to learn. I dropped my fear of making mistakes with her and welcomed her corrections.

"*¿Cómo se dice leepsteek en inglés?,*" she asked me. I told her it was the same, lipstick, and we laughed.

Our meals were prepared by two women hired by Sara to cook for her family and guests. The food was delicious, more European than the Mexican dishes I was familiar with in California. Curious and wanting to learn how the food was prepared, I asked Sara if I could help the women in the kitchen. She was somewhat stunned by my request and immediately answered that guests should not be doing menial work. I got the idea that it would make Sara look like a poor hostess if she were to allow that. It just wasn't done.

I persisted with my plea, saying I could broaden my Spanish vocabulary by learning the names of foods and spices and conversing with the women while we prepared the food. It wasn't an easy decision for Sara, but she finally relented. At first, the cooks were shy, but they saw that I wanted to help in an unassuming way. I enjoyed it! I needed to be useful.

We had a light breakfast before the girls and I left for our classes. As in many Hispanic cultures, the main meal was enjoyed mid-afternoon. A very light snack, like pan dulce with milk or hot chocolate, was just enough to satisfy before retiring.

The first day I attended the classes at the university, I wondered what I had gotten myself into! Most of the students were local and Spanish speakers. The professors did not make any concessions for us second language learners. The cadence was rapid fire. While I tried to process one sentence, the lecture raced on, sometimes leaving me in the dust. My goal had to be slightly adjusted by realism. I would glean all I could, get the gist of the lectures, and produce the assignments to the best of my ability.

In the history class, I was initiated into a perspective I had never encountered in any of my classes at home. The presentation of Central American history was blatantly anti-United States.

For instance, The United Fruit Company, born in Boston in the late 1890s, was portrayed as a predatory rapist of the fruits of their lands, coffee, and bananas. History confirms the company's power spread in Central America, starting in Costa Rica, where government contracts exchanged land for The United Fruit Company to build a railroad from San José to the port city of Limón. The railroad was purported to transport the government's coffee, but The United Fruit Company soon used it to export huge amounts of bananas to the United States.

Using Costa Rica as a model, United Fruit stretched its greedy tentacles into Guatemala, Honduras, Nicaragua, and Panama, becoming known as *El Pulpo*[4]. Commerce, real estate, and politics intertwined to the detriment of the local people of the "banana republics," whose governments reduced or eliminated other crops to increase banana production.

We were told the United States Central Intelligence Agency covertly interfered with Guatemalan politics in 1954 and was instrumental in removing a democratically elected president, Jacobo Arbenz. Carlos Castillo Armas was installed and became the first of several US-backed dictators to rule Guatemala. This incited a long period of civil war (1960 to 1996). When I was there in 1968 and 1969, a sign of the general political unrest was the requirement that interior vehicle lights must stay on when driving after dusk.

To sum it up, the professor likened the arrows in the claws of the US eagle to the countries south of the United States. Although it was a novel educational experience to listen to the vitriol spewed against my country, it did not incite anger in me. I had to realize that the

---

[4] The Octopus

lectures contained historical facts as well as interpretations, which invited more objective study and critical thinking.

The conversation class was somewhat easier because I was more familiar with some conversational vocabulary. With a smaller class size and interaction, I benefitted more in that class than I did in the lecture setting of the history class. There, too, I completed assignments to the best of my ability but received only a C in history and a B in Spanish conversation. However, most of my learning could not be measured by grades. Subconsciously, I absorbed language tempo and word combinations almost by osmosis.

After a couple of weeks of living with the Barrios family and attending daily classes, I noticed a marked improvement in my Spanish speaking and understanding. It was like learning to roller skate when I was a child and plunked on the sidewalk until, finally, one day, I learned to glide.

When I arrived in Guatemala, trying to converse in Spanish was belabored, searching for single words and trying to remember verb conjugations. Simple phrases became subconsciously familiar in an immersion setting as I heard them repeatedly. Verbs and nouns found each other, linked naturally into phrases, and surprised me when they exited my mouth without me having to visualize verb conjugations or pass my words through the grammar sieve. I decided to consciously count in Spanish instead of in English, and I've kept that habit. I realized one day that I was thinking in Spanish, too! One night, Spanish sentences even debuted in my dream. It was a euphoric mark of progress.

On weekends, Sara enhanced our knowledge and enjoyment by taking us to visit nearby attractions. She had friends or family who lived close to Lake Amatitlán, where we were invited to swim, eat, and spend the day. The weather is usually perfect, with highs averaging 77 degrees, in the "land of eternal spring." A rain squall may appear suddenly, but it lasts only long enough to maintain the verdancy and blooms everywhere. Then, the sun returns after the brief intermission.

Another weekend, Sara drove us two or three hours to Lake Atitlán, which is known worldwide for its spectacular beauty. Towering over the sparkling water are the three volcanoes that formed the lake. It is a quiet place, surrounded by 12 Mayan villages where native languages are prevalent, and Spanish is used only when necessary. Spectacular sunsets over the lake are the norm.

In Panajachel, the town most visited by tourists, an array of unique souvenirs typical of Guatemala are sold. I was fascinated by the patterns of the intricately woven fabrics. The indigenous people in each village wore distinct fabrics by which their origin could be identified. I bought a huipil (a piece of woven fabric with sides sewn up to armholes and a neck cut from the fold to form a blouse), a corte (a very long piece of material wrapped several times for a skirt), and a faja (sash) to keep the skirt in place. The colors and designs of the fabrics qualified them for veritable works of art.

Then, as Sara promised, the time came for us to spend the weekend in Champerico, Retalhuleu, where her husband, Manuel, was Port Director. For three hours, we traveled two-lane roads walled by tropical vegetation, mostly banana and coffee plantations. I thought of the professor's accusations about United Fruit and wondered about the current status of their formidable political power. Had the company been brought in check by worker strikes and/or the current dictator? One thing was indisputable: the area was ideal for growing bananas and coffee.

The house where we stayed at Champerico resembled a two-story tropical hotel. The grounds surrounding the white structure were meticulously manicured, and plants with flamboyant flowers contrasted nicely against the whiteness. There were plenty of rooms for everyone to relax and enjoy their privacy. We were shown to our rooms on the second story, where we had fabulous views of the black volcanic sand and the Pacific Ocean.

We spent the weekend lazily, walking on the deserted beach, swimming, and eating delectable kinds of seafood. On Saturday, a priest who was a close friend of the Barrios joined us for the main meal. He and Manuel took their time assembling an amazing paella in an outdoor cooking area while conversing, joking, and drinking *jaibolitos* (highballs). I was surprised to witness the open, unashamed mix of alcohol with religion and gained a new-found respect for the seeming broad-mindedness of Catholicism. Even the weddings in the churches I attended as a child were dry, and the punch held no punch.

When it was time to return to Guatemala City, Sara, being the resourceful woman she was, filled a large ice chest with fresh fish and seafood to take back to the city. There, she would sell it to schools and restaurants.

Back in Guatemala City, we settled into our weekly routines, which I found interesting, never boring.

One night, after supper and studying for my classes, I washed my face, dampened my long hair, and wrapped it as usual around large cylindrical rollers, trying to coax a wave. I quickly fell asleep at the end of another day of constant learning.

At 12:01, I was awakened by Mariachi music directly outside my window. Sara told us to get up and get dressed quickly. The party was here, and it was to celebrate my birthday! In the adrenaline of the moment, I could only wonder how she knew. I detached the rollers from my hair, threw on the skirt and blouse I had planned to wear to classes, and ran a brush through my hair.

I entered the kitchen, crowded with friends and family, food, and decorations. The Mariachis continued to play. Everyone joined in the Happy Birthday song:

Estas son las Mananitas These are the dawns

que cantaba el rey David That King David sang about

Hoy por ser día de tu santo We are singing because

te las cantamos aquí. today is your saint's day.

Despierta mi bien despierta Wake up, my dear, wake up

Mira que ya amaneció See what dawn has brought

Ya los pajaritos cantan The birds are singing

La luna ya se metió. And the moon has set.

Que linda está la mañana How beautiful is this morning

en que vengo a saludarte on which I come to greet you

Venimos todos con gusto We come with happiness

y placer a felicitarte! and pleasure to congratulate you!

El día en que tu naciste, All flowers were born on

nacieron todas las flores the day that you were born

Ya viene amaneciendo Dawn is arriving and

ya la luz del día nos dió the light of day is upon us.

Levantarte de la manana Rise up this morning and

mira que ya amaneció. See what dawn has brought.

Y en la pila del bautismo At your baptismal fountain.

cantaron los ruiseñores. The nightingales sing

Levantarte de la mañana Rise up this morning and

mira que ya amaneció. See, that dawn has come

…and the song continues for five more verses, giving time for the honoree to get dressed, maybe.

The kitchen table was laden with many tamales stuffed with sweets and meats. There were other foods I can't remember, cake, and all kinds of drinks. The Mariachis played people's requests, and there

103

was spontaneous dancing where space allowed. *Quetes* (fireworks) were set off outside on the street. The party continued until dawn when the guests had to go home and get ready for the day's commitments.

I had given my temporary address in Guatemala City to my family in California because that was the only way to communicate and share experiences before email and texts besides very expensive phone calls. In July, I received birthday cards from my parents and some siblings but tried to keep them under the radar. Or maybe the registration for the program required my date of birth? However, they became aware of my birthday, and the Barrios gave me a beautiful surprise for my 20th birthday!

As the end of our summer program approached, Sara invited me to come back the following summer just to visit. I was honored by the invitation and told her I would love to return. In the interim, we agreed to write letters - in Spanish of course.

I returned to my job at Marie Calendar's with a much-improved ability to communicate in Spanish and with stories from the summer.

As promised, we wrote quite regularly, both of us assuming I would spend the upcoming summer in Guatemala. One of the letters from Sara included various pages from the Sears Catalog on which certain items were marked, complete with sizes and details. She asked if I could buy the items in the US and bring them with my luggage when I came to spend the summer. Acknowledging it was a huge favor to ask, she explained that she could avoid the cost of shipping and taxes and possible tariff complications. Of course, I told her it would be no problem and that I wanted to pay for the requested goods as partial compensation for their hospitality.

The Sears products were mostly clothing for her and the girls, with a few items for Manuel. The Barrios were impressed with United States culture in general, diligently learned English, and wanted to emulate even our clothing styles. All of the items fit nicely in a large cardboard box, which did not cause a problem for me when I went through Customs at the airport.

*****

Before I arrived in the summer of 1969, Sara had written that she had arranged for me to apply for a summer job at the Colegio Mayor de Santo Tomas de Aquino in Antigua, where her parents lived. Sara's parents, Dr. and Señora Betancourt were an affable retired couple whom I had met the summer before. Working and living in the small town of Antigua would be another great experience.

The job opening was for an interpreter for a summer school group from Florida. Although I considered myself underqualified to be an interpreter, having never worked in that capacity, my hosts were confident I could do it. At least I would be interpreting from Spanish to English, which is a more forgiving and less stressful task for a native English speaker than it would be from English to Spanish. Also, the interpreting style was consecutive rather than simultaneous, meaning the professor would say a few sentences and then stop while I interpreted what he said to the group. Simultaneous interpreting involves both parties speaking at the same time, with the interpreter trailing a bit. I don't remember much about the interview, but it wasn't a very extensive assessment of my skills. I think they just needed someone.

Antigua, where I stayed with the Betancourts, was well preserved from the time when Spain conquered the Americas in the early 1500s. Quiet cobblestone streets, lined with colorful colonial-style houses, were in stark contrast to where I had stayed in Guatemala City the year before. Women still balanced huge baskets of food on their heads with only a donut-shaped padded disk underneath to buffer the weight on their heads.

On the street, a series of high wooden doors in a wall concealed and protected the beauty on the other side of the doors. Opening the huge door of Betancourts' home revealed a central fountain surrounded by a garden of lush blooming plants. Circling the fountain, which was open-air, was a covered patio with clusters of comfortable seating. In openings from the patio, there were several rooms and a kitchen.

In the evenings, the sounds of opera filled the patio. Dr. Betancourt sipped a ritual glass of port and savored the music while Sra. Betancourt taught me to finish woven pieces and blankets with decorative fringe types. For me, it was a welcome way to relax for a while before going to sleep. Once inside the door of their home, the feeling was always peaceful, private, and protected.

On the first day of my job at the Colegio, I was nervous, of course. I worried about meeting the expectations of the professor, the attendees, and myself. However, I was soon relieved by the relaxed atmosphere. The professor encouraged me, and we agreed that he would pause every few sentences for me to interpret and communicate as accurately as possible. The group of about 15 students was older than me and tight knit, seeming to have known each other before their trip to Guatemala. The brain strain that interpreting inevitably causes lessened slightly over time, and I became more comfortable with the task. Details of the course material have slipped from memory, but it concerned local history and was interesting.

Sometimes, I would walk with Sra. Betancourt when she bought food items in town. We always stopped at the catholic church on the way, a brief ritual she never missed. After shopping, we carried the groceries in bags the short walk back to the house, as we were not adept at balancing loads on our heads.

I was surprised that Dr. Betancourt still received patients at his home, although he was retired from his former practice. There would be a timid, unexpected knock at the large wooden door, and his wife would answer. She would relay to her husband the simple request to be seen for treatment and invariably invite the person inside. The would-be patient humbly gifted the Señora with a chicken, some eggs, a hand-embroidered piece, or some small token of appreciation for the doctor's generosity.

The Doctor led the person to one of the rooms off the patio, where he kept the basic sterile equipment for diagnosis and treatment and where privacy was respected and maintained. When the consultation ended, the patient expressed his gratitude effusively to both the Doctor and his wife. Dr. Betancourt remained useful, serving patients who possessed few resources and for whom paid treatment was out of reach, without openly competing with younger doctors currently practicing medicine. He seemed to find fulfillment in being able to treat the less fortunate.

On July 20th of that summer of 1969, the Betancourts and I were invited to a friend's home. Family and friends packed their small living room to watch the first humans ever to land on the moon. All of the chairs and sofas were occupied, and we younger ones sat close together on the floor. Of course, there were tasty finger foods and drinks to quell our anticipation for the momentous event we were about to witness. All eyes were trained on the small television screen, an impressive possession in Antigua at that time.

The mood was slightly tense and almost incredulous as Neil Armstrong exited the space vehicle and took the "small step for man, one giant leap for mankind." Then Edwin "Buzz" Aldrin followed, and both astronauts planted a United States flag on the powdery surface of the moon. We began to celebrate and realized that we had witnessed the landing and planting of the flag because a small camera transmitted the event from the moon to Antigua. It was amazing!

I completed the six-week course and gladly gave my meager earnings to the Betancourts despite their repeated reluctance to accept them. I tried to convey my gratitude for their kindness, all I had learned from them, and my experience at the Colegio. They said I was always welcome to stay with them whenever possible.

I could not even imagine the opportunity that would present itself for next summer.

Part Two - Routes

Wings

"I'm sorry. You do not meet the weight requirement," the perfect woman told me when she read the scale. Her Barbie body was impeccably dressed, and her ample hair was caught up in a sophisticated bun. Enhanced by an arsenal of carefully applied makeup, her porcelain complexion did not show evidence of frequent smiles. So, I did not expect she would waste such a rarity on me. Even though I still suffered occasionally from residual naivete, I knew my shortcoming was not only about the numbers on the scale.

I was so tempted to play her game, ask what the magic number might be, and how far off I was. I knew I wasn't over the weight requirement. Maybe she could give me a little time to plump up a bit? But the finality in her voice, followed by silence, told me my interview time had expired. I decided to lock the questions inside, give her an insincere thank you, and leave.

I had responded to an ad for United Airlines, which was hiring stewardesses. My Dad, always supportive, offered to drive me to apply. I had been driving the family car since I was sixteen but did not yet own a car. A few weeks earlier, he had taken me to Trans World Airlines to apply there, but I had not received a response.

The next day, I reported my experience to my employers at Marie Calendar, who planted the idea that I would be a great candidate for stewardess. We laughed about my failing the weight requirement, and they encouraged me to stay positive.

A few weeks later, Jack brought me an ad in the LA Times classifieds for Pan American Airlines, which was hiring stewardesses to staff a fleet of new 747s. Instead of the seven flight staff used on 727s and 707s, the new 747s would require at least sixteen. Pan Am had only international routes, and the ad noted that all applicants must be fluent in English plus another language. Having studied Spanish for two years in High School, another two years at Pepperdine

College, and spent two summers in Guatemala, I felt I might have a chance. Cautiously excited, I called the phone number in the ad. I was told the interview date, time, and location - a hotel near the Los Angeles International Airport.

Now, it was time for me to prepare for success. The interviews were scheduled for a weekday morning when Dad would need the car for his work. So, I rented a car, which proved easier than I thought.

Dressing for the interview proved more difficult for me. Using the Pan Am uniforms as a guide might give me a clue. Compared to Pacific Southwest Airlines (PSA) uniforms, neon pink and orange hot pants with matching knee-high boots, Pan Am landed at the opposite end of the spectrum. Head to toe, Pan Am was different. To my knowledge, its sky blue or tan felt bowler hat was distinct. The uniforms were conservative suits, which hit slightly above the knee, a white blouse, and a long-sleeved blazer. The look was cosmopolitan and monochromatic, sky blue or tan, except for the modest white blouse with the high neck and white ascot. Practical walking heels were worn but could be replaced inflight by comfortable flats.

My wardrobe then and since high school was not only limited but mostly composed of hand-sewn dresses, skirts, and blouses. After leaving Pepperdine and VISTA, it seemed I usually wore Marie Calendar's uniform.

Nothing I owned would do. Not a practiced shopper, and with budget concerns, I looked for a simple, conservative interview dress, remembering the somber Pan Am uniforms. When I have to shop for clothes for myself, the experience usually starts with optimism, even excitement occasionally. While shopping, as the options in my size dwindle due to ill fit or plain dislike, my level of frustration rises. After a few hours of desperation, my pattern is to buy something that a saleslady says is perfect for me. Or, when feeling strengthened by faith in my taste, I thank her for her patience with me, admit to being a challenge, and flee the store. I don't remember how many attempts it took to end up with my interview dress, but it was a case of classic acquiescence. It was not my style or even the colors I typically wore to showcase my eyes, but it was safely conservative. The color was rust brown with a white collar, cuffs, and belt. Of course, the length was at the knee, and the collar circled a high neckline.

As the interview day neared, anticipation and self-confidence increased. I read everything I could find (in pre-internet times) about Pan Am. I learned they had no domestic flights unless they connected to their international routes. Pan Am was the most prominent international airline in the US. It was founded in 1927 and called itself the most experienced airline. The early planes carried airmail, then passengers could purchase a sleeping berth for long flights. Pan Am was the first airline to purchase 747s in 1970, which resulted in requiring many more stewardesses. Because of the urgency to hire more stewardesses, I was allowed to interview in the fall of 1969.

Driving an unfamiliar car to the unknown areas surrounding Los Angeles International Airport (LAX) required some pre-trip research. Long before GPS was available for the masses, paper maps and bulky street atlases were the resources available. Dad had atlases in the car for many areas, which he used during his career with Southern California Edison Company. Together, we found the best route to the hotel where the interviews would be held. Then, I wrote down the succession of freeways and turns on surface streets to the destination. I was feeling prepared, as well as excited.

When the interview morning arrived, I allotted plenty of time to shower, wash and dry my hair, and dress. As I had for most of my life, I wore my blonde hair long and straight with simple bangs. A narrow ribbon, tied at the nape of my neck, held my fine hair out of my face. Makeup was minimal and self-taught. I dressed, making sure no runs had appeared in my new pantyhose, and I was ready to leave with plenty of time to arrive at my 11:00 am interview.

I was extremely alert and cautious while driving on the older freeways going to Los Angeles. The lanes seemed extra narrow, and other drivers were more daring and impatient than in Orange County. Finally, I arrived at a large parking area for the hotel and found the specified room.

I felt positive and confident until I opened the door. The room was packed with young, hopeful, lovely women. They sat quietly in rows of chairs not configured to promote conviviality. All the chairs faced the door to an adjoining room, which would open intermittently to announce the name of the next interviewee. These women were not in a gregarious mood; We were in ruthless competition for a dream job. The air was heavy with rival scents of feminism—perfume, hair spray, and lotions. It was overwhelming!

I sat in a back row, where chairs were still available, while I studied the various hairstyles on the backs of the heads in front of me. The sea of heads in front of me oozed and defined sophistication.

I was attentive to *the* door that opened and closed repeatedly. Breaking the pattern slightly, the door opened, and an interviewer walked to an obscure table on the side of the room to retrieve a paper there.

It hit me mercilessly! We were supposed to sign in when we arrived. Wishing I were invisible, I got up, sidestepped to the end of my row, and then turned left, having to pass the ends of all the rows of chairs where the hopeful beauties sat until I got to the small table. I was the last to sign in.

How did I miss this crucial step? I'm not sure if there is an excuse. But I think it had something to do with the innate female compulsion to compare ourselves with other females. This goes on, consciously and subconsciously, all our lives. This reflexive mental action is rarely beneficial, often distorts reality, and is a real confidence killer. It can detour or prevent positive action. In a situation like this, with mile-high stakes, all my senses were immersed in the process of deciding if I could measure up and be a winner or if I should flee the room.

Having written my name at the bottom the list, I was committed to staying. I snapped to the realization that some positive and practical thinking was overdue. I had to overcome the comparison coup and regain my calm confidence before entering the interview room. Nothing had changed. I hadn't changed; I had only made the mistake of comparing.

I determined to use the waiting time to recall my relevant experiences, skills, and perspectives, anticipate questions, and prepare some possible answers. They needed to be lined up and waiting in the wings when the questions started.

My beauty was not my standout feature, so I would sell them on my ability to work tirelessly while serving others' needs, my language skills, and my desire to experience other cultures. I would make the interviewers see all my values as the whole package and conclude that I was a match for Pan Am.

One by one, the candidates were called in from the door, interviewed, and left. I was the only one in the room while the next to the last candidate was being interviewed. It was well past lunchtime. The interviewers must be fatigued and peckish, having endured the nonstop stream of hopefuls.

When they called me, I told them I would be happy to wait or return after they got something to eat. They said they wanted to finish and invited me in. I felt ready to interview after all the angst and anticipation.

Now, over 50 years after the event, some details of my interview are vivid and clear, while others have become fuzzy. To start, I think I had to field the unimaginative "tell us about yourself" request. I remember telling them I enjoyed working and living with people of diverse cultures, that I had developed stamina while waitressing in high school and college and enjoyed serving people, that I had spent two summers in Guatemala living with families, and that I spoke conversational Spanish.

At some point, they asked me to describe the room in Spanish. It was a common hotel suite with beds, lamps, faux art on the walls, and mostly neutral colors. They stopped me while I was still describing. I wasn't sure if they were satisfied with my fluency or were just hungry and wanted to wrap up the last interview.

Lastly, they asked me to walk across the room to the window, then turn and walk back toward them. Stiffening at the thought of them critiquing my gait and body, I saved myself by imagining I was walking purposefully to deliver an order to a table. On the return, walking toward them at the same enthusiastic pace, I just smiled. The familiar, well-broken-in shoes were an excellent choice.

The interview team told me I would be notified by telegram within a few days whether I was hired. It was impossible to pick up any clues about my chances. I thanked them for their time and for considering me.

After successfully reversing the directions on the way home, I arrived feeling slightly proud but mostly relieved.

It was about three days later that our doorbell rang, and a telegram addressed to me was delivered. Apprehensively, I opened it. It instructed me to arrive in Miami on a certain date in April to begin my five-week training course for Pan Am stewardess. More details will be sent to me...

In the next weeks and months, anticipation increased. My bosses and coworkers at Marie Calendar's were delighted at the news of my good fortune. I received specifics from Pan Am about what to pack for training in Miami – dresses for classes and meals, casual clothes, and bathing suits for training and exploring Miami during free time. I learned how much my entire uniform would cost, with all its components. I had about five months to save as much money as possible to arrive prepared. Motivated was too mild a word to describe my enthusiasm for this new goal!

Welcome to Miami!

The balmy Miami climate in April of 1970 made it ideal for training, including outdoor simulations of emergency procedures. The accommodations for our class of 24 women were comfortable dormitory style. There was an onsite dining room where we served ourselves from an ample buffet.

The first item on the training agenda was Grooming. For me, it involved a near makeover. Each of us had to choose one of three hairstyles: A Bob, a Pixie, or one I can't remember, but it was a short style. Our hair could not touch our collars. We all started with short hair, but we could grow it after graduation if we wore it up in a bun while in airports and on planes. Hair could not be loose. I quickly learned how to manage my Bob. Vision correction could only be done with contact lenses, not glasses. We were each given a magic number of pounds we could weigh, more than which would warrant a written warning and more frequent weighings. Skincare and makeup were also a new frontier. Moisturizer, mascara, and pale lipstick were my former routine. The grooming instructor was incredulous that I didn't pluck my eyebrows regularly. I thought I was lucky to have blonde, fine brows that were self-maintained and weren't oversized, but I learned how to shape them. However, the mandatory requirement to wear false eyelashes was a challenge. For the five weeks of training, I struggled with the glue and the fear that one end would break free and flap or completely detach.

One day, when I was practicing the demo about the emergency equipment on board, the life vest hit a faux lash as it went over my head, sending the black fringe down to the aisle floor. I had to retrieve it and reapply it when we broke for lunch.

Many of us were dealing with new haircuts, required makeup, and lots to learn. It was a commonality that created more camaraderie than competition. We were excited and ready to do whatever it took to prepare for this dream job we were lucky enough to be offered.

We memorized and were tested on the three-letter abbreviations for all of the airports in the world to which Pan Am flew. We became familiar with the 24-hour clock, our default time-telling method. In the evenings, we studied and quizzed each other on abbreviations, first aid procedures, and other pertinent facts we needed to know.

We received multiple immunizations in both arms on one of the first days. Routine vaccinations were updated, and we received protection against yellow fever, tetanus, cholera, and other diseases I've forgotten. After initial training, every six months, we attended a full-day session to review emergency procedures and got another Cholera shot.

Our trainers filled each day with hands-on experiences. We spent most of our time in the simulated cabins, where we practiced cooking and serving in galleys and cabins identical to those we would encounter after graduating. There were both first-class and economy-class simulations of galleys and passenger seats. The cabin configuration, menus, and service for each class were disparate, creating separate worlds.

First-class seats were at least double the width of those in economy class. A passenger could sink into them or curl up if their size permitted, don Pan Am-provided eye shades and disposable slippers, and take a nap with a pillow under a warm blanket. All this after a spectacular five-course meal.

All first-class service was delivered from a double-shelved cart. The liquor service was first, soon after reaching cruising altitude, when it was safe to open latched cabinets and load the cart. The array of top-notch wines, liquors, and liqueurs was amazing. Although we were not bartenders, we had to know the components of basic popular drinks.

While drinks were served, another cart was artistically arranged in the galley with an assortment of irresistible hors d'oeuvres. All servings to passengers were done from the cart using large silver spoons and fork pairs, overlapping them to pick up the food items. It was a trick to be learned, akin to handling chopsticks.

Passengers could choose an *entree* from at least three, among which were chateaubriand, roasted inflight from its raw state using an oven thermometer, and carved on the cart according to the doneness preference of each passenger. They also selected accompanying side dishes. There was always a generous bunch of parsley among the garnishes for each course. We were encouraged to occasionally munch a bite of it in the galley to ensure fresh breath. I was told that the salad course followed the entree course, adhering to the European sequence.

Then came the cheese and fruit cart, offering a collection of cheeses with a variety of tastes and textures, from soft to hard and mild to pungent. Almost all of them were new to me. There was a wide array of fresh fruits and crackers from which to choose.

Last was the dessert and liqueur cart. Every item served in first class was excellent, with five-star quality. First-class leftovers were plentiful and up for grabs by the flight crew.

I should note that during my second year flying, we noticed some changes in the first-class offerings when other international carriers became a competitive threat. Whereas Moet champagne and French wines used to flow freely, we started to pour wine from California vintners, and the frequency of Turkish caviar onboard diminished and then disappeared. Although the first-class meal remained top-notch, passengers noticed these small changes, and some were not reticent to complain.

The beverage service in economy class was served from a cart carrying soft drinks, coffee, tea, and liquors in single-serving miniature bottles for purchase. We delivered the meals two trays at a time right after adding the hot entree. There was usually a salad, bread, and dessert already on the trays that the commissary had slid into their cold storage shelves in the galley. It was a veritable feast compared to the tiny bag of peanuts served on today's flights, if you are lucky.

In training, we served real people who volunteered to eat what we cooked, making our training more authentic and enjoyable. We practiced the "Clipper Dip," which involved bending our knees while reaching to serve someone in a window seat to avoid overexposing our backsides. It was not easy at first. What we lost in reaching distance was gained in decency, I guess.

*****

In addition to the study and memorization that filled our evening hours and the extensive training focused on food service, we practiced simulated ditchings in the swimming pool and land emergencies that required getting volunteer "passengers" and ourselves safely down the inflated shoots in a certain number of seconds. The drills were repeated until we reached that goal.

At that time, hijackings to Cuba were quite frequent. On the 747, in the upper first-class lounge was the entrance to the cockpit. A plain-clothes security guard sat in the lounge, appearing like a first-class passenger throughout the flight. If a highjacker asked us to take him to the cockpit, we were instructed to do what they asked without being confrontational. I never experienced an attempted hijacking, but the security guard and the cockpit crew knew the protocols they would enact if it happened.

How to deal with an unruly passenger was also addressed. Examples given were a passenger who would not extinguish his cigar (cigarettes were permitted; cigars were not), a passenger who would not vacate the galley (passengers were not allowed in the galleys), or a passenger who had too much to drink and became belligerent. We were to exhaust all types of finesse first, including gentle urging and even humor. If all our polite attempts failed, especially if the passenger's conduct had to be stopped immediately, a surprise blast of cool from the CO_2 extinguisher was recommended. We were trained on how to use it and practiced its use on each other.

The notion of refinement overarched our training. We were told we were a select group, unlike the stewardess stereotypes at that time. Despite various books like *Coffee, Tea, or Me?* which had been published recently, and the clever innuendo many airlines were pushing in their advertising, we were to demonstrate superior classiness. Expectations for us may have been the highest industry wide. We were hired because we met various Pan Am requirements that were not mandatory for employment in other airlines, such as being able to speak English and another language and having some college education if not a degree. Even our uniforms connoted a cosmopolitan air. Because Pan Am had only international routes, we would become world guides and "ambassadors." We must model impeccable behavior in all the countries to which we flew. It was a tall order, and we were eager to comply.

However, some Pan Am restrictions would never be tolerated today. Until the year before I started, stewardesses could not be married. That mandate had been changed, but the maximum age for a stewardess was still 35, the arbitrary age for retirement. A shameful restriction was that there were no Black stewardesses until the 1960s and the ban was lifted slowly, only through individual lawsuits.

As an exclusively international Airline, Pan Am's goal was to appear diversified. Around 1970, when I was hired, the cover of Wing Tips magazine featured three models debuting the new 747 stewardess uniforms. The three models were a blonde, an Asian, and a Black. In the years I flew, from 1970 to 1974, I never flew with a Black stewardess on any of my flights. At the time, I thought my schedules didn't happen to coincide with those chosen by Black stewardesses. The reality was that only a few were hired.

By 1965, and forced by lawsuits, it is estimated that only 50 Black stewardesses were employed across all airlines. Airline executives openly admitted they feared losing their mostly white passengers if Black women served them. The executives' admissions were rich with irony, given the US history of Blacks serving whites. With the advent of the 747s (Pan Am being the first to add them to their fleet in 1970), the number of Black stewardesses still rose to only 1,000 industry wide.

*****

Besides the incredible opportunity to travel the world, we had paid health insurance and paid vacation. Our families also benefited from our employment. Employees had an unlimited 90% discount to travel on Pan Am during our time off, and there were discounts offered to us by reciprocating airlines. Our parents and husbands (the restriction against being married had just been overturned) enjoyed an unlimited 80% discount on flying Pan Am and reciprocating airlines. My siblings could take an annual trip at a 90% discount. I was ecstatic to tell my family! Most had never flown in an airplane.

At graduation, after five weeks of training, we received a certificate, a photo of our class members, and an assignment to the base from which we would work. I was assigned to New York City. We were issued two complete sets of uniforms, one light blue and the other tan. They included a skirt of each color attached to a camisole, two white blouses, an apron of each color with my name embroidered on it, blazers of each color, and a long wool blue uniform coat. We had earned our wings to be attached to the lapel of our blazer!

A Bite of the Big Apple

Linda Rennick, a friend from my class, was also based in New York. So, we decided to team up to find housing together because we wanted to be near Greenwich Village in Manhattan, an area of the Big Apple we had only heard about but neither of us had experienced. Many stewardesses chose to live in Queens, which was closer to John F. Kennedy Airport, where we would report for flights and further language training. I met a friend from another training class, Liz Vandercappellen, who decided to room with other stewardesses in Queens.

After verifying the rules for requesting a transfer to another base, Liz and I agreed that we would try to transfer to Los Angeles, where our families lived in neighboring towns, as soon as possible. We submitted our requests within days of arriving in New York City and were told it would be a minimum of six months and only if Pan Am needed additional flight staff there. If the variables worked in our favor, we would escape an East Coast winter and be back in California close to our families.

*****

Scouring the rental ads in the newspaper, Linda and I were awakened to the shocking prices. A two-bedroom furnished apartment with one bath, several stories up, went for $250 a month! And that was one of the least costly! We took a cab from the hotel where we stayed temporarily to the rental address. There, we met three other young women who were trying to break into New York modeling or theatre or whatever their current dream was. If we rented it together, it would be only $50 each per month.

The couple who had placed the ad told us they had just been offered an opportunity to live and work abroad but were unsure how long they would be out of the country. Meanwhile, we could rent the apartment. They gave us details about where to send our rent check, and we chose rooms and settled our few belongings. I opted to sleep in the living room on the fold-out sofa. There was only one bathroom, but we made it work because we all had differing schedules and trips.

All was roses until the owner of the apartment contacted us. He was furious! We learned the couple had tried to sublet to us, which was illegal, and he seemed ready to throw us out. We pleaded that we were completely unaware that we were subletting and begged him to let us stay. He relented, kept the rental price the same, and we signed a valid agreement.

It was May in New York City. None of us had many belongings, but Linda and I had only clothing for Miami and our uniforms. That's all. We wore our long, blue, wool uniform coats everywhere, over everything, just to be comfortable until the weather warmed up.

We were to report to John F. Kennedy International Airport for orientation and to meet individually with the linguist who would polish my Spanish and teach distinct airline vocabulary. He was amazing, fluent in 15 languages, and had a definite no-nonsense teaching style. We had homework and were expected to have an individual session once a week.

As I was leaving my first session, walking outside the building, I saw a small, private plane take off, gain insufficient altitude, and suddenly crash back down to the tarmac in a ball of black billowy smoke. Emergency equipment rushed to it, but I did not want to watch. I increased my pace in the opposite direction, searched for a cab, trying to forget what I had witnessed, and chased away ominous thoughts.

We learned how to bid on a schedule for the month. Each numbered "line" listed the dates and destinations, which added to the total number of hours for a full month's work, and we could choose three lines. We would be assigned a line if none of those could be awarded to us due to our zero-seniority status. At first, I flew mostly turnarounds from New York City to San Juan, Puerto Rico. The good thing was that every line had at least one extensive trip to compensate for all the turnarounds.

My first flight was to Paris, where I was initiated as a real stewardess on a flight to Europe, and I practiced all I had learned in a simulator! I worked in economy class on the way to Paris and felt quite competent – thanks to the extensive training. During the layover, which was probably only one day, other stewardesses showed me the Eiffel Tower, Champs Elyse, etc.

In the briefing before the return trip to New York, I was assigned to work the first-class galley. Hastily trying to quell the panic of that responsibility, I tried desperately to remember the components of the most requested drinks, the temperature for the chateaubriand and how long it should cook, the decorative cart presentation for the various courses, and all the endless details designed to make the first-class passengers feel special. I reminded the Purser that this was my first flight and welcomed all the tips and prompts she and the other stewardesses could give me.

When I successfully calmed the butterflies in my stomach, I realized the value of repeated simulations in training. Most of the learning had stuck. My fellow stewardesses were wonderfully supportive, and I enjoyed giving superb service.

When we were chatting in the galley, a stewardess asked me how I got my first name. I admitted my mother had read the name in a magazine, thought it was different, and liked it, although she had no idea how it was pronounced. All my life, my family had accented the first syllable. The European stewardess told me the name was quite common in France and Germany, but it was pronounced with the second syllable accented. On other flights, crew members pronounced it correctly. So, from then on, I introduced myself with the proper pronunciation. The silver lining was that it seemed slightly easier for people to remember.

Most likely, that Paris trip was the highlight destination of the month. As the most junior member at the base, my schedule was filled with one-day turnarounds to San Juan, Puerto Rico. Although report times varied slightly, I was in front of our apartment building in the dark, well before dawn, in full uniform with my flight bag, asking the "Super[5]" to please get a taxi for me.

The taxi took me to JFK airport, where I reported for briefing two hours before flight time. The captain attended at the start of the briefing and told us if anything unusual, like adverse weather conditions, was expected for the flight. Next, the pursers in both first-class and economy class gave more detailed information about which stewardesses were assigned to work in each class and any passengers' special needs.

The flight time to San Juan was three to four hours, during which we served drinks and a full meal in both classes. On my first flight, I was instructed to present the kosher trays to passengers who had requested them before we unwrapped or heated them. On some flights, most economy-class passengers had chosen kosher meals.

We were on the ground in San Juan only about 20 minutes after the passengers disembarked, which was barely enough time for the ground employees to exchange used food trays for fresh ones and give the cabin a quick cleaning.

Soon, we were greeting passengers bound for New York City. After take-off, when we reached our cruising altitude, we started the beverage service, followed by the hot meal. After landing in New York, the morning routine was reversed. I caught a taxi that accelerated, jerked, and braked until it arrived at my temporary home. A shower, something to eat, and time to relax felt great! I would be

---

[5] A building superintendent or building supervisor

off for a minimum of 48 hours before my next flight, which provided time to explore the city.

Speaking of New York taxis, one driver comes to mind. He picked me up outside the apartment building, where the Super motioned him to pull over. As usual, I told him my destination was JF Kennedy Airport. Traffic seemed heavier for whatever reason, and I was a little nervous that I might be running late. After snailing for several blocks, he suddenly pulled to the right, left the vehicle running, and said he would be right back. He returned in a few minutes, explaining that he had to buy some cigarettes. Of course, the meter was running while I waited for him to make his urgent purchase. When we reached the airport, I paid him the fare without including a tip, grabbed my flight bag, and quickly walked away from the taxi. He started yelling at me when he discovered I had not tipped. I could hear him as long as I was in earshot but hurried forward without glancing back at him. I figured he got his tip when he stopped to shop on my dime and time!

*****

On my time off, I tried using the subway to visit stewardess friends in Queens. It was imperative to know which stop to exit and be quick about it. But I never felt comfortable using the underground transport, especially after seeing a man exposing himself to those of us waiting. Another time, someone lit a fire in a trashcan in the boarding area. I preferred walking around Manhattan; staying above ground felt safer, even though I was part of a massive flow of people always rushing.

Pan Am's benefits for flight attendants seemed quite generous to me. We had paid health insurance, ample per diem, well-compensated overtime, and paid vacation with the opportunity to travel at very little cost. At each city where Pan Am flight crews stayed, a cost-of-living calculation determined the amount of per diem we were given during our trip. No receipts or other evidence that we ate the meals were required. We received a generous allotment of gifted money with our pay.

At the time I flew, the most expensive cities in the world were San Francisco and Tokyo. In the summer months, the time when the 747s were often full and we earned overtime frequently, I earned $1000 per month in salary alone. It was more than I had even dreamed of making! I felt rich, and it made me happy to be able to buy unique things for my family members.

There was one annual requirement that was temporarily restrictive. Out of the 12 months, one month was spent in the Pool, which meant being available 24/7 on call. Important to remember is that cell phones did not exist then. So, if I needed to run downstairs for a few groceries, I had to call a number at the airport to say I would be away from the phone for 30 minutes. I wouldn't buy much because there was no way to know if I would be home or away. My suitcase was ready, packed with clothing for all climates around the world. We were allowed one suitcase, so clothing and toiletries were thoughtfully chosen. I became an expert packer, with practicality as my guide.

When I got the call to report, I had to be at the airport in two hours. Those of us in the Pool were last-minute substitutes for stewardesses who became ill. We also filled in when other unforeseen changes happened, such as an extra stewardess needed for an unaccompanied minor passenger who required one-on-one supervision. Upon returning from a Pool trip, there was a mandatory 48 hours off, regardless of the length of the trip. Pool trips could sometimes be advantageous to junior stewardesses, allowing them to fly to coveted destinations usually awarded to the more senior crew. All stewardesses served a month in the Pool, and despite the adventure, we were happy to return to a relatively predictable schedule when the month ended.

*****

One of the places I flew from New York was Rabat, the capital city of Morocco in Northern Africa. My memory of Rabat is tinged with an unfriendly, very foreign feeling. In 1970, the airport seemed primitive, surrounded by jungle. After we disembarked from the plane, right onto the tarmac, we went inside the airport to claim our luggage. Our passports were requested and collected by a serious-looking official. We were told they would retain our passports until our departure. The welcome mat was nowhere in sight. It was disconcerting to have our identification taken away, and I don't remember venturing very far from the modest accommodations. Also, we had to take huge white anti-malaria pills. I went there only once. It was an opportunity to relax and read.

Twice, I was lucky enough to fly with famous people on board. Ironically, their inflight demeanor could not have been more disparate. Gina Lollobrigida boarded, settled into her first-class seat, donned the eye covers and light blanket provided by Pan Am, and requested not to be disturbed even for the meal. In complete contrast, The Platters boarded noisily, gregariously interacted with other passengers, and gave the flight a party feeling. They were open, convivial, fun people. I don't remember the destinations of these celebs, but it was a pleasure to have them on board and serve them.

One flight of special significance to me was to Panama. Although time wouldn't permit a trip to the Canal, it was a chance to experience the tropical humidity and resulting blooms and vegetation. This was where Pops worked on the construction of the Canal and where Grammie and Pops honeymooned and began their married life!

West to the Nest

In October, just as Liz and I started to fear being stuck in New York and having to buy winter clothes, we received notice that our transfer requests to Los Angeles had been accepted. We and our families were ecstatic! Suddenly, I needed to buy a car and look for housing. I would stay with my family in La Habra for a short time. Liz decided to live with her family in (the city of) Orange and commute to LAX.

Solutions came quickly. My sister Trisha's friend, Cathy Gerber, had started her first year at UCLA and was looking for a roommate to share her apartment. Perfect. I knew her well, and we were quite compatible. I bought a new compact, no-frills Nissan for about $2,000 with savings from New York earnings. Very soon, I could drive to the airport (no more taxis) and began flying the routes out of LAX.

The lines awarded to junior stewardesses were much more exciting than those flying out of New York. We usually flew one round-the-world flight a month. Depending on whether the flight started eastbound or westbound, the trip took either nine or ten days. Our layovers were in Honolulu, Tokyo, Hong Kong, Bangkok, New Delhi, Beirut, Frankfurt, and London, returning to Los Angeles via the polar route. Or we started with the polar route eastbound, making mostly the same layovers. To make up the rest of the required flight hours, I was awarded other trips, including trips to Tahiti, Auckland, New Zealand, Sydney, Australia, the Philippines, Guam, and other destinations.

When asked my favorite place to fly, it was difficult to give just one answer. But Beirut stood out to me. We stayed at Pan Am's Intercontinental Hotel, overlooking the Mediterranean Sea. In addition to the surrounding clear blue water, the sprawling central marketplace with its variety of shops was unlike any shopping experience I had. Gold jewelry chains hung like long fringe on display bars, and multitudes of gold bracelets and rings were displayed in front of each vendor. The prices were relatively low, generating gift ideas for family and friends. Leather goods were also of good quality and very attractive. As we shopped, a man, somehow wearing everything needed for coffee service on his body, offered demitasses of his concentrated, potent product. I liked the rich, slightly sweet sips.

Of course, stewardesses with Israeli passports were not awarded flights that landed in Beirut. Israel and Lebanon had been in perpetual conflict for decades. We were warned not to go anywhere alone in Beirut because there were reports of "disappearances." Some of the cockpit crew would accompany stewardesses who wanted to shop or eat away from the hotel.

Hong Kong was the mega mecca for shopping, and dining was a close second in popularity. Even senior stewardesses would occasionally bid a line that included an around-the-world trip to visit their favorite tailor, who would transform individual design ideas into precisely measured, perfectly fitted clothing. Using an amazing array of high-quality fabric, the tailor would create a one-of-a-kind masterpiece. A second trip was necessary for a final fitting when any adjustments were expedited in time to continue the trip.

In Hong Kong, I went once with several crew members to the border where China met Hong Kong, which had been leased by China to the British for 99 years, ending in 1997. It was marked by an unimpressive chain link fence through which I remember seeing nothing but uncultivated land.

Tokyo was the "yes" city. No one wanted to tell you your request could not be granted or that it had to be modified. Yes, yes, it was reinforced by head-nodding, but only time would confirm whether the petition was fulfilled.

Stewardesses let me in on the tip that Tokyo excelled at pampering, recommending massages, nails, and hair care. I had my first massage ever, and it was wonderful and affordable.

Before one trip, I had not found time to fit in a periodic body wave for my fine hair, so I asked the upscale hotel salon if, by chance, they could wave my hair that day. Yes, they could, and they got started. True to the tip, I was made comfortable and enjoyed the pampering. However, there was one detail neither the salon nor I considered. My fine hair overreacted to the onslaught of chemicals meant for coarser Asian hair. My hair was kinked just short of nappy, and I had to cut it short. I hoped it would grow out fast! It was a short, blonde afro upon which I set my uniform hat.

Shopping in Tokyo was fun in skyscrapers where everything from watches and electronics to clothing and perfumes were found. But taking a break to eat was even more interesting. Outside each eatery, in an enclosed glass case, were wax models of all the menu items, so meticulously replicated that they looked exactly like food. Seating was communal at the tables, where workers stopped for a hurried refuel. They ordered, were served immediately, and ate with chopsticks, holding their bowls under their chins. They shoveled and slurped the noodles directly into their mouths. The table where I was seated turned over its customers at least four times as I enjoyed my lunch.

In Hong Kong and Tokyo, on the busy city streets, I saw many people wearing surgical masks. It was the first time I had seen public, non-medical use of masks, and I assumed their purpose was to filter the polluted air when they had to be outdoors in the city. Maybe some had colds or flu and didn't want to share.

Bangkok left its impression, too. Almost as soon as the door of the plane was opened, a distinct aroma met my senses. It was not unpleasant but unique. Tropical places, by nature, were characterized by the humidity that fed the verdant green life and exotic blooms, but Bangkok's abundance of teak trees exhaled a damp, musky, predominantly masculine smell that hung in the heavy air.

The hotel advertised a boat tour along the Chao Phraya River that sounded interesting. Since ancient times, the river has given life, transport, and commerce to the communities that flourish along its banks. It runs through most of Thailand, nurturing the land and providing rich soil for agriculture.

As our boat cut slowly through the murky water, the shore dwellers performed their daily activities at the river's edge: washing clothes, brushing teeth, bathing, and children playing as they bathed. I felt almost embarrassed as we tourists gawked, invading their privacy. But they seemed well-accustomed to it and went about their routines, ignoring us.

Apart from round-the-world flights, there were trips to Pacific Island destinations. My memories of my only trip to Papeete, Tahiti were the noisy motored bikes and the American couples of a certain age dressed in matching tropical fabrics. In the crowd, the husband's shirt and the wife's muumuu identified them as a couple. They seemed to be ecstatic to have finally arrived in paradise. I was grateful for the opportunity to visit while I was young.

I boarded a boat from Papeete with some Pan Am crew members to spend the day on the nearby island of Moorea, where we enjoyed a luau at Club Med and swam in the crystal-clear water.

The Performing Arts Opera House, overlooking the harbor, had just been completed in Sydney, Australia. It was an amazing acoustical accomplishment consisting of a series of white pointed arcs of graduated size, half nested into each other. The beaches of Sydney reminded me of the familiar California coastline.

Even in English-speaking cities like Auckland, New Zealand, certain words were unfamiliar or had different colloquial connotations. For instance, a swimming suit was a "cossie," short for a swimming costume. After a delicious meal of delectable fresh seafood, someone said she was "stuffed." A more experienced crew member advised against using that word because it carried a sexual connotation far different from what she intended.

It may have been the same trip from New Zealand that we stopped in Pago Pago, American Samoa. During the brief transit, huge barrels were loaded into the cargo area, and ample-bodied passengers embarked into the cabin. They were jovial and excited to be going to Los Angeles. We learned they were taking Samoan specialty food to relatives in LA. During the flight, one of the oversized ladies came to me in the galley. Giggling to mask her embarrassment, she showed me the split side seam of her dress, whose stitches had succumbed while she maneuvered down the aisle to the restroom. I always carried a tiny sewing kit in my tote, along with an extra apron, my other shoes, a pair of pantyhose, and a toothbrush and paste. The sewing kit had the essentials: Needles, a threader, a thimble, mini scissors, and a few small spools of neutral-colored thread. There was not much surplus fabric to crudely stitch the gap together, and I had to be careful not to stick her with the needle. Her grateful smile was enormous.

I had trips to both Fairbanks and Juneau, Alaska. Outstanding memories include dining on the freshest of seafood, touring an old mine, and having to use blackout curtains to sleep at night. Summer in Alaska was light 24/7!

There were two times that mechanical issues interrupted my scheduled flights. On the polar route, we made an unplanned stop in Iceland at Keflavik Airport, where a part was replaced during a brief delay. Passengers and crew had the choice of staying on the 747 plane or going to the terminal to look around. Not dressed for the extreme cold, I stayed onboard. When the plane was ready to resume our route, the few who remained onboard laughed at the black stream of fur hats exiting the terminal and winding on the tarmac toward the plane. Without a doubt, it was a record-setting number of hat sales for one day.

The second mechanical delay necessitated a stop in Istanbul, Turkey. There, we all deplaned but were told to wait in the terminal for a status update. It was a "rolling delay," meaning one of indeterminate length. I remember the airport air being hot and stuffy as we waited for word. Finally, we were notified the crucial replacement part would be flown in from Frankfurt. All passengers and crew would be put up in local hotels for the night.

By the time we reached the hotel, it was too late to begin sightseeing. Cooling off in the nearby water of the Black Sea was more tempting. Amazingly, I was swimming (with the jellyfish) off the coast of Turkey's largest city, what used to be Constantinople and the capital of major historical empires. The next day, we were back to our flight schedule, but I enjoyed the bonus break.

We lay over in New Delhi, India, on many round-the-world trips, depending on whether they originated eastward or westward from LAX. We arrived around 5:00 a.m. after a night flight from Beirut or Bangkok. For whatever reason, the customs officials found pleasure in delaying and detaining crew members, especially stewardesses, with their baseless, embarrassing, and harassing questions about items in our suitcases. It was just something we had to endure.

On one trip, upon arrival in New Delhi, the security guard (who sat in the upper lounge of the 747 in plain clothes) asked if anyone would like to share a taxi to see the Taj Mahal in Agra. I was the only one who either hadn't been there or was too tired to make the trip. Usually, I would try to sleep a couple of hours and then start the day when the locals were awakening. But we were anxious to get on the road because the drive to Agra took two and one-half hours, one way without stops. I showered and dressed in cool clothes to be able to tolerate the 120°F (48°C) temperature that day, and we found a taxi.

I don't remember ever being so miserably hot in my entire life! It was oppressively humid, we were beyond thirsty, and there was only Coke to drink at each roadside mini attraction where the taxi driver stopped. We watched the obligatory shows featuring dancing cobras, bought more Cokes, and continued the trek through the desolate landscape.

When we finally arrived at the Taj Mahal, it did not disappoint. The construction included precious stones and gems from Sri Lanka, China, Tibet, and India. More than 1,000 elephants were enlisted during its construction to transport the gems and building materials. The Taj Mahal was a symbol of love and the burial place of Shah Jahan's favorite wife[6], who died giving birth to their 14th child in 1631.

Despite the unique construction, historical love story, and amazing beauty of the Taj Mahal, something else I witnessed near the entrance where all the visitors passed left an indelible impression on me.

Two young Indian children carried a heavy brass pot, one on each side holding the handles. Inside the pot was a younger child whose legs had grown circular, forcibly conformed to the contours of the pot. The siblings (presumably) of the intentionally crippled boy were begging tourists for money. Even now, more than 50 years later, remembering the atrocity overwhelms me with a wave of revulsion.

---

[6] Izz-un-Nissa

A Brief Break

Every seat was filled on the flight departing from Bangkok, Thailand, destined for Saigon, Vietnam. The Pan Am 727 was returning the uniformed, all-male passengers to Vietnam after enjoying five days of R & R in Bangkok. It was 1971. We were five stewardesses, a purser, and three cockpit crew. Our job was to make this flight as pleasant as possible for our passengers, which sounds like our mission for every flight, but everyone aboard knew this was different.

Our individual views about the Vietnam War meant absolutely nothing on this flight. Each crew member had bid this line (schedule for the month) as one of three choices awarded by seniority. We had chosen to make the trip to Saigon, transporting approximately 106 humans back to the jungle they knew too well, back to being ever-alert, extremely uncomfortable, and always vulnerable. Many of the passengers were younger than I was. Many had not volunteered to serve. All were gentlemen.

As I looked over the mass of neutral, khaki uniforms, I tried to process their plight as individuals, but their faces revealed little, just quiet resignation. I could only imagine the emotions they had recently locked away. Some had met wives and girlfriends in Bangkok for a brief respite from their constant longings and fears while serving in Vietnam. They had relaxed, danced and drunk, and celebrated their love. Too soon came the inevitable, dreaded wrenching apart and goodbyes.

Of course, I knew many of my classmates had been drafted; however, it was only factual knowledge. On this flight, I felt the tragedy of war embodied. These servicemen were too young to be conscripted into war, in which some would inevitably die. What a waste of our nation's youth or human wealth of any age! I thought of my brother Tim, who was only 12 then, and hoped the draft would be eliminated during the six years until he was 18. If not, I even considered arranging for him to live in another country.

The United States Government had contracted with Pan Am since 1966 for these R & R flights. A Pan Am captain originated the idea, which found its way to the appropriate government decision-maker, who accepted the offer immediately. It was implemented within days. Pan Am charged the government $1 monthly for the first four months of service. After that, a more remunerative contract was initiated, with the condition that the airline would not profit from these flights. In the first year, 100,000 servicemen were transported to eight resort destinations. Pan Am flew 18 R & R flights daily into Vietnam during the second year.

The men were welcomed on the PA by the captain. The flight was to be less than two hours, during which he hoped they would enjoy a drink and the inflight meal. As standard on other flights, the purser reviewed emergency procedures and asked that no one smoke until the captain extinguished the "no smoking" sign. Then, we would start the beverage service.

Almost every man lit a cigarette as soon as the "no smoking" signs were turned off. Seeing the clouds of smoke filling the cabin, the purser politely reminded the men on the PA that they had air vents above their heads. In unison, 106 arms responded by reaching up to open the vents. We should not have been surprised because they were a disciplined group. But it was humorous to us. Bourbon and coke was the favorite drink, although Pan Am had stocked a full bar of liquor.

Near the end of the beverage service, the captain came on again with updated flight status, the altitude, the approximate local time of arrival, and the news that we would soon be serving the meal. He stated that after the meal, there would be a topless coffee service. Like me, the passengers may have thought they misheard the announcement. I asked Ana, a stewardess, what he meant. Not wanting to be a spoiler even for me, she only smiled and said, "You'll see."

Ana and Osa were twin Norwegian stewardesses with whom I had flown at least once previously. Unforgettable, they were both beautiful, curvy, identical blondes, but their attraction transcended the visible. Both demonstrated a quick wit, contagious laugh, constant helpfulness, and compassion. Every purser would love to have them on her crew.

We served a hot meal consisting of steak, home fries, green beans, milk, and ice cream. Being a well-trained and efficient crew, we soon had the trays and trash collected and stowed. Only the coffee service remained.

Ana or Osa – I couldn't tell them apart – started a slow, pseudo-seductive slink up the aisle from the back galley while easing off her apron. She would flick it gently on a man's neck, move another step, and flirtatiously brush another man's cheek. The men responded with clapping, whistling, and laughter. With all eyes on her, she continued to the cockpit, gifting numerous light touches as she went.

As Ana entered the cockpit, Osa started from the back, pleasantly surprising the spectators again. The applause increased as she began leisurely unbuttoning her white uniform blouse, bestowing playful strokes as she made an unhurried stroll up the aisle. She entered the cockpit as Ana was exiting, laboriously unbuttoning her blouse with one hand while bestowing gentle caresses with the other. Finally taking it off completely, she wore only a camisole underneath. She swirled and dragged the blouse lightly over the men. Their total attention was on her, and the anticipation was palpable as the clapping and whistling reached a crescendo. They were so distracted that they did not notice that our uniforms had the camisole sewn to the skirt.

It was not easy to be sure where each of the identical beauties might be at any time. Then, the cockpit door again opened slowly. A tall figure emerged carrying a pot of coffee. It was the flight engineer, and yes, he was shirtless!

Upward

When I had flown for Pan Am for one and a half years, I became eligible to apply and train for a purser position. Liz and I both wanted to expand our responsibilities, pay potential, and flight assignments. The training proved extensive and fascinating because we had little knowledge about all the behind-the-scenes duties. We both passed, became pursers, and started a new chapter in our Pan Am experience.

The supervisory hierarchy of the 747 was slightly different from that of smaller aircraft. The flight crew on a 747 included a Flight Director who occasionally was male, but many were females. Under the supervision of the Director were two pursers. One directed the first-class service and the stewardesses who worked there that leg of the trip, and the other performed the same duties for economy class. On smaller planes, there was no Director; the pursers supervised the stewardesses in each class and usually rotated classes on each leg of the trip.

A purser's duties began when she reported for a flight at least two hours before flight time. She checked with the cockpit crew and ground staff to know about the expected flight duration, weather conditions in the air and at the destination, special needs passengers, special meals requested, unaccompanied minors, celebrity passengers, and anything else unusual.

At the briefing, which included all inflight crew, the captain said a few words to everyone, highlighting atypical details, if any. Then, each purser met with the stewardesses assigned to the class she would supervise that leg of the trip. She relayed information from the ground and cockpit crews and outlined the service details: who would work the galley, who would offer drinks, who would sell headsets for the inflight movie, etc. Also noteworthy on long flights was the conservation of water and soft drinks. There were times, on full polar flights, that we ran out toward the end. If it were a night flight, the purser would signal when to lower the window shades and offer

141

blankets and pillows. First-class passengers were also offered eyeshades and slippers.

Especially on long or overnight flights, the purser would oversee a rest rotation. Like me, some stewardesses did not feel comfortable sleeping inflight, but some had no problem catching up on lost shuteye when most passengers were resting and the cabin was quiet. There were usually unsold seats in first class where the crew could rest. The purser needed to know where her crew members were resting and if they would like a wakeup.

Conferring with the cockpit crew about the updated remaining flight time, she determined when to raise the shades and distribute warm, damp towels to passengers to freshen themselves before breakfast was served. Apart from the initial welcome aboard salutations and flight details, which stewardesses gave in their qualifying languages, the pursers made all other pertinent announcements inflight.

When I flew for Pan Am, all passengers and crew were allowed to smoke. But we had the discretion, with the backing of management, to ask a passenger smoking a cigar to extinguish it. When meal service was over and any time when duties lessened, especially during night flights, stewardesses could smoke in the galleys. Even though I disliked my introduction to cigarettes, I did take it up for a short time while I flew. It was common among stewardesses and kept me from nibbling on the tasty, tempting leftovers from the first-class meals. But after I had a 24-hour bug in London on one trip, cigarettes just did not appeal to me, and I have never smoked since.

Whereas stewardesses shared a room with another stewardess on layovers, pursers were given a separate room. In addition to our suitcase, which was checked when we reported for a flight, we had a large tote bag that contained real silver utensils for first-class meal service. We were also accountable for all currency collected for sales of headsets and liquor, which were inventoried at the start and end of each flight. We accepted all currencies and had to know the current exchange rates for each.

Due to the volatility of rates, I made a durable chart listing Pounds, Francs, Marks, Lira, Rupees, Quetzals, Pesos, Yen, Rubles, etc. Before each flight, I updated the exchange rates at home with small removable stickers, as needed. I posted the chart in the galley for all of us to use as a resource. To my knowledge, I was the only purser with a chart like that. Other pursers verbally stated the rates of currencies most likely to be used on the flight. Collecting revenue was not an exact science because we could not possibly carry change for every currency, but we tried to come close. Before we began the descent to a destination, if I were the economy class purser, I began inventorying small liquor bottles and headsets. The revenue also had to be categorized, counted, and documented. These were turned over to ground personnel upon arrival.

I had a double room to myself on every layover, a perk that gave rise to the idea of my sister Sheri taking a round-the-world trip with me when she was 21. Her Pan Am benefits allowed her one trip a year at a 90% discount. She stayed in my room, and our meals were easily covered by the generous per diem I received. So, she went around the world for $275.

Although I would never have suggested it, other crew members upgraded her to first class on each leg if seats were available after everyone was aboard. Although she probably remembers more details than I do, I know we didn't waste much time sleeping. By the time we reached New Delhi, arriving early in the morning, we had planned to sleep for only a few hours, then go shopping, etc. We slept through all the daylight hours and awoke startled to have just enough time to shower and dress for the next flight. The overdue rest gave us a second wind, and we continued Sheri's once-in-a-lifetime experience.

In other years, my siblings and Sheri used their discounts to go to Hawaii. When Tim was about 12, his best friend Bret moved to

Hawaii. Because of his Pan Am discount, he could fly to Honolulu and spend half the summer there with Bret. Then, he and Bret flew back together and spent time on Lemon St.

Parents of employees had amazing discounts on Pan Am and other reciprocating airlines. They could fly Pan Am unlimitedly at 80% off the standard fare. Other airlines also gave various discounts. Dad took advantage of his discount several times. He flew to Germany and returned to Munich, where he had been stationed in WWII. I wish I had taken the trip with him to learn more about his time there during WWII. He also went to Yucatán, México, to explore.

I assume Mom did not want to travel with him, so he went alone. I arranged a trip for Dad, Mom, and me to see some of the places in Guatemala that I had visited. We were to stay at an all-inclusive *posada* by Lake Amatitlán. We thought Mom would go, but she backed out as the trip time neared. Ironically, she said she didn't want to miss a reunion with some of Dad's family. Dad and I went anyway. I was happy he was able to see some of the scenic spots I had seen because of his generosity in paying for my first visit. He may have gone to other destinations that I don't remember now, but Mom did not use her discounts to venture even once.

*****

I decided to commute to LAX instead of living in the Los Angeles area, so I moved back to Orange County to live in Corona del Mar. Although Corona del Mar was farther from the airport (about an hour's drive time, depending on traffic), I preferred to live away from the Los Angeles metropolitan area. Flying out of LAX, my flights were longer; therefore, they were fewer. So, I had the luxury of living near the beach and could afford the $175 monthly rent.

My one-bedroom apartment in Corona del Mar was perfect for me. There was a small kitchen with the basics and an adequate bathroom. I bought a new bed and made floor-length curtains of white islet fabric. It gave the apartment a feminine touch, I thought. There was an ample carport outside the back door, so parking was not a problem. In most beach areas, even residents must compete for parking with beachgoers. Walking a few blocks and descending the cliff via a long set of steps brought me to the shoreline. It was a workout going back up to the apartment.

My sister, Denise, and her friends liked visiting when I was off between trips. They were about seven years younger, but we all got along well and enjoyed the proximity of the beach.

It was they who introduced me to marijuana. Pan Am had a rule about no alcohol for eight hours before report time, and marijuana was illegal. Period. Many times, I had several days between flights. My first time to smoke it was with some of Denise's friends, and it turned out to be an experience completely out of my comfort zone.

We smoked some, relaxed, and got hungry. I offered to walk a few blocks to Kentucky Fried Chicken and bring back food. I told them I would be right back, having walked there many times due to laziness or lack of time to cook. I arrived at KFC in minutes, ordered plenty of food, and started home. By that time, my overly relaxed brain had gone on strike. Details were taunting me, but I couldn't remember exactly how to get home. I wandered on several streets looking for landmarks, went too far in one direction, and became increasingly frustrated with myself and my foolishness while carrying the bags of previously hot food. Forcing myself to focus, I eventually got home, unintentionally taking the scenic route. The kids probably had no realistic guess about how long I was gone. I'm not sure I knew either. The lapse of control was extremely distressing, and I vowed that it would be the last time for me!

Destination and Destiny

Deciding how to spend a vacation would seem effortless for stewardesses, except there were so many choices. We could choose to visit a place for the first time, accompany family members while they used their discount, or stay home, renew relationships, and relax.

We had been flying for about three years when Liz and I sought something different. Liz's cousin, Margot, was coming to visit from Holland. Of course, she did not have the discounts to fly like we did. Heads together, we came up with a train trip to Mexico! Although we considered destinations such as Guadalajara and Vera Cruz, we decided on Acapulco.

In those years, Acapulco was a destination for celebrities, college students on break, and anyone else who enjoyed the beauty of the tropics. It was a safe vacation destination, exactly the opposite of today's cartel-ruled most dangerous city in México it became around 2006.

We learned about the "Express" train, on which we would have two roomettes with fold-down berths. Liz and Margot would share one, and I would have a single. There was also a toilet and sink in each room.

Liz's parents and a brother or two took us very close to the border with Mexico, where we camped overnight before boarding the train early the next morning in Mexicali. Her family was fun to be with, and I had gotten to know them when we got together between flights. We all enjoyed the camping night before we boarded the train.

I don't remember how many hours the trip from Mexicali to Acapulco took, but the train route went inland, then down to the Gulf of Mexico, hugged the scenic coastline, then inland to Guadalajara, and on to Acapulco. At night on the train, after getting in our berths, we raised the huge window shade as it was during the day, and it felt like we were sleeping under the stars. Meals were eaten in the Dining

146

Car, and we read and talked to fill the hours. Traveling by train was peaceful and relaxing.

Arriving in Acapulco, we took a cab to the hotel where we had reservations. From there, we could easily walk to Playa Caleta, a calm cove on Acapulco Bay, which was a favorite for locals and tourists. In the evening, we met a small group of local men of various ages who were singing informally with guitars. We were invited to join them, and they ordered beers for us from the nearby outdoor palapa-roof bar. Besides us, another female tourist from Canada seemed to be with one of the men.

Introductions were made, but it was Javier whose name we remembered. We learned he was an entertainer at the Acapulco Princess Hotel. His charming voice and how he effortlessly accompanied it with his guitar induced his friends to sing along. The songs were not typical tourist favorites. They were classic, romantic Spanish songs and ballads, and I could recognize enough of the words to understand the emotions they conveyed. We newcomers sank comfortably into the warm, relaxed atmosphere. At the end of the night, Javier invited us to be his guests at the show at the Princess Hotel the next evening. We accepted, of course.

The Princess Hotel, on the outskirts of town, was the most luxurious in Acapulco at that time. Frequented by jetsetters, the eight-story towers, restaurants, nightly entertainment, lush gardens, pools, and golf courses were impressive even to Liz and me. We stayed in Pan Am's Intercontinental Hotels in many places, but it was easy to see why the Princess in the Mexican Tropics along the Pacific was an alluring resort. The show was enjoyable and included some classic favorite English songs, like "You Are My Sunshine" as well. We were Javier's guests and attention was lavished accordingly.

Very soon, a magnetic mutual attraction between Javier and Liz became apparent. They were inseparable during the rest of our trip, seemingly trying to make the most of the incredible magic. Margot and I understood and were happy to explore on our own or hang out at the beautiful beaches. We may have all gone together to La Quebrada to watch the Cliff Divers plunge with torches at night from one of two ledges, either 40 or 80 feet above. To avoid disaster, the daring jumps must be made in perfect sync with an incoming wave. From the second the diver left the safety of his perch, spectators held their breath in silence. He was rewarded by enthusiastic applause when he submerged, then surfaced in triumph.

One night, Margot and I slept on lounges at the hotel pool after night swimming, leaving our room to Liz. The warm, humid Acapulco weather was conducive to round-the-clock activities. I don't remember curfews, closures, much less caution. But we were young and in vacation mode. It was a pleasant trip, both relaxing and adventurous.

We flew back to California, but not before Liz and Javier promised to continue seeing each other. For Liz, the agreement was easier because she could fly frequently for little cost from LAX to Acapulco between working her flights for Pan Am.

Downside

After recounting the innumerable, diverse, and unforgettable experiences afforded me as a stewardess and purser, I hesitate to detail the disadvantages. However, describing my job as purely pleasurable and without challenges would be unrealistic.

Time changes between destinations require adaptations, as anyone knows who has flown even within the United States. Usually, as flight time increases, so does the time disparity. So, a 12-hour polar flight to or from London, which I flew frequently, would result in an eight-hour time difference at the destination. Crossing the International Date Line was especially confusing, as you would be on a different calendar day after crossing. Areas to the west of the Date Line are one day ahead of areas to the east.

Stewardesses needed to wear watches. We had to listen carefully to the captain's announcements concerning the local time at the destination to be able to give announcements in English and our second language and answer passenger questions. Our watches seemed like toys that we were constantly setting and resetting.

After arriving at our destination, going through Customs, and riding in a van to the hotel, we would try to assimilate to local time as closely as possible. For example, if the layover was to be 24 hours, as it was on all round-the-world trip legs, I needed to plan mealtimes and sleep to be nourished and rested for the next leg of the trip. That meant often staying up even though I had flown all night, waiting for local mealtimes, and/or going to bed extra early, using blackout curtains. Planning was imperative.

Even though we were young, round-the-world flights were exhausting! Some stewardesses slept and ordered room service during layovers. I never wanted to let time pass like that and waste the opportunities to see and learn. But nine or ten consecutive-day trips did cause cumulative fatigue and fuzziness.

One time, I got dangerously drowsy during the drive home from LAX to Corona del Mar. It was a warning that I needed to take small measures, like getting more air, chewing gum, and listening to my favorite songs to avoid slipping into drowsiness for even a couple of seconds. I didn't expect to be at peak performance the day after returning, so not much was planned. It was enough to wash clothes, buy groceries, and let the jet lag subside. We had a minimum of 48 hours after a flight to recuperate.

One of the facts of flying as a junior stewardess and purser was that I was never at home on major holidays, like Thanksgiving, Christmas, New Year's, Fourth of July, Memorial Day, etc. More senior stewardesses and pursers could bid and be awarded lines to be home on some holidays, but there were unknown variables even for them. So, holiday celebrations had to be shifted to before or after the day. When we were in flight on those days, there was a festive feeling, and sometimes, there were surprise holiday tokens for the crew and passengers, which I appreciated.

Also, future planning for appointments, reunions, and birthdays was almost impossible due to the unpredictability of our schedules, which were different every month. We bid for three package deal schedules for the month and usually were awarded one of them. This made it a challenge to maintain relationships, but friends and family had to accept the fact that I may not be able to attend a future event, regardless of my intentions.

However, without a doubt, these small sacrifices were well worth the opportunity to travel the world and expand my horizons!

Out of the Blue

My great uncle Jack, Grammie's older brother whom we visited in Staunton, Illinois, did not have children with Aunt Alice. By the time he died, his sisters had children and grandchildren, of whom I was one. Unexpectedly, I received $3,000, as did each of my many cousins. A surprise monetary gift can seem like a bonus that generates thoughtful consideration for its use. Of course, I put it in the bank, but it nagged to be spent on something special.

My younger siblings were lucky enough to need orthodontic treatment at a time when my parents had two fewer dependents because my sister Sheri and I were out of the family home and on our own. Having noticed and disliked my slight overbite seemingly forever, I decided to go to an orthodontist to discover solutions. Clear plastic braces affixed to the teeth and connected by a single, thin wire were a novel, popular alternative to the traditional, all-metal predecessors. While detectable, they were much less conspicuous. At 25, I was fortunate enough to have this state-of-the-art option available.

I briefly considered Pan Am's grooming rules and how some had relaxed in the last couple of years. For instance, when I started flying, stewardesses who needed corrected vision had to use contact lenses. I remember complaints of dry, bloodshot eyes and even infections caused by the airplane cabin air and smoke. Although glasses were not allowed then, some stewardesses would take out their contacts in flight and resort to glasses for relief. Finally, probably thanks to union negotiation, glasses became acceptable. So, I rationalized that if frames and lenses could be worn on beautiful faces without diminishing that beauty, clear, inconspicuous braces covering less area of the face would be even less objectionable.

I was excited to start the process. At that time, extractions were common in a crowded mouth, followed by slow, steady closing of gaps, eventually creating a more perfect bite and smile. After each tiny cranking of the fine wire, my teeth would be slightly tender for a few days. But the result would be worth it!

I performed my job as a purser exactly as I had for the last two years. I had developed methods to make the extra responsibilities easier and always had the support of excellent stewardesses whom I supervised. Several passenger letters were in my file at the flight supervisor's office, commending me and the crew on the flight they had taken. No crew or passenger seemed to notice and did not comment about my braces.

After I had flown over three months with braces, I was called into Grooming before a flight one day. I rarely was asked to weigh in, but they did weigh me occasionally, probably to maintain equity. Some stewardesses had been put on a monitoring schedule and told they must lose weight if they wanted to continue flying. The grooming supervisor weighed me and was happy with the reading. When I turned to go to the briefing, she said, "What is that on your teeth?" I told her they were clear braces for correcting my overbite. She dismissed me without commenting, but her displeasure was obvious, quite in contrast with her demeanor when she weighed me.

My thoughts and actions returned to trip mode, gathering information and briefing my crew. It was no time for worrying about the interaction with a mere grooming supervisor.

The trip was most likely round-the-world, lasting nine or ten days. When I returned and was easing into my normal at-home routine, I got a call that summoned me to my flight supervisor's office. I thought it must be evaluation time again. For a stewardess, time passed in spurts and drags, erasing normal cycles and distorting the length of interim periods.

Mike Spurgeon was my flight supervisor. On some level, his family was involved in Orange County politics, but I don't know if that had anything to do with Mike landing a job at Pan Am. He was affable and relaxed, more like a friend, although he conducted our routine evaluations.

I don't doubt that he took his job seriously. When he received a letter from a passenger praising our service and attention, he passed on the encouraging compliments to the stewardesses he supervised. The only comment on any of my evaluations that barely could qualify as "room for improvement" was that I could be a little more assertive. (I'm not sure if Pan Am had an unidentified employee onboard one of my flights to evaluate me or just how Mike got the idea that I didn't assert myself.) I told Mike that if I needed to be assertive, I would, but I was lucky to work with exemplary stewardesses without exception. They knew their duties, demonstrated friendliness with passengers, were voluntarily helpful to both passengers and crew, and we all appreciated our jobs. Besides that comment on that single evaluation, the others were glowing.

Mike invited some of us to a party on a huge lot at his (parents'?) beautiful family home in Santa Ana. Liz and I accepted the invitation. I remember seeing Ana and Osa, who had been on my flight to Saigon, also there. It was an evening of classy, "good, clean fun," with abundant food and drink.

So, I arrived at his office in a lighthearted mood, having had no experience to the contrary. But he seemed pained for some reason I could not guess. The heavy atmosphere was ominous.

"Why would you do such a thing? Why did you think you needed braces?" he asked me. Pan Am loved my smile, which was one reason I was hired. He also reminded me of the many complimentary letters in my file.

"They in no way affect my ability to perform my duties. Besides, I have flown for over three months with the braces affixed, and no one has even commented," I told him.

I could have asked if there were any negative letters in my file concerning the braces, but I didn't want to seem smart-assed. I mentioned that stewardesses could now wear glasses and that my braces fell into the same category of corrective measures. I didn't say it, but it wasn't like a precedent-setting, door-opening thing. I doubted everyone would want to go right out and have braces affixed to their teeth.

It was unstated, but he seemed to have received a directive from above his position that he was powerless to change.

"Can't you please just take them off?" he pleaded.

I told him the four extractions in preparation for the braces made that an unfeasible option. So, he laid out the ultimatum: Remove them or resign.

The protocol that followed right then was shocking and rapid-fire, literally. I was led to a barely lit empty conference room, monopolized by an enormous oval table, and asked to have a seat. Papers appeared on the table in front of me. Sign to resign. Then, I was taken to a tiny cubicle for a hearing test. Not surprisingly, they quickly determined that my hearing had not been diminished by boarding and deplaning directly on the tarmacs in many parts of the world while plane engines roared. I must return my uniforms and coat to receive my last paycheck; I could keep my aprons and wings.

It was too late to remind myself that logic and common sense are scarce in the world of regulation. I was determined to contact the union as soon as I got home. There was still an avenue of hope for a reversal. I paid dues for almost four years, and surely someone with a modicum of common sense would guide my grievance through the channels. Wrong again! I was told they could not take my case because there was no rule about braces. Precisely! *My argument exactly*. But, it was useless to try to convince them. They refused to go into the great uncharted.

I've since wondered if, subconsciously, I wanted to play roulette, if I was tired of the aloneness, and if I craved more stability and predictability. I'm not sure. Consciously, I learned that you don't play roulette unless you are prepared to lose.

Part Three - Roads Taken

Reality Hits Hard

I wasn't prepared to lose my dream job. Nor was I prepared to reintegrate full-time into Southern California living. Flying for nearly four years prevented me from fully understanding the realities of what was happening at home. The hours I spent in the air and other countries predominated my time, interests, and concerns. Time at home was for seeing family, resting, and packing for the next trip. I admit to being rather oblivious about the state of the job market.

After relating the story to my family about how I suddenly joined the unemployed, a question from Mom was disconcerting, and I don't know how or if I answered her. She asked why I had not warned her that I was "quitting." Either she hadn't listened to me or, more likely, did not want to accept responsibility for the consequences of her procrastination. As my parent, she had unlimited 80% discount on Pan Am and reciprocating airlines to go anywhere in the world for almost four years. She had not once taken advantage of my employee benefits and backed out when I booked her to take a trip with Dad and me.

With no hope of reinstatement by Pan Am, priority one was to look for a job just to pay the rent. Any job would be an interim means to earn money while I worked on a plan. I wanted to continue living my freedom in Laguna where I had moved from Corona del Mar. I had become accustomed to my independence, so returning to Lemon St. was unthinkable for multiple reasons.

Waitressing had dominated my job experiences before Pan Am. I would do that until a better plan fell from the sky. I thought any restaurant would be happy to hire me, a former stewardess and, before that, a waitress at Marie Calendar's. I was ashamed to let the owners know about the swift demise of my Pan Am career, so did not consider a job there again.

Before the Internet, employers advertised in the Classified Section of newspapers in the mid-seventies. Reading the ads, calling a phone number, or just showing up at an advertised time was the way to be interviewed and hopefully hired.

The Crazy Horse Steak House and Saloon in Santa Ana had an ad for waitresses that caught my eye. At that time, it was an upscale western (if that's not an oxymoron) restaurant where I imagined I could make good tips. I arrived at the time specified in the ad and joined a long queue of hopefuls that had formed at the restaurant entrance and spilled almost to the main street.

As I stood outside in the sun, I thought confident thoughts. More accurately, I was smug. The line to get inside to interview seemed almost stagnate, but patience became easier during the wait because of my secret advantage: my experience. Finally, it was my turn to come into the coolness and sell myself. I filled out an application and then spoke with someone. Having had an abundance of time to collect a mental list of my perceived strengths, I laid them out succinctly. We thanked each other, and they said they would call if I were selected.

I wasn't. Trying to solve the mystery of my non-select status consumed me because I needed to know why. Knowing could direct my next steps to employment. There were only questions: Did they consider me overqualified? Did they think I would be disappointed with minimum wage plus tips and leave soon after being hired? Were they afraid that having been a union member might make me a troublemaker? Did they picture me in their short-hemmed, low-necked, ruffled uniforms and disqualify me due to that image?

The short answer was that the 1970s featured high unemployment, high inflation, an oil embargo and resulting oil shortage, and a flood of baby boomers like me looking for jobs. Others my age who had managed to earn degrees were disappointed at the lack of opportunities after sacrifices of time, expense, and persistent study. My cushy job at Pan Am had buffered me from those realities.

Relating my woes to my hairdresser in Fullerton brought a surprising, if unfulfilling, solution. He said he could use someone in the salon to shampoo and clean up after clients. As he thought more about it, he offered to send me to a cosmetology school to train to be a licensed manicurist in his shop. I decided to disregard my lack of enthusiasm for a career in cosmetology and the commute (about 25 miles) from Laguna and accept his offer. It was something.

Grateful, I tried to make the best of it. Days at the salon dragged on, interspersed with putting in hours at cosmetology school. To qualify for the state test, it would take a seemingly interminable 1,000 hours of study and practice at the school.

I think the salon owner convinced the school to count my salon hours or gift me some hours so that I could finish earlier. I began to study for the test for which Mom volunteered to be my client. It went well. I passed and started to use all I had learned for the regularly scheduled salon clients who must keep their nails beautiful. Listening to the two-week segments of their life sagas and trying to comment appropriately was taxing. I continued because I was earning my existence. Although devoid of motivation in that occupational setting, I was friendly with the salon operators, and customers seemed pleased with my services.

I had kept in touch with Liz regularly, visiting her family, especially after getting to know them when they took us to the train in Mexicali. Of course, I had told Liz about my forced resignation. She was incredulous but confessed to a little envy, saying that flying was taking its toll on her. In addition to her Pan Am flights, she was weaving in trips to Acapulco to see Javier. Not long after, she announced their engagement, gave notice to Pan Am, and started making wedding plans.

Javier's parents would travel from Chilpancingo to Acapulco, about a one-and-a-half-hour drive, and then fly to Los Angeles. The wedding would be in Orange, where Liz and her family lived. I was honored to be asked to be one of her bridesmaids.

The Vandercappelens were a close-knit Dutch-Indonesian family who had survived major life changes together. Liz and her two brothers were born in Indonesia, where her father was employed in law enforcement until the Japanese invaded the island in 1942, a few months after Pearl Harbor. Although quite young, Liz retained the memories of fear, danger, and family upheaval. She confessed to residual enmity for the Japanese in general from then on. Her family fled to Holland, where they had relatives. Eventually, although I didn't know the details, they were all cleared to come to the United States.

Javier was adamant that they would live in Acapulco. Liz liked Acapulco but had mixed feelings about being away from her family again, indefinitely this time. She knew I had not found my niche since leaving Pan Am. My days were drawn out, void of passion or any sense of progress. Liz began lobbying me to come live in Acapulco.

The idea sparked various positive emotions in me. The dominant one was hope, which had been in short supply. My disenchantment with Southern California living was implanted even before flying with Pan Am. The ubiquitous conspicuous consumption, an overemphasis on the importance of appearance, and general materialism seemed increasingly shallow. I didn't want to play or compete any longer.

By now, I had observed and experienced life in many cultures, worked with stewardesses from numerous backgrounds, and was impatient to continue my progression. Thankfully, those experiences increased my independence and self-confidence.

Living in Acapulco would offer another immersion experience in a Spanish-speaking country where I could continue improving my conversational ability. Always ready to taste and learn to prepare new foods, that opportunity was also exciting. My best friend, Liz, would live there, and we would support each other and assimilate.

I seriously considered the idea quietly before announcing the possibility to my family. But the spark was being fanned, glowed, and motivated me.

When I told Liz I was excited about her idea, she was happy too. Of course, Javier was consulted, and he was enthusiastic about it. He was always friendly and an easy person to be around. After the wedding, I decided to go to Acapulco on the same flight as his parents and the newlyweds. We joked about me being their chaperone.

Although I had saved money, I hoped to find employment there, preferably with a US-based company. I researched hotels in the downtown area where I could walk to work. I think it was the Hilton I wrote to, now that I had an arrival date, and included my resume. I received what seemed to be a promising answer but not an actual job offer. It gave me the name of one of the managers I was to contact to set up an interview.

It was time to prepare to leave the country with the wedding date approaching. I would "lend" my car to an older friend of Mom's who would get around better in my small compact than in her old boat of a car. She agreed that I could have it back when I returned. I gave notice at the salon and started giving away things in my apartment that I would never need in Acapulco. I sewed a few more clothes for the hot tropical weather.

Packing only clothes and toiletries, I prepared to live in another country, not just spend a day or two there. Employment with Pan Am had implanted a yearning for adventure and new challenges, which had been involuntarily interrupted for several months. Also, my Spanish skills would be honed every day. A fresh start was intriguing, away from the hyper-materialism of SoCal and my current state of stagnation. Hope was on the horizon again.

Assimilation

My new home was a room above the post office, reached by climbing a flight of stairs. It would be fine. It had the essentials: a bed, a bare-bones bathroom, a mini fridge, a two-burner *parilla,* and a chest of drawers. Javier warned that it was best to spit out shower water; don't swallow while showering.

There were high windows on the outside wall and open, narrowly spaced cement louvers on the wall where a staircase ascended just outside the room, leading to other rooms. The immobile louvers were angled precisely to offer both privacy and air current. A chest of drawers was centered on this wall, under the louvers. In the back corner of the room was a rod on which to hang clothes. It was time to unpack my belongings.

This didn't take long. I placed my wallet and a few items on top of the chest for easy access. It was the only piece of furniture. I don't know when or exactly how my wallet disappeared from the chest top. It must have been a small hand that slipped through the louver at the level of the chest top. Luckily, most of my money – the majority in traveler's checks – and valuables were stashed in my suitcase on the opposite wall. However, it served as a warning for me to be more vigilant.

Javier had found a small home for Liz and him to start their new life. It was a three-bedroom, had a fairly ample kitchen and living room, one bathroom, and an outdoor clothes washing station. The floors were all tile, which is most practical for the tropics. In the front yard was an *aljibe*, a large, covered subterranean tank of water. It was a reserve of water in a rectangular cement receptacle.

One of the first things on my list was to phone my contact at the Hilton to arrange an interview time. The administrator who had signed my letter invited me to a meal. The food was good, but the conversation was stilted, atypical of what I expected for a job interview, even an informal one. The uncomfortable silent intervals made me wonder if one of us had misunderstood the purpose of the meeting.

Being patient, thinking it might be a cultural courtesy not to jump right into business, I wondered if he would furnish job details after we finished eating. He stood, signaling that the meal was over, led me toward the elevator, and then invited me up. I thanked him for the meal and left. His motive was no longer a mystery. I had hung my hopes on a positive-sounding letter that now stank like bait. When I told Liz and Javier about it, Javier said he didn't know the guy, but he was not surprised.

*****

Knowing that the room above the post office was spartan by any standards and that my perceived offer of employment fizzled, Liz and Javier invited me frequently to eat and spend time with them. I was constantly mindful of their newlywed status and did not want to interfere with their initial bonding. However, they both convinced me that I should come to live with them.

Although it seemed unusual for newlyweds to have a tenant, I believe there was something in the arrangement for each of us. Liz was missing her family, spoke little Spanish, and could use female companionship. From the time I met Liz, I liked her practical, honest, down-to-earth manner. I could be myself with her. I imagine Javier wanted his new wife to be happier in her adopted country. And he could go about his daily business without worrying that his wife was lonely.

We would learn to thrive in Acapulco together. Although Liz had visited Acapulco many times since she met Javier on our vacation, it was different to be married and a resident now. For me, the beauty and warmth of Acapulco, the complete lack of clothing style consciousness, and the freedom to skip makeup were all refreshing changes. I had long felt like an outlier in Southern California, whose inflated importance on women's appearance irked me. Our lives were much simpler in Acapulco than our former lives in Southern California.

We began to explore and learn. We became familiar with Comercial Mexicana, which was very similar to US grocery stores, and approached big-box size. We cleaned the house, washed clothes, planned meals, and then went to the beach to swim and relax. The first time a tropical storm passed by Acapulco, we put on our swimsuits and shampooed our hair in the warm rain. We welcomed the healthy, low-maintenance lifestyle we had chosen. However, when Javier relayed an invitation to model at the Princess Fashion Show, we accepted. The experience was novel and fun.

*****

Liz was confronted with an unexpected prefab bias that put her in a defensive position from the start. She appeared to have the *café con leche* Moreno skin like the locals, but when they discovered she spoke no Spanish, they derisively asked her, "*¿Qué pasó con su español?*" (What happened to your Spanish?) Of course, they had no idea she spoke English, Dutch, French, and some German. The common assumption was that she, like some Mexicans with the means to do so, had spent time in the US, learned English, and returned to Mexico afflicted by amnesia about her native tongue. Based on this assumption, they diagnosed her with an acute case of superiority.

To make matters worse, Javier's parents, who were aware of Liz's background and capabilities, found it easier to talk with me in Spanish. It wasn't intentional exclusion; it just required less effort.

The unforeseen issue was unfortunate and had no immediate remedy. Fortunately, and much to her credit, Liz absorbed a fifth language, Spanish, as her assimilation progressed.

Visitors in Paradise

Acapulco, in the 1970s, held a magical allure for visitors. The jagged coastline offered a variety of bays, inlets, and open ocean, perfect for recreation and relaxation. In unique, non-chain restaurants, all kinds of fresh seafood and beef, chicken, and exotic delicacies were served. Midday, after the main meal, life crawled to the speed of relaxation. Humid afternoon heat could best be tolerated in a hammock, with a drink, and near water for intermittent dunks. Refreshed by a shower and the slight coolness of evening, tourists revived to revel in the nightlife of their choice. All were available at a whim: music, movies (with Spanish subtitles), dancing, cliff divers, shows, bars, night swims, spontaneous gatherings, supper, and finally breakfast when the night ran out too soon. Acapulco life was 24/7, a charming coastal resort.

During the time I was in Acapulco, all my immediate family members (except Mom) visited Acapulco to see me and for other reasons, like getaways and honeymoons. Liz's parents also visited a few times, and it was good to see them again and get caught up on what was happening.

Although I cannot relate family visits in strict sequence, I'll mention some well-remembered times. Trish and her new husband, Rich, honeymooned in Acapulco, and Sher and Mike (her fiancé) came for a getaway at the Princess Hotel. Captivated by the tropical ambiance, Mike joked that he would be happy to live in one of the huge flowerpots at the entry to the hotel.

When I made short returns to the California nest for rare visits and Christmas one year, there were two occasions when a family member accompanied me back to Acapulco on the train and then flew home. I had told my family about my first trip to Acapulco on the train with Liz and Margot. Impressed with the unequaled sense of travel by train, I described the unhurried freedom to absorb towns and territories from the enormous windows of our sleeper while tracking the path of the sun from dawn to dusk. At night, before pulling down the bed to sleep, we again raised the huge, rolled shade to enjoy the night sky. Without competition from manmade lights, multitudes of stars splashed the sky, and rays of moonlight slanted into the cozy cabin.

Dad returned with me on the train one time to experience Acapulco firsthand. A sun lover and somewhat of a foodie, there was little for him not to like. However, he interrupted a pickpocket, whipping a half circle to confront the would-be thief of his wallet on a crowded standing-room-only city bus. The lesson learned was that front pockets are safer for valuables. No wonder women carried money in small soft pouches safely nudged into bras between their breasts.

*****

For most of my life, a sewing machine had been an essential appliance. It was good insurance against unraveled hems and split seams. Besides, sewing hot weather wear, bathing suit coverups, and curtains were easy, custom, and inexpensive. I got the impression that bringing my machine on the plane and getting it through Mexican Customs might be problematic and/or costly.

When I went home for Trish and Rich's wedding, Denise and I devised a plan. She and I would take the train instead of flying back to Acapulco alone. The thought of her coming with me to see Acapulco and experiencing train travel was exhilarating. Overconfidence and excitement probably caused my error, which cost us a few days of discomfort and extreme tests of patience.

The train I booked for us left at a different time of day than previous trips, which should have been a red flag to me, but it was advertised as "Express," so I thought the daily departure time had changed. Another advantage was that its scheduled departure would allow time for us to take a bus from Orange County to Mexicali.

There was nothing "express" about that train! We had only seats, no sleeper, no diner car, no water, and a heavily used restroom. The train stopped in every tiny village along the roughly 1,500-mile route. At each stop, eager, agile vendors hopped quickly aboard, laden with a variety of foods carried in large baskets they could barely shove above our heads through the narrow train aisle. I don't remember what edibles we selected, but we had to sustain ourselves with something. Luckily, we didn't get sick. Trailing the vendors, serious-looking officials asked for our visas and IDs at each stop. Invariably, they took a suspicious interest in the sewing machine stowed on a rack above us. I reiterated a short schpiel in Spanish, assuring them it was for my personal use, not for sale.

The hours dragged, punctuated only by slowing, stopping, and pulling forward again. Entire days and nights seemed stretched past the actual numbers while we remained captive in our seats. Our skin became sticky with grime, our teeth grew fur, and our hair grabbed the humidity, mixed it with stale body oil, and clung to our heads. Denise said she boarded as a blonde but became a brunette.

A welcome surprise awaited us in Mazatlán. We would change trains and board a Pullman with all the amenities I had described to Denise and thought I had booked. Ecstatic, we could clean up, eat in the dining car, and get some rest. Finally, our ordeal ended. We arrived in Acapulco, ready to savor the tropical paradise.

*****

Javier had introduced Liz and me to a novel Thursday ritual. On this day of the week, a local family opened their home to sell their famed green *pozole*. The advertisement was by word of mouth, and seating was on a first-come, first-served basis. The house had a spacious adjoining patio covered by shade tarps. Several long tables filled the patio to accommodate as many clusters of guests as possible.

In the unhurried atmosphere, for it would be the height of rudeness ever to hurry guests (especially to deliver a bill before it was requested), the diners set the pace. Of course, beer was available, but *mezcal* was the common accompaniment to *pozole*. It was the real deal

167

and contained a worm to prove it. Being well-primed for *pozole* meant a few rounds of *mezcal* in the company of friends who brought an offering of fresh *chisme* (gossip) to share. If beer was the beverage, empty bottles were lined up on the table to tally the amount owed when guests were ready to leave.

It was up to guests to signal the hosts when they were ready for *pozole*. Then, several bowls of enhancements began to crowd our section of the table: sliced radishes, chunks of avocado, quartered limes, sliced green onion, sliced jalapeños, shredded cabbage, and *chicharrónes* (fried pork rinds). As with many Mexican soups and stews, *pozole se guisa en la mesa* (*pozole* is made at the table).

The laborious process of pozole-making begins several hours before the addition of the final garnishes. It starts with a large pot or several in this *pozolería*. Pork shoulder, ham hocks, and pig's feet are accompanied by onion, carrot, celery, garlic, bay leaves, and salt. These are covered with water, brought to a boil, then simmered for two to three hours. The meat should fall apart and be easily shredded with forks. The stock is strained, discarding the solids, and continues to simmer.

Onions, peppers, and pepitas (pumpkin seeds) are *sautéed* in a separate pan. More garlic, thyme, cumin, salt, and pepper are added. These ingredients are put in a blender, to which some stock, tomatillos (small green tomatoes), and radish leaves are added. The blended concoction is then returned to the pan and simmered to thicken.

The green mixture is swirled into the stock along with the shredded pork and white hominy. After simmering for a few minutes, it is served, and diners add the finishing touches to the table. Of course, a stack of hot corn tortillas is at the table and replenished as needed. It is a rich, delectable meal. When Denise was visiting, she, Liz, Javier, and I spent a good chunk of one Thursday at the *pozolería*. As we chatted and relaxed, the slightest twist of Javier's wrist and the circle of his index finger would cause another round of *mezcal* to appear magically. Mid-afternoon, fully satiated, ecstatic to be alive and enjoying each other's company, we walked to a nearby dock and jumped into the lukewarm ocean, clothes and all. Memorable, fun times!

Angel of Iguala

Denise got another chance to visit me. She seemed to want to assimilate into Méxican culture more naturally than my other siblings. Whether she loved Acapulco, missed me, or both, she visited when possible. I was still living with Liz and Javier, so I asked them what they thought of the idea. They knew her easy-going nature and sense of humor. "Yes, tell her to come! We have room, and it would be good to see her again."

Denise retains many indelible memories of that trip; most are happy, but some are just unforgettable.

She remembers us making quesadillas from delicious Manchego cheese for breakfast and helping Liz and me sweep and mop the tile every morning. She memorized *"Medio kilo, por favor"* when she took a clean dish towel to the *tortillería* before the main meal and returned with a tightly wrapped piping hot stack of soft white corn tortillas. Of course, Thursdays were for visiting the *pozolería*.

Also, during this visit, a slanting blasting rain powered by hurricane-force wind happened to roar into and through Acapulco. Surrounding Liz and Javier's house were a few other well-built homes, but farther up their inclined road, the residents lived in makeshift dwellings that their meager earnings afforded them. It was sad to witness their sparse possessions being fiercely forced down the street by the flood of water. The pavement of La Costera, the main coastal road, severed, leaving one side on an angle while the other side sloped into a sinkhole.

*****

My visa would expire soon. Six months had passed quickly. Javier proposed that we all go to México City, renew my visa, get a glimpse of the capital, and eat at a restaurant famous for its *cabrito*.

170

It would be just a day trip. Javier was familiar with the road and the five-hour drive each way. Besides, we were young. We expected to get home sometime that night.

The trip to the capital was pleasant and uneventful. We never seemed to exhaust our capacity for conversation and stories. Arriving in México City, we went to the U.S. Consulate, where a long line snaked from the entrance. We were not even sure it was possible to extend my visa without returning to the U.S. and reapplying. The line was too long to wait for an answer, so we began the second purpose of the trip: sightseeing.

After Javier pointed out some of the capital's landmarks to us, hunger took precedence, and we headed to the famous restaurant whose name escapes me. It was an immense place with high-capacity seating. Visible just inside the entrance were large hunks of raw meat hanging. The sight was startling to Denise, but I was accustomed to it at the Mercado Central.

The menu was ample, but Javier praised the *cabrito* (meat of young, milk-fed goats) and its savory sides, which were served family-style. Javier, Liz, and I had a drink, and Denise had a soda while we waited for the feast.

A platter piled high with grilled-to-perfection meat appeared, followed by tortillas, beans, salsas, pickled vegetables, etc. We ate unhurriedly, refueling from the drive and sightseeing. The generous portions were almost gone when we decided we should head home.

Leaving the greater metropolitan area, we traveled the same route we had come, winding through many towns that were not considered map-worthy. Observing residents in these villages, I imagined the details of their daily lives at such a distance from the conveniences we considered necessities.

Suddenly, Denise told Javier she was feeling sick. Could he pull over? She barely got the rear door open in time to vomit violently onto the road. She apologized, saying she had felt fine until it abruptly hit her. She settled into the seat, and we all hoped that whatever offended her digestive system had exited. But sadly, the intestinal revolt continued.

During our second stop, when she felt sick, Liz kindly offered to switch places with me. My pallid face must have conveyed my aversion to upchucking. I was embarrassed by my squeamishness but beyond grateful to her. As I switched to the shotgun seat, she tried to make Denise as comfortable as possible in the back seat. Liz was a natural nurse. I think she may have found a bag or blanket to contain the mess.

All of us were alarmed by the fierceness of Denise's sudden illness. Her body seemed to be on a single-focus mission to exorcize whatever demon she had ingested. Expeditiously, it began to employ both exits. Entering each of the many towns and villages en route, Javier immediately looked for a bus station or anywhere we might find a public restroom. The trip seemed interminable, stretched by the numerous stops, while Denise's condition only worsened. We feared she was becoming severely dehydrated. Darkness had surrounded us, closing in tightly, especially in the smaller villages where the thick night was pierced only occasionally by electricity.

Only half of our homeward journey was behind us when we rolled into Iguala de la Independencia, famous for ending the Mexican War of Independence from Spain and considered the birthplace of the Mexican flag. Disregarding the town's importance in Mexican history, we focused on the plight of our patient. As we searched for a restroom, we saw a two-story, narrow, stark-white building with a red cross painted on the side. Although it was late, the light over the front door was lit. Javier parked and knocked on the door. In a minute or so, an older man opened the door. Javier returned quickly to the car with good news. We accidentally found a clinic, and the resident doctor invited us in.

From his downstairs humble residence, he escorted us upstairs to his clinic. We helped Denise, who was thoroughly debilitated, up the stairs. The doctor helped her into his clean hospital bed and calmly gathered details as he started an IV of *suero* (serum) to combat the dehydration.

We told him we all ate family-style food from the same serving platters. He asked Denise if she drank anything alcoholic. Underaged by US standards, she had only soda while the rest of us indulged in a couple of drinks. With a smile, the doctor surmised that she might have been wise to have had a couple of drinks too. He conjectured that maybe a fly had chosen a particular piece of meat to lay her eggs on, and Denise was the unfortunate consumer of the fly's progeny.

As the *suero* circulated in Denise's veins, it was miraculous how quickly her symptoms started to abate, although she was very weak. We expressed our gratitude to the doctor and experienced surges of profound relief, knowing we were in good hands. None of us, least of all Denise, gave any thought to the sterility of the needle, any of the equipment, or the doctor's credentials. We were only thankful that she was getting the lifesaving *suero*.

The doctor advised that we spend the remainder of the night while the *suero* rehydrated Denise, giving her healing strength. He would be downstairs if we needed him. The stress drained from our bodies as we relaxed into comfortable chairs to rest and doze.

When the first pale light of dawn entered the high windows, we descended the stairs. Although we fully expected to pay for the care and hospitality, the doctor would not accept it. Again, overwhelmed with his generosity, we expressed our gratitude. As we resumed our journey toward Acapulco, we were amazed at the beneficence of a doctor we happened to find in Iguala.

Denise continued to improve after the onslaught on her system, but it took a few days to return to normal. Goat meat will never pass her lips again.

Caleta Beach

Some evenings, I went with Liz and Javier to Caleta Beach, where we had gone as tourists and where they met. The same cluster of friends gathered to sing, joke, and exchange profanity, proving their level of closeness. As the beer expanded emotional expression, the singing became increasingly heartfelt. Maybe the words and beer opened channels to experiences in their lives and freed their voices to release emotions. Seeing this uninhibited masculine behavior, especially in a stereotypically macho culture, was interesting and novel to me.

I vaguely recognized one of the men, Gilberto, who was with the Canadian companion when we visited on vacation. She was not present, and he seemed to be interested in me a bit. Possibly Javier had told him that I was Liz's friend and had come to live in Acapulco. I don't know. He started talking to me in accented English, markedly educated and fluent. As we spoke, I think he noted that I was following the group's Spanish conversation and sometimes commented in Spanish. The realization that I was somewhat bilingual may have upped the attraction.

Gil, as everyone called him, was an affable addition to any social gathering. He listened and contributed equally well, had a frequent contagious high-pitched laugh, and seemed to be an integral, charismatic part of the knot of friends. Physically, his skin was dusky, further tanned by the tropical sun. He had ample dark hair with shallow *entradas* (recession) beginning above the temples. His thick, bushy eyebrows and mustache, which he fingered involuntarily, could make him appear stern or at least pensive when he was not laughing or talking. Intermittent work as a longshoreman at the port and occasional swimming kept him in shape, appearing slightly younger than his years despite regular imbibing.

Javier told me Gil had been married and still was, but his wife had lived in California for many years with their two sons. They visited

174

Acapulco very infrequently. She had never endeared herself to the *Acapulqueños*, but they were politely courteous when she visited. I did not interpret Javier's objective information as a warning. He offered the background to me, a friend, about another friend. So, I knew those facts from the start.

However, that knowledge did not prevent me from accepting an invitation to go with Gil to see a popular Mexican band perform a few nights later. He renamed me Mara (sometimes evolving to Maramarú, Marushka, Marika, etc.) because Marlys didn't roll off a Spanish speaker's tongue easily. We conversed comfortably; he was easy to be with, and assimilation was rapid and pleasurable with a local guide.

Los Martinez

I wish I knew more, but what I write here is what I remember from information gleaned from conversations with Gil over the years and what I could glean from the internet. Unfortunately, no one is alive now to corroborate my memory or offer more details.

Surprisingly, his mother, Dolores de Martinez Rivera, and his father, Constancio Martinez, met in California sometime in the 1920s. They happened to work together in a cannery in San Francisco. I don't know how Constancio or Dolores left Mexico and came to the United States, but Gil told me his mother was an orphan who went to California when she was 14. She learned English quickly and could still remember some English in the 1970s when I was in Acapulco. But she and I always spoke Spanish.

I imagine the couple had a civil wedding, rented a flat, and continued working until their first daughter, Irene, was born. A couple of years later, Ana was born. Having been born in the US, the two girls were United States citizens, which Acapulco natives alluded to kiddingly.

I am unclear about what sparked Constancio's unease about staying in the US, but it was probably a mix of reasons. He and Dolores likely had illegal immigration status, and between the World Wars, public sentiment concerning such immigrants was largely unfavorable. I was told by Doña Lola (Dolores) that her husband felt such an urgency to return to Mexico that she was told they could not take many belongings. She had to leave behind her sewing machine and most of the conveniences they had acquired with diligent work.

They came (or returned?) to Acapulco to live in a house with dirt floors. In 1933, Gilberto was born into this circumstance of poverty. His mother told him she slept lightly to protect her family from scorpions.

Upon arrival, Don Tancho (Constancio) worked as an *estibador* (longshoreman, dock worker). Gil said (and the internet confirmed) that his father established the La Confederación Regional Obrera Mexicana (CROM) union in the port of Acapulco. I understood that union members in Acapulco worked port-related jobs, but La CROM also represented agricultural, textile, and other workers in México. La CROM had an office in Acapulco, and its members and their families had access to a medical clinic and a hospital when I was there (1974 to 1978).

Don Tancho was revered in Acapulco for his constant efforts to protect and fight for workers' rights. He also acted to protect some of Acapulco's shoreline, conserving it for local fishermen when touristic ventures were quickly devouring it. A street named in his honor, Calle Constancio Martinez, connects two major streets, Benito Juarez and Costera Miguel Alemán.

Dual-cultured and bilingual, Irene and Ana continued school in Acapulco. While both were excellent students, Ana was selected to be part of an advanced program in Chilpancingo, the capital of the State of Guerrero. Because of the distance, I'm not sure if she attended daily, but the designation allowed her to advance beyond the academics offered in Acapulco. When I was there, she was the secretary to the mayor of Acapulco. Irene worked in the offices of La CROM and took over its administration after her father's death. She also opened and ran a small eatery in their neighborhood, conveniently located for dock workers on short breaks. Gil took me there occasionally.

Irene and Ana were both married, and each had a son; Fernando was Irene's, and Mario, who was adopted, was Ana's. Neither of Gil's sisters was still married when I came to Acapulco.

The Martinez women, Doña Lola, Irene, and Ana were outliers in the town. Apart from their uncommon female independence, their nutritional knowledge and culinary expertise were extensive and

177

unusual. Doña Lola had diabetes, and she and her daughters shared the goal of feeding the family as healthfully as possible. As I got to know Gil better, I suspected that all three women had enabled him to become markedly less ambitious than they were.

Although the family was not Catholic, nor did they practice any religion to my knowledge (another anomaly in their community), they always attended friends' milestone events and funerals in religious settings.

After arriving from the US, the Martinez Family had proven itself to be a cornerstone of the community and a positive, contributing element for the people of Acapulco.

Integration

Whether my views about marriage resulted from the social revolution of the times or close-range observation of family members' deteriorated unions, I no longer revered the institution as I was brought up to do. As an adult, I witnessed my parents living under the same roof, traveling solitary, seldom intersecting paths. Conversation between them became increasingly minimal and utilitarian. As their children became more independent and less reliant on their care and guidance, I wondered if their union lacked purpose.

I considered Gil's long-distance marriage, which had stagnated for many years. It seemed to be one of convenience only. Because of his marriage, he acquired temporary resident status in the US and possessed a green card, which allowed him to travel and work there. Although he visited California infrequently, Acapulco was undoubtedly Gil's home, his base, and his comfort zone. Some years at Christmas, the estranged family spent a few days in Acapulco. Later, I learned the marriage was unplanned and was mandated when Charlotte became pregnant with twins.

In short, I deduced that a marriage was not defined by the existence or absence of a certificate.

I find the following irony interesting as it runs contrary to stereotypical ideas about stewardesses' sex lives: During the time I was employed by Pan Am, ages 21-25, I was approximately 99% chaste. The 1% exception was not in serious relationships but at home and not on trips.

Yet, after living in Acapulco for a while, I began living with an older married (long-distance) man and suffered no qualms. Gil and I got together to swim, see movies, enjoy musical bands, indulge in late suppers and early breakfasts, and take day trips when there was no ship in port to load or unload.

However, early on Gil gently explained the repercussions of local mores on our relationship. I could not visit his family's home because of his marital status, even though reality and his actions openly belied the legality. The Martinez home, across from the *Malecón* (wharf), consisted of several dwellings that Gil's father had built over time for his wife and adult children. They were contiguous but not connected, like private apartments separate from the main house.

One of his sisters, Irene, had a small-scale eatery adjacent to their houses where Gil took me to meet her, have a light supper, and catch up on the neighborhood gossip. Physically, she was matronly and stout, with a natural air of leadership and strength. After her father's death, she assumed his authority in La CROM, the local dockworkers' union. Despite this responsibility, she remained unpretentious and industrious.

While she bustled to fill the customers' orders, they volleyed comments, joking and laughing. However, I sensed polite restraint toward me. I felt I was on the fringes of the friendliness she showed her customers. It was to be expected. I imagine, in retrospect, she might have silently asked herself when her errant younger brother would reform and mature.

I didn't meet Ana, his second sister, for a while. When I did, I felt more acceptance from her, which may be attributed to her personality or the passage of time. Her slimmer, softly feminine appearance contrasted with Irene's; she was physically prettier than her sister. Her extraordinary intelligence was evident when she spoke, and her quick witticism could be both humorous and sharp.

Gil described his mother as a typical Mexican matriarch whom I would not meet in person for a few more years. The widow of Don Tancho wore her gray hair in two long braids that lay over her ample bosom. The soft rounds of her body were a testament to her abundant culinary knowledge and skills utilized daily to prepare delectable "*guisos*" (dishes) for her family. She asked her son if I was a hippie.

He told her no, adding that I was very clean and orderly. We laughed when he told me about her concern.

Soon, Gil found a place for us to live, which was a lot like a motel room but had a communal kitchen and clothes washing area. Huge trees shaded outdoor tables for eating and socializing. Gil brought a collection of essential pots, pans, plates, and utensils from his house, assuring me they were extras. Grateful, I was anxious to start cooking.

*****

My introduction to *Mercado Central* (Central Market) was a novel experience. With sturdy shopping bags in hand and a minimal wallet discretely hidden, we boarded a standing-room-only bus destined for the immense outdoor shopping area. Gil owned a fairly reliable, beaten-up compact vehicle (a Renault?), but he usually walked or boarded buses in town.

A symphony of smells waxed and waned as we passed by myriad vendor booths where I learned to buy the ingredients for our meals. In the absence of price labels, the potential buyer had to ask, "*¿A cómo es?*" (How much is it?) "*¿A cómo son?*" (How much are they?)

All animal parts considered edible were draped over rods or lay on naked display. Rice, beans, and assorted dried chiles were offered in bulk, scooped, and weighed. Artistically exhibited, every imaginable vegetable, fruit, and fresh herb was available, including unfamiliar ones I had not yet learned to use. Gil bought tamales of iguana for me to try. I reminded myself that they were seasoned and fully cooked like any other meat, as I tried not to visualize their live appearance. I had seen vendors circulating carrying iguanas hung by their long claws tied to a stick. The tamales were tasty, like chicken.

I bought a *molcajete* (heavy stone pestle and mortar), which would be my blender for a while. The curing process of a molcajete, using dried corn kernels, took time and persistent wrist-twisting effort to smooth the rough stone. The inner bowl had to be perfectly smooth to prevent food particles from lodging in stone pores and endangering food safety.

Gil accompanied me this first time to the *Mercado Central* as I absorbed the learning experience. After that, I shopped alone and enjoyed the adventure. Once in a while, I still shopped with Liz at Commercial Mexicana.

In Acapulco, near the *Malecón*, was the place to buy marlin filets that were cut from the enormous fish that were rolled on flat wagons from the boats. It was a mild, inexpensive fish best fried quickly to retain its tender texture. There were also delicious *guisos* that required lengthy simmering in sauces to bring the flesh full circuit back to tenderness.

Working irregular hours as a longshoreman, Gil would appear at any time of the day or night when he had a break or had finished a ship, sometimes bringing a friend or two. His friends respectively addressed me as *"Señora,"* connoting a married woman. I gave them whatever I had made to eat. The chance to practice hospitality made me feel happy and increasingly integrated.

Gil began to bring containers of food with generous portions of the day's main meal, *la comida. "Mi Mama te manda este guiso para probar,"* (My Mom sends this dish for you to try) he would tell me. Without exception, the ample samples were delicious! I asked Gil, who was also interested in cooking and culinary experiments if he knew how the dish was prepared. He said, "Call my Mom."

Even with his permission, I was apprehensive about making the first call, knowing the restrictions he had outlined and not knowing how she might react. However, my fears were unfounded. I told her I thoroughly enjoyed the *guisos* she had sent me and thanked her for her thoughtfulness. Would she have time to explain how some of them are made at her convenience? Of course. Which one would I like to learn first? Doña Lola was open, humble, and unassuming. I felt she wanted to be accessible, even though local decorum dictated it had to be by phone.

Doña Lola instructed me by phone in Spanish and with full details on how to replicate her *guisos*. She freely gave tips and wanted me to be successful. However, a noticeable omission was the exact measurements of ingredients. Instead of cup, tablespoon, and teaspoon, she used measures such as *manojo* (handful), *tantita* (a little bit), *pizca* (dash, pinch), and *una quarter*, meaning the size of a quarter in the palm of your hand. I jotted the Spanish quickly as she explained, adhering to the required sequence. The collection of recipes grew to include seafood (marlin, red snapper, octopus, squid, etc.), meat (beef, kidney, heart, brains, tongue, and armadillo), chicken, vegetables, and salad dishes.

Had her legitimate daughter-in-law been unwilling to taste Doña Lola's culinary offerings, much less cook them? Naturally, many questions existed, but I resolved to suppress all questions concerning Carlota, believing that asking even Gil would demean me. Listening and internalized deduction seemed more fitting.

After making each *guiso*, Gil and I ate my version, and he took some of the leftovers to his Mom and sisters, who encouraged me with praise. I transferred my sketchy recipe notes to complete Spanish sentences written in a notebook that increased in size and diversity. Today, over 50 years later, I have that handwritten notebook. I plan to type Doña Lola's instructions in Spanish and translate them into English as well.

*****

We ventured in Gil's car to nearby coastal destinations frequented mostly by locals. At La Laguna and beaches like Barra Vieja, there were hammocks hung from and shaded by *palapas* (round thatched roofs made from palm fronds). It was a peaceful spot to relax, swim, have drinks, and eat seafood made to order at your leisure.

Sometimes, raw oysters and/or turtle eggs were offered. I learned not to try to divide an oyster into two bites, no matter how large it was. They were plump and not easily parted. After adding a squeeze of lime and a dash of hot sauce, the most effective way to eat them was in one slurp from the shell. Turtle eggs could be legally harvested when they were not in "*Veda*" (a prohibited time or a place where they could not be harvested due to scarcity or their reproductive cycle). The egg size and color mimicked a ping pong ball. Lime and hot sauce could be inserted after poking a hole in the shell which was thin and pliable. A swift, strong suck brought the rich contents to your mouth.

After swimming in the warm, inviting water, we lay in open-weave hammocks, the breeze cooling our wet bodies. When hunger revisited, we ordered fried whole fish or other types of seafood served with salsa, corn tortillas, and fresh herbs. Delicious! It doesn't get any better!

Downtime

Something was off. My energy and appetite were flagging. We had always joked that if a Harper lost their appetite, something was seriously wrong. Intermittent waves of mild nausea passed over me, making me wonder if maybe I was pregnant.

At Gil's suggestion many months prior, we agreed I would stop using contraceptive measures. As my malaise continued for days without becoming much worse or resolving, pregnancy seemed the most likely cause. I continued to cook and clean but did not have much appetite. I tried to eat minimally, knowing I should, pregnant or not.

It seemed there was a leak in the fuel tank; my energy was in increasingly short supply, replaced by weakness. As my condition progressed, I was alarmed by the Coca-Cola color of my urine. We finally went to the doctor, carrying a specimen jar in a bag. The doctor looked at the yellowed whites of my eyes, heard my complaints, and told us I had Hepatitis A. He assured us it was not chronic, as is the case with other types of hepatitis.

The virus causes inflammation of the liver, affecting its ability to function in its energy-storing role. Despite my white seersucker dress, twice I had to sit down anywhere I could find while walking to the doctor's office, so his explanation for my lack of energy made sense. He told us the virus was usually transmitted by contact with food or drink contaminated by an infected person. Even swimming in an inlet where water was incompletely flushed out to sea could have been the cause. We would never know.

Complete rest (meaning bedpan, sponge baths, etc.), nutritional foods, and frequent spoonfuls of quick-energy honey and *cajeta* (*dulce de leche* – milk caramel) were prescribed. He advised me not to even read until my strength returned. Time and rest were my only options. The doctor did not need to see the specimen to diagnose and asked us to throw it away elsewhere.

Gil deserves credit for the way he cared for me as I recuperated! He brought light meals that his Mom and sisters made for me: *gelatinas* (milk-based gelatin molds made from scratch), *ensaladas de berros* (watercress salads), fruits, *aguas* (blended fruit drinks), and teas. I took a spoonful of honey or cajeta every couple of hours. Gil checked on me when he had a break from work and, yes, emptied the bedpan. The extreme weakness subsided slowly, and my appetite picked up. On day 10, I took a shower and washed my hair, marking a turning point in my recovery. After that, every day was better than the previous. Although Hep A is contagious, Gil did not contract it, thankfully.

A huge morale booster was the news that my siblings, Denise and Tim, were coming to visit. At that time, there was no vaccine for any type of Hepatitis, but they received immunoglobin, which was the only protection at that time. I was approaching good health when they arrived and enjoyed the reunion immensely.

Soon after, Gil found us another rental that became home for me in a deeply sensed way.

Sharing Nature's Space

Our rented lodging on the outskirts of Acapulco was nudged securely into a cliff, high above a narrow U-shaped bay. The bay had no beach approach, and I considered it my private source of beauty and peace. It was crowded with water-rounded rocks, whose voices varied with the moods of the ocean. At its angriest, the rush of water slammed the rocks against each other with the fierce din of natural drama. But usually, the rocks merely rumbled hypnotically. In the calm times, the rocks slept, motionless. These sounds of Nature, which always permeated our living space, created a sense of continuity despite the changes.

The apartment hugged the cliff in a straight stretch, without a hallway, from the street entry door through the kitchen, a small living area, the bedroom, and finally to the bathroom. Opening a metal door outside the bathroom and descending a few steps, there was a cement area, a ledge without restraints. From there, the cliff tumbled steeply to the bay below.

The ledge was where I washed clothes on a ribbed stone sink. Adjacent to the ribbing, the other half of the sink was a stone reservoir, which I filled with fresh water for rinsing. A half gourd carried the water from the reservoir to the scrubbing area to wet the clothes and rinse the detergent. The daily wash included sheets, towels, and clothes.

The apartment did not need a water heater because the temperature of the piped water was always tepid in the tropics. We showered and washed dishes and clothes with the naturally warm water. On the lower ledge, I hung the wash on lines stretched parallel to the dwelling, where they dried rapidly in the breeze. If a sudden squall threatened, I raced down to the ledge to retrieve the clothes before Nature could spot them with her oversized drops.

The kitchen had only a low wall to separate it from Nature. There were no screens or windows in this part where we cooked and ate on a table by the half wall. On the other side of the wall was the pristine cliff, clothed with thick tropical vegetation and home to an assortment of nonhuman life.

All of Nature's creatures considered themselves invited into our dwelling. We welcomed *cuijas* (small geckos), mosquito-eating guests who traveled walls and ceilings freely, occasionally making kissing sounds. Once, an over-curious iguana accidentally entered under the metal door outside the bathroom. It looked confused, then panicked, clicking its claws on the slick tile floor as it scrambled clumsily to find an exit. It quickly discovered a drainage hole in the kitchen area and slithered down into its familiar habitat.

The list of unwelcome guests, besides mosquitoes, included cockroaches and mice. I kept the house as clean as possible, trying to eliminate attractions. Also, I strung a thin wire high across the kitchen, from which I hung food items in bags. Dried chiles, herbs, pasta, and rice dangled from the wire, so mice could not get them. Regardless of the precautions, the unwanted visitors entered. I guess humans were the intruders in Nature's realm.

An increasingly pungent smell, which the sea air could no longer hide, alerted us to a problem. The odor was of death, unmistakably. We looked everywhere as the stench became intolerable. Finding no clues, we assumed a rodent had gotten trapped inside a wall and died. Then, mysteriously, the stench lessened, but its source remained unknown until I decided to thoroughly clean the stove. When I lifted the cover over the burners, the sight startled me. A mouse had found its way into the flat space in the center of the burners, where it was trapped, died, and was roasted. It was completely dehydrated by then and splayed as if stretched for a science project display. I had to dispose of it, trying not to think it had lain beneath our food while I cooked every meal since its demise.

188

Next, in the linear floor plan, after the living area, was a door to the bedroom. Here, the opening above the low wall was covered by screens inconsistently attached and only partially effective at keeping out mosquitoes. We built a second line of defense, called a *pabellón,* a rustic hanging canopy over the bed for our protection while we slept. I sewed netting to the square of wood that hung from the ceiling, leaving an overlapping slit in the net for a door. We tucked the netting under the mattress at bedtime and felt safe from the buzzing menaces. A fan hummed every night to mitigate the humid tropical heat, and pajamas were non-existent. I gathered the net cascade each morning into a twisted knot over the bed and removed the sheet to wash it.

The furniture in the bedroom was minimal: a low chest of drawers on which the TV set and a tiny table for the fan. A hammock hung from the ceiling attached to large S hooks, parallel to the screened windows, at just the perfect height.

The sparse furnishings made it easy for sweeping and mopping, an everyday chore due to the openness of the apartment. The cleaning didn't take long. Once I got a routine using a wooden T mop draped with an absorbent clean *jerga* (rag) and a bucket, the tiles got a once-over. The reward for washing and cleaning was going to the beach to swim and relax before preparing *la comida,* the main mid-afternoon meal.

One impediment to my cleaning regimen lasted for many irritating months. Gil had acquired some surplus wood from someone and dropped the disordered pile just inside the street entry door against the wall. Its intended use remained a mystery; It was for something, someday. I didn't like the idea that a variety of unwelcome creatures could hide there, propagate, and call it home. Although I complained about its unsightliness and not being able to clean the area, the response was always indecisive and procrastinating.

One day, my tolerance reached an abrupt limit. Leaving the apartment, I walked down the hill toward town without a feasible plan for how to get rid of the wood. Along the way, I noticed shacks and houses that could be repaired if only there were money for materials. I asked a couple outside their home if they could use some lumber. They accepted the offer immediately. They recruited two friends to help carry the unexpected donation, and we all walked uphill to the apartment. They were grateful to be the lucky recipients, and I was happy to be rid of the mess. I cleaned and mopped the area, which made the entry of our home more pleasing.

My solution was immediately noticed when Gil came home. He was furious! Red, heated, yelling, furious! He couldn't believe I dared to disregard his wishes. Nothing had broken the peace between us until then. But the anger and resentment were nonviolent and short-lived. And the wood was gone for good.

The method of trash collection was another lesson for me. It didn't happen on a consistent day of the week or seem tied to any schedule. If I heard a loud cowbell ringing farther up the street, it would be my chance to get rid of the trash. Quickly, I grabbed the bags and some pesos for a tip and went out to the street to wait. The tip was obligatory. Leaving the trash on the street for pick-up was not an option.

The refilling of propane tanks was equally unpredictable. When I heard someone yelling "gaaas" repeatedly, I went to the street with pesos in hand to ask them to check the remaining amount and refill the tank. At the mercy of the deliveryman's level of honesty, I learned that trust must be nurtured, and a healthy tip helped.

The proximity of our apartment to the ocean was a huge advantage for reasons besides its alluring beauty. Exiting the apartment and following the street downhill brought me to an open beach, where small fishing boats launched every night to test their luck. They fished all night, hoping to sell their catch at dawn.

Several times a week, I got up before it was light, washed my face, and threw on a shift to go down to the beach to meet the nocturnal fishermen. I carried a broad, flat kitchen knife to clean the fish, a plastic bag (which locals called "a nylon") to bring them home, and pesos in my pocket.

As I descended to the beach in the balmy predawn, the glaze of silent water, dotted with twinkling lanterns of small row boats, stretched to meet the barely visible horizon. The boats were well-spaced as if they respected each other's chosen proprietary area. As the dawn steadily crept to conquer the night, the boats turned to row toward shore. The tiny vessels thudded themselves into the sand, and a fish or two, still alive in the boat bottom, flipped rebelliously.

Usually, there was ample choice of small fish to make a delicious breakfast, fried whole and served with rice and salsa. I paid whatever they asked and marveled at their endurance and patience. After buying only the fish we would eat that day, I descaled and gutted them at the water's edge, as Gil had taught me. Inserting the knife point in the mid-belly hole, I cut a straight line upward toward the head and removed the innards in one handful. Hooking my fingers into the circle of gills, I yanked them from the head. The heads were left intact to crisp in the oil when fried. I placed the guts and gills where the next soft swoosh wave would coax them into the water. Circling seagulls swooped down for the guts even before a wave could swallow them. Then, I would trudge uphill with the fresh, odorless fish to make breakfast.

I made this predawn trek countless times without incident until one morning. I was descending to the beach in semi-darkness, enjoying the stillness and watching the constellation of rowboat lanterns below, when I was startled by the noise of a vehicle that had suddenly crested the hill behind me. As the vehicle sounds let me know it was slowing, my sense of peace was shattered. My feet froze in their gait as the noise stopped beside me. Rotating my head to the right, I saw it was a police jeep.

"*¿Adónde va?*" (Where are you going?) one policeman asked.

191

"*Voy a la playa aquí abajo para comprar pescado.*" (I'm going to the beach below to buy fish), I answered.

"OK. *Ándale pues,*" (OK, go ahead), one replied. Seemingly satisfied with my answer, they drove on.

Relief and gratitude washed over me as I continued to the beach. The sudden appearance of the police had put a protective numbing spell on all thought processes. Now, I tried to look at the incident from their perspective. The police saw a "*huera*" (light one) openly carrying a large kitchen knife (or could they have missed the knife at my side?), walking by herself at almost dawn. It was not an area visited by tourists, and there were no hotels nearby. Lucky for me, they didn't seem curious about my immigration status, if I worked, or where I lived.

Nor did they know my visa had expired. When my initial 180-day visa was near expiration, I made the long trek by bus to Allen, Texas, to cross the border and renew it. With a new visa in hand, I boarded a bus the same day to travel 30 hours back to Acapulco. It was a grueling, lonely trip, after which I decided being illegal was preferable.

Of course, I had no permission to work in México, either. But, sometimes, when Mariscos Pipo Restaurant (owned by Gil's uncle) was crowded with tourists, I waitressed there, earning only tips.

I was grateful for the policemen's lack of curiosity and that they mercifully did not want to harass me to amuse themselves. It could have gone much differently!

Gil contacted a friend who worked in the *Instituto Nacional de Migración* (INM) (National Institute of Migration. We met with him, and he extended my visa by another 180 days. In the future, his assistance would again be invaluable.

Hablando

There is a saying in Spanish, *"Hablando se entiende la gente."* (People understand each other by talking.) If implemented, this simple truth could prevent or solve problems. At the very least, perspectives and opinions can be exchanged if not adopted.

Frequent conversations with Gil were open, interesting, and sometimes raw in their honesty. We shared backgrounds, incidents, and confessions. Of course, our cultural and religious histories contrasted sufficiently to result in fascinating exchanges. Then, the matter of our ages – Gil was 15 years older than me – and past experiences made for disparate perspectives. He had fathered three boys; I was still childless. As more memories were related, the gaps in our dissimilar life stories began to fill in. I think the intense listening and telling proved cathartic for both of us.

On some topics, despite the sharing, we each remained on parallel tracks. Reasons for the inability to connect on those issues may fall under the broad category of culture.

Take celebration of birthdays. Gil explained that the person whose birthday it was hosted the party. On one of his birthdays, we decided to invite guests to celebrate with us. We planned what to serve, even inventing some *botanas* (appetizers), an original salad, and *guisos* we thought the guests would like. Gil invited acquaintances by word of mouth. There was plenty to drink, but I got the message much earlier that women were to imbibe sparingly, if at all. That was fine with me because I wasn't accustomed to drinking much. The guests complimented us on the food and welcoming atmosphere. Although we worked together planning, prepping, and cooking, Gil gave me the credit, saying, "¡*Mara es como la chingada*!" (Look it up. Despite its crude sexual definition, it was meant as a compliment.) So, the *reunión* (get-together) was a success, and we enjoyed hosting it.

193

Just for contrast, I'll relate an exchange. Although we were aware of each other's birthdays, there was no mention of my birthday before or on the day. He did not come home to eat midday but arrived well into the night and *en sus copas* (he had been drinking, and not a little). I assumed he had forgotten it was my birthday and calmly reminded him. He said, "Yes, but unfortunately, your birthday happens to fall on the *Santo* (Saint's Day) of all the Enriques. Can you imagine celebrating with all the Enriques?" And he went on to describe the festivities.

*****

Gil repeatedly voiced remorse about how he had failed (past tense, as if the opportunity already expired) to fulfill his role as a father. As I understand it, one of the twin boys died in infancy in Acapulco. Although I don't know how long Carlota remained in Acapulco after the death of one boy, it may have been a brief time until she returned to the US with the surviving twin. Gil and Carlota remained married, living in separate residences and different countries from then on. After some interval, another son was born, presumedly conceived during someone's visit to the US or México.

The younger son, Ari, was nine years old when he flew alone to visit his father while we were living on the fringes of Acapulco. I assume Ari first went to the Martinez home to see his grandmother and aunts. Then, Gil brought him to our apartment and introduced him to me, telling Ari he would stay with me. Gil said he would be with us when he wasn't working. I was happy to have Ari's company for a week.

Ari spoke no Spanish but curiously asked how to say a few words in Spanish. He would hear the response and without trying the pronunciation say, "Right." We laughed about that, but it revealed a perception that the language and culture of his father's family were not considered a priority to learn.

194

We headed to the beach on our first day, and Ari and I set some important precedents. He had an inner tube and a couple of beach toys. I took a large bag containing towels, drinks, toys, and snacks. Suddenly dropping the inner tube, his only item to carry, he implemented a test. I stopped and waited for him to pick it up, thinking maybe it slipped. He refused. Without reprimanding or guilting him, I explained that I needed his help. He stood his ground while I turned and walked toward the beach. When he saw I was not going to even look back at him, he picked up the tube and ran to catch up with me.

After that, we were buds. Pizza and hamburgers topped the list when I asked about his favorite foods. We boarded the bus to shop at Commercial Mexicana because Mercado Central would have been an overdose of culture shock for him. We bought ingredients for his favorites, sandwiches, and other foods for the week. Like his father, he was interested in cooking and liked to help me prepare meals. The highlight of the week was making pizza from scratch, mixing the dough, smoothing the marinara, placing the toppings, and baking it in the oven. We cooked hamburgers another day, and I think he may have tried fish, rice, and selected foods his Dad brought from his grandmother, Doña Lola. Gil checked in on us occasionally and seemed happy to see that Ari was having fun.

Exhausted after walking, swimming, meal preparation, and showers each night, we fell asleep in clean bathing suits on the one bed, under the *pabellón* with the netting securely tucked under the mattress. The fan on the little table whirred.

After Ari returned to California, I encouraged Gil numerous times when he bemoaned that he was an uninvolved father. It was not too late, I urged. Ari was fun to be with as well as impressionable. Although Gil blamed only himself, he seemed satisfied with frequent confessions and residual regrets.

Wedding at San Nicolás

Just past twilight, it was a high-pitched human whistle that stopped the truck in which we had been riding for about four hours. The truck was huge, with a wood railing around the oversized bed. A real "beater!" The man who was driving swung nimbly down from the cab and walked unconcernedly toward the rear of the truck. Curious and needing a chance to stretch, we followed. A figure was herding four young goats toward the back of the truck, where they would share the spacious truck bed with a huge water tank, a guitar, and the baskets containing our changes of clothing and a few provisions. The unwilling hitchhikers, pitifully voicing their insecurity, would be received at a spot along our way that the driver knew. I suspect that any vehicle making the trip from one remote village to another was open to transporting, if possible.

We were on our way to the village of San Nicolás, in the Costa Chica, south of Acapulco, having been invited to a wedding there by the godparents of the groom, Dr. Eduardo Diego, and his wife, Chelo. Dr. Diego and his wife made regular trips from Acapulco to give medical treatment to the people of Costa Chica.

In a Volkswagon following the truck were Eduardo's brother Pepe and his wife Yolanda. They had lived for five years on the ranch where we would stay. When we came to the end of the paved road, the VW had to be left with friends, and we all piled into the truck, the three women in the cab and the men in the company of the four goats. We three women and the driver could fit, although tightly, in the extra wide cab.

Shortly after leaving the pavement, our senses were aware of a delectable foreignness. The invigorating air, moving subtly, brought us sweet, pungent smells of the brush and trees. In mud-lined gullies and on sudden inclines, the truck struggled to maintain equilibrium and laboriously continued in the two ruts that stretched across the plain.

It was hard to accept the geographical fact that we were on the west coast of Mexico when our senses said this was Africa. Someone said that the only thing lacking was the lions. Most of the people of Costa Chica are descendants of the Africans who were forcibly transported and brutally transplanted on this continent. It is not surprising that when these people attained freedom, they settled in an area that resembled their native land.

At first, the purity of the atmosphere permeated us, producing tranquility into which conversation would have been intrusive. But after a while, curiosity collaborated with imagination, and I began to ask Yolanda numerous questions about the five years she and her family had lived on the ranch.

Along our way, a distant lightbulb competed with the moon and stars, but Yolanda said electricity is a novelty here; no one had it until just a few years ago. By the time we would reach the ranch, she told me, we would have traveled two hours since we left the paved road, slowly tacking across the plain. They used to make this trip by tractor, which is still the most practical means of transportation in this area, to buy provisions every 15 days. In the rainy season, there were times when the trip was impossible, or once started, the tractor had to be abandoned, and they went back to the ranch on foot. They were partially self-subsistent, having a herd of milk cows, raising chickens, and growing corn and other vegetables.

I was fascinated by some of the local beliefs that Yolanda related. One requires that a newborn child be placed on a pile of ashes immediately after birth. The first animal to pass by donates its soul to the child, and this animal's characteristics will always be evident in that person.

The truck rolled to a quiet stop. Quickly, I stowed my imagination and entered the present reality. We had finally arrived at the ranch. The soothing sensation of tranquility was even denser, like a rolling enveloping fog. Relaxing in the hammocks hung from the high porch surrounding the ranch house, we sipped water filtered in an earthen pot and listened as the caretaker couple spliced together recent history. Soon, we went inside to sleep. The knot in the net *pabellón* over the bed was left tied; in this season, not even the mosquitoes dared interrupt the peace.

At about six the next morning, fully rested, we arose with a feeling of quiet excitement. Yolanda had already started the fires in the hollows of the hewn-stone outdoor cooking area. Chelo and I chopped *chile*, tomato, and onion, then ground them to *salsa* in the *molcajete* (stone mortar). A bucket of pure, freshly ground corn appeared, which had been deftly kneaded on the *metate* (inclined stone plane where a long, stone cylinder is rolled to crush the corn to *masa* for *tortillas).*

Almost immediately, the combined odors of baking *tortillas,* spicy *chorizo,* and coffee drew the men. Our breakfast was complete with a moist, homemade white cheese, *queso fresco*, and a bucket of fresh milk.

After breakfast, the pump that brings water from the storage tower to the house was turned on. We each showered hastily, careful not to waste water, and put on our other change of clothing. Knowing that weddings usually start at about 10:00 a.m. and allowing for a one-hour drive over the same route we traveled the night before, we took our places in the truck and were on our way before 9:00 a.m.

In the Costa Chica, the mere knowledge that there will be a wedding constitutes an invitation. Our truck automatically converted to a communal transport, making stops at farmhouses and small communities just long enough for passengers to scramble aboard. A mother with her baby wedged herself into a corner of the truck bed in such a way as to minimize the erratic jolts of the truck and offered a full breast to her little one. Anticipation for the day's festivities became epidemic by the time we arrived in San Nicolás.

We were greeted on the main road of the village by the groom's mother and were invited into the welcome coolness of their block house. In San Nicolás, there is still a remnant of round, thatched roof dwellings made of branches and earth, but most have been replaced by more modern construction. Another detail of the groom's house, by which the level of family prestige could be judged, was a giant speaker on the roof. On this day, the village communication system broadcasted locally popular music of tropical tempo.

Inside the house, a temporary curtain on one side of the room formed the dressing room for the wedding party. At closer and closer intervals, the music was interrupted by a loudspeaker summoning the bridesmaids to come and start dressing. Sitting opposite the dressing room, we chatted and watched the curtain become alive with protrusions caused by the excitement and inevitable minor catastrophes of such occasions.

As we followed the wedding party out of the house and into the baking sunlight, the other villagers, alert to an inaudible signal, flowed from their houses. We walked the short distance to the church slowly and with dignity as one body. The church had no walls, only a roof of palm fronds that sheltered its modest altar and a small table covered with a white cloth. Strings of intricately cut, white paper flowers streamed from various points in the thatching. A few chairs had been brought for the parents and godparents, but it was obvious that the participants were accustomed to standing in ordinary religious exercises. There was room for almost all the guests to stand in the shade of the fronds.

While waiting for the bride to arrive, many children and some adults sucked popsicles to counteract the heat. We watched some boys nearby meticulously arranging firecrackers on crude tripods made of sticks. With that, the preparations were finished.

As soon as the bride arrived, escorted by her father, the simple ceremony began. Using the unsophisticated language of the people, the priest gave the couple the most basic counsel concerning the practicalities of everyday cohabitation. While he talked, some young girls, still licking popsicles, meandered among the crowd, distributing rice packaged in handmade, miniature heart-shaped pillows.

The atmosphere was one of naturalness, completely lacking the artificial reverence typical of some weddings. The ceremony ended with the godparents placing a circular string of flowers, twisted once to form an eight, over the heads of the bride and groom. Immediately, it rained rice, and the cannon-like booms of consecutive firecrackers marked the beginning of the celebration.

Almost considered part of the religious ritual is the partaking of hot chocolate and *pan de mujer* (bread of woman, literally). Under another frond-covered area near what I thought must be the center of the village, two long tables had been set. A complete and eclectic collection of the villagers' chairs and benches lined the tables. Because we were with the godparents of the groom, we were in the first group to be invited to have bread and chocolate. The *pan de mujer*, a coarse, barely sweet, raised bread with an incomparable flavor, was served from barrel-sized baskets. The hot chocolate was also delicious and made from fresh milk and locally grown cocoa.

About this time, just as several young men were carrying cases of iced cold beer to be served soon, we became aware of a serious problem. The *conjunto* (band) had not shown up. The groom's family, who is responsible for the wedding, was extremely embarrassed and tried to compensate by offering to play records over the loudspeaker. That way, at least, the guests could still dance. Maybe the *conjunto* would arrive later. Unfortunately, the predicament was not so easily remedied. Although various cajoling emissaries were sent to him, the father of the bride, indignant and determined that the groom's family be duly shamed, declared that there would be no music at all.

The crisis had passed, and the murmurings quieted, but we did not lack entertainment. Spontaneous laughter erupted from various integral groups as jokes and stories were shared. The children sifted unnoticed through the adult atmosphere and amused themselves in the immediate outskirts. The young men who volunteered to serve the guests were so attentive that one beer was never finished before one replaced it.

But, for Matatoros, all this conviviality was still lacking something. He knew that a few more *tragos de mescal* (sips of mescal, a liquor less refined than tequila made from the maguey plant) would bring inspiration. And his prescription produced results. With his head cleared, it was obvious that this occasion merited an infusion of beauty, fine art, and an expression of human sentiment.

And so, Matatoros, the village poet, recited and extemporized. He was a volcano of arduous feeling. Sometimes, between eruptions, he felt the need to re-clear his head with a few swallows of *mescalito*. I think it was after one of these intermissions that I realized he was addressing me with a poem that started something like, "*¿De dónde apareciste? ¿Del cielo?*" (From where did you appear? From heaven?) It continued flatteringly and respectfully. Self-consciousness hindered my memory from capturing all the words, but I told him I was honored by his poem. Of course, such outbursts of spirit are extremely exhausting, and after a few brave attempts to continue, even Matatoros had to lie down to rest for a while.

At about three in the afternoon, the unpretentious tables where we had eaten the bread and chocolate held huge containers heaped with food for the feast. I was amazed at the organization that must be required to serve such a party with so much attentiveness and efficiency. There were no audible commands; no one seemed to be in charge. Yet, there was a smooth, if invisible, coordination among the wedding couple's neighbors who served us. From various contributory ovens, the food was brought steaming hot to the table, and numerous consecutive shifts of people were served with every attention.

There were deep pans of chicken in dark, rich mole sauce, which contained several types of *chile*, chocolate, cinnamon, and at least 20 more ingredients. It is a tedious dish to prepare but a delicious specialty. The pans of chicken were alternated with mountains of fluffy, plain white rice, tall stacks of hot *memelas* (thick, handmade *tortillas*), salsa, and platters piled with *barbacoa*.

Barbacoa, or Mexican barbecue, involves an exotic technique completely distinct from the North American concept. The meat (usually lamb, goat, or beef) is wrapped in the leaves of the maguey plant, banana leaves, or those of other plants, depending on the desired flavor. Then, it is slowly roasted all day in a pit in the earth. The flavor and moist tenderness are indescribable.

Each group of feasters took their places at the table. Unhurriedly, they ate while talking and laughing. The pans of food, miraculously, did not noticeably diminish. As the chairs were vacated and refilled, the cycle began anew.

Late in the afternoon, a previously underground plan emerged. Because of the irreversible decision of the father of the bride, barring music, we would all continue the festivities in Colorado, the next village past San Nicolás. There, the celebrants could dance to music as the occasion required. The remaining cases of beer and all the wedding guests that the truck could hold were loaded into the back of the truck, and we again began the cumbersome maneuvering across the plain.

In the late afternoon, Nature ridiculed man's clumsy transport even more by masking gullies and shadowing inclines. Several times, the overburdened truck leaned precariously to one side, leaving its human cargo breathless for a second. Then, it would regain its balance and hobble on. During the hour and a half that we rode like this, I felt a closeness, besides the physical proximity, with my fellow passengers in the back of the truck. The ceaseless flow of stories and jokes, the uninhibited laughter, and spontaneous songs were now intensified by alcohol and other more abstract spirits.

Colorado was even smaller than San Nicolás and showed fewer signs of modernization. Except for the house at the village entrance, with Colorado's record player and speaker on its roof, there was no other evidence of electricity. Lanterns provided light after dark.

The village skirted an oblong clearing, which was the predecessor of a road. An irregular line of round, earth, and twig huts bordered the relatively modern part of the village. After those dwellings, the interruption in the plain ended, surrendering to its natural state, and herds of milk cows grazed freely on the wild land.

The love and esteem the people had for Dr. Diego, who had made numerous trips over the years to treat the villagers, was evident wherever we went. Upon arrival at the house with the record player, we were offered a hearty soup of tender goat meat and tortillas. Although we were still feeling quite satisfied from the midday feast, there was no inoffensive way to decline.

Meanwhile, the festivities were instantly resumed with a second-wind vigor. A ceaseless succession of 45 records was played at maximum volume, interrupted only by short but sincere dedications. The majority were for Dr. Diego and his wife, and they were accompanied by an indeclinable request that they dance. In a concentrated group, we danced and celebrated in an area lined with benches and a few tables. The intrinsic rhythm of the dancers and the originality with which they released their feelings were beautiful to watch. With envy, I saw that their bodies were possessed by the music. It shook, twisted, rolled, and jerked them exactly to its beat; the movements were reflexive, devoid of conscious effort.

We drank the warm beer courteously, although it tasted harsh and was not very refreshing. The local people, for whom refrigeration was still a luxury, were accustomed to it and made no apologies as we were constantly offered another from the inexhaustible supply.

Suddenly, the music stopped. There was a hush, followed by a deafening rally of firecrackers. When the music and dancing resumed, it was with frantic, wild abandonment. Without knowing why, I assumed this must be the climax of the celebration.

With a strong, proud voice, the mother of the bride said, "I know what I have in my house!" Yolanda must have read my confusion and explained. The groom, having initiated his new wife, was happy to announce that, by local social norms, he had found her to be a virgin.

The other dancers filtered to the perimeter as the couple approached the dance area. The music was changed to a slow, romantic song (perhaps out of deference to the bride), and they danced in dreamy oblivion, swaying smoothly as one body. But, as soon as the wedding dance finished, the tropical cadence music again took precedence.

A mood of healthy hedonism reigned. The day and night of uninhibited celebration was a welcome and deserved respite for the villagers. Daily, they struggled against nature; at best, they developed a delicate cooperation with their natural habitat. At the height of a wedding celebration, the serious realities of life were forgotten or talked about in jest.

A wiry little woman, vivacious despite her years, offered *una copita* of brandy to Yolanda. Graciously, Yolanda explained she was drinking beer. The woman poured the brandy and placed it next to Yolanda's beer. Laughing gaily, she said, "*¿Qué importa? Todos moriremos o tarde o temprano.*" (What does it matter? We all die sooner or later.)

Yolanda was rescued when one of the men with whom we had ridden in the truck approached, motioning to us. "*Vengan a comer.*" (Come and eat.) We found out that upon our arrival, he had hurried to his hut and ordered his wife to kill two chickens – there would be guests for late supper. Surprised, and again without alternative, we followed him away from the light and noise of the fiesta.

I felt the humble, unlimited hospitality as I entered the circular dwelling. A lithe, young black woman, standing in the background, simply nodded her greeting. Her husband spoke for both of them. He quickly made Chelo, Yolanda, and I comfortable at a small table and bench, the only furniture pieces. The men were accommodated on the floor on a *petate* (woven mat).

Immediately, the silent woman placed a bowl of steaming *caldo* (soup) in front of each person. The rich broth had whole chicken parts, chiles, and various herbs and was served with a continuously replenished stack of handmade *tortillas*. The young woman's complete obedience to her husband was somehow compatible with her self-respecting dignity, evidenced by her erect posture and demeanor. We ate quietly, following the example of our hostess, while the men talked and laughed among themselves. As we finished the warm *caldo* (soup), increasing tiredness crept over us. We expressed our gratitude to the couple and returned to the festivities.

Although the party had diminished, the music had not ceased, and the remaining dancers were indefatigable. Then, we announced that the truck was ready to depart for all destinations on our route. There were fewer passengers, so we did not have to stand in the truck bed. Each one settled himself, his woman, and children and dozed or talked softly. After numerous short stops to unload sleepy children and exhausted parents, we finally reached the ranch around 1:00 a.m. I remember hearing a guitar played softly by the caretaker as I fell heavily into bed, easily surrendering to sleep within minutes.

We awoke refreshed early the next morning. Perhaps the gentle coolness of the nights or the sweet air of the Costa Chica makes it possible to be renewed with just a few hours of sleep. Each of us chose our form of relaxation for the first part of the day, as we had decided to wait until after the heat of the day to leave for Acapulco. We spent the day exploring the area, chatting, and singing.

We had all sworn the night before that we would not need anything to eat after the marathon consumption of the wedding day. But, in the early afternoon, two unsuspecting chickens met their fate. During the quick killing, I was only a spectator. But, from that point on, the women extended my urban education. I was taught to dunk the chickens in hot water, pluck the quills, dismember them, and discard the refuse. Then, we boiled them with several spices and added vegetables when the chicken was almost cooked. Rice and fresh cheese complemented the meal.

Reluctantly and with a pleasant sadness caused by the coming twilight, we placed our few belongings in the truck. We also loaded bags of sesame seeds and two prize cocks destined to fight in Acapulco onto the truck bed. Riding in silence as the twilight slipped into night, I collected and reviewed the events of my short introduction to Afro-México. Although I knew this experience had considerably expanded my perceptions, my impressions and abstract feelings were not yet ready to evolve into words.

Reluctant Return

I had lived in Acapulco for about three years when Gil suddenly suggested that I return to the US for a few months to earn money. Initially, it seemed strange because I still had money, and he generously gave me varying quantities of pesos for food when he was paid. Like our relationship itself, finances were completely nebulous and undefined. The amount of rent paid or who paid it to whom was unknown to me. There may have been arrangements, but it was not for me to ask—a discussion of who would pay for what never happened and seemed unnecessary. Life was lived day by day, unplanned, to be relished.

Had he resented that I wasn't contributing enough? If so, there had been no hint. My pride would not allow me to probe the why of his suggestion.

OK, I could go home, get a meaningless waitress job (more plentiful since I left), visit family, and return in a few months. The thought of staying to live stateside did not tempt me in the least. I longed to be back in México before I left.

My memories of this trip are murky. I stayed at the Lemon St. house, and my parents seemed happy to have me there, if only temporarily. The atmosphere in the house was dampened because we children had left, and the distance between my parents had broadened. I took a waitress position at a nearby restaurant. Thanks to my parents, I was able to save almost all my earnings.

Of course, I helped with cooking and cleaning. Dad was interested in some of the culinary things I had learned in México. I stuck to the less exotic dishes and went easy on the hotter chiles.

During my temporary stay, while visiting Sher and Mike's home, there were questions and discussions about my life in Acapulco. My answers were as honest as my privacy allowed. After all these years, I recall a comment from my brother-in-law. He unequivocally said that a man in his forties (referring to Gil) would not change. I heard the warning, advice, or prediction with my ears, but my heart silently clung to hope. Interestingly, in the future, Mike's own life disproved his statement.

Back to Paradise?

At the end of four months, I left a message for Gil and booked my flight, happily anticipating my return to Acapulco. Again, the details are fuzzy, but I think Liz and Javier picked me up at the airport. Gil may have been working.

They broke the news of a reality I never imagined. Gil and the woman who owned the Jeep rental business had been enjoying a fling and using our apartment and bed for quick trysts. I could not process what they were telling me, much less accept it. It couldn't be true!

Liz and Javier drove me to the apartment. Everything was surreal. The emptiness echoed. Our home was dead, devoid of signs of life, abandoned except for brief entrances for convenience. Dirt had drifted onto the shiny tiles, piled up, and dulled them. There was no evidence of food, no aromas of black beans boiling, salsa ingredients roasting, or *guisos* patiently simmering. No one had cared for the place I loved.

Liz and Javier were thoroughly disgusted with Gil's actions in my absence. I think it may have been then that Javier shared Gil's local nickname, *perro vago* (stray dog), with me. They both generously urged me to live with them again.

Reeling from the revelation, my thoughts were not lucid. Emotions bubbled up like a boiling soup, but I would not let them be demonstrated with tears or ranting. They jostled for dominance, from anger toward Gil to self-loathing for my gullibility to sadness and the greater fear of thwarted independence.

What did I expect? My belief that an unspoken trust existed was exposed as unilateral and painfully naive. The belief died, leaving me feeling robbed by the deceit of my mind. There were no rules, and there was no recourse for assumptions.

My answer to Liz and Javier's offer was that I did not want to be a burden, especially on friends of *confianza* (trust, mutual reliance, closeness) adjusting to a newcomer in their young family. While I was in the US, their first son, Christopher, was born. On the contrary, they assured me I could sleep in Chris's room and that Liz would love my help with meals and daily chores. Also, she was missing female company. The offer was sincere, and I gratefully accepted it for the time being on the condition that I contribute to household expenses.

Gil called Liz and Javier's landline, which was the only communication at the time. He asked for me, but I told them I had no desire to talk, nothing to say to him. They relayed my message, but he continued to call.

*****

I enjoyed sharing baby Chris's room. Most of the time, he was an easy-going baby. I knew he was awake in the morning when happy, unintelligible sounds rose from the crib. I smiled down at him, lifted him from the crib, and changed his diaper. We would let his parents get a bit more rest. He rode my hip to the kitchen, where I made him a bottle and began our day.

Liz and I together made short work of the daily sweeping and mopping. We shopped at Comercial Mexicana, prepped meals, cared for Chris, and sometimes went to the beach. We talked nonstop, catching up on happenings in our lives and those of our families.

I had missed Liz's Indonesian foods, which were interspersed with Mexican foods that Javier had taught her to prepare. Liz made Gado Gado (Indonesian), which became my favorite. It was simple. A variety of colorful vegetables and potatoes are slightly boiled, cooled, spread on a large platter, and served with an Indonesian peanut and chili sauce (*sambal*). It was perfect for an unhurried meal interspersed with catch-up conversation.

Both *salsa* and *sambal* were always on the table. I liked them both and introduced Liz to some of the things I had learned from Doña Lola. Javier was easy to please.

Finally, I consented to talk to Gil. We went somewhere to eat.

"¡Ay, Mara! ¡No fue nada! No duró nada." (¡Oh, Mara! It was nothing. It didn't last.") he told me repeatedly.

In my judgment, it sounded more like an admission of his failure to woo her and fell far short of an apology to me. Was she married? Did she tire of him quickly? Was she shocked by our humble home? Was she too sophisticated for him? Did his interest in her wane unexpectedly? No details were forthcoming, and I didn't want answers.

I weakened my stance about not seeing him but made it clear that I would continue to live with Liz and Javier. He asked if I would like to go with him on a road trip to Oaxaca if he could plan it around ships' schedules. I consented.

The trip in his car was a long day's drive on an interesting route because there was no good crow's flight road from Acapulco to Oaxaca. We headed north from the state of Guerrero, circling into Puebla through its capital of the same name then headed south to the mountainous state of Oaxaca and arrived at its capital.

The city is studded with cultural gems, most notably a plethora of museums and art galleries. The museums exhibit specialty types of art: contemporary, prehispanic, textile, Oaxacan, and there are complete galleries of single artists' works. Most museums collected no fees, and we wandered unhurriedly from one museum to another until hunger provided a welcome break. The eclectic beauty of the city was amazing!

Besides the myriad museums, Oaxaca is known for its rich *moles* of every hue and flavor. *Mole,* a sauce made from about 30 ingredients, is the national dish of México, and all seven varieties are specialties in the states of Puebla and Oaxaca. They vary in color, sweetness, tartness, and savory heat. There is *mole rojo* (dark red), *mole coloradito* (red, like enchilada sauce), *mole amarillo* (yellow), *mole verde* (green), *mole negro* (dark, black), *mole chichilo* (corn), and *mole manchamantel* (of caramelized fruits, literally meaning tablecloth stainers) We did our best to sample as many as possible, never encountering one we didn't like.

Perhaps the trip was an attempt to mend a severed relationship. Reality showed it had always been loosely cobbled only by consent, completely devoid of expressed commitment or any timeline. Still, for me, scars remained, and trust was slow to recuperate. However, our history of sharing enjoyable times came to the forefront again.

La Escuelita

John Homer, the British General Manager of the Princess Hotel, where Javier was employed as an entertainer, happened to mention to Javier that he was seeking an English-speaking school teacher for six children at the hotel. He and his wife and two other sets of parents had decided not to enroll their children in Mexican schools that year. They had arranged for a woman to come from Arizona to be their teacher. She ordered and sent all the necessary textbooks for the children whose ages ranged from third to eighth grade. In September, just as the school year was to begin, she notified John that a death in her family would prevent her from accepting the job.

Javier encouraged me to talk with John. However, there were numerous reasons for my hesitation. I had a valid visa, but it did not permit me to be employed in México. Javier said not to worry about that; John would take care of it. More importantly, of overwhelming concern was my lack of experience and education. Javier said, "Just go talk with him. He's a good man." I said I would but vowed to adhere strictly to the bare truth about my background.

John warmly invited me into his office, the size and lushness of which befitted the man responsible for every aspect of the smooth operation of Acapulco's best hotel. Despite his position, he was down-to-earth, unassuming, and possessed the gift of making others comfortable in his presence.

He explained the sudden need of the three families who had chosen to take their children out of the local Mexican school. Although the children spoke Spanish and English, the parents decided it was time they were instructed in English.

The hotel's chief landscaper (a Columbian) and his wife had a boy and a girl, and the pastry chef (from Holland) and his wife had a son and a daughter, as did John and his wife. The parents had planned for everything. The textbooks arrived, and a small building on the hotel grounds was converted into a schoolhouse. They even purchased balls, jump ropes, and other recreational equipment for activity breaks. A Plan B for the teacher was never considered.

Then John deftly began to transition the conversation to focus on me. He listened leisurely and attentively. Thinking he needed to know about my academic experience first (as it might be an instant disqualifier), I began with my two years at Pepperdine College, briefly explaining my premature departure. He encouraged me to continue. I breezed over my summers in Guatemala and how I became a stewardess for Pan Am, where I had met Javier's wife. I told him we traveled with her cousin by train from California to Acapulco for vacation, and Liz met Javier. Honestly, I related how and why I came to Acapulco to live. Although I aimed for brevity, he asked for more details as he absorbed my history. His ability to put me at ease made me almost forget it was an interview.

I was astonished when he expressed his confidence in my ability to perform the job, adding that I was the right person for it. He reassured me that the parents were hands-on concerning their children's education and would assist me. Of course, he would speak with them before he could offer me the job. Suddenly, l was almost mute, grateful that he would consider me. Various emotions jostled, and fear was among them, but gratitude triumphed, and I managed a few words. Buoyed by his confidence in me, I told him I was excited about the prospect and looked forward to hearing from him.

*****

Liz and Javier expressed their confidence and congratulations, although still a bit premature. Very soon, John Homer called to offer the job, saying the other parents were relieved that a solution to their dilemma had materialized.

John laid out the details of the opportunity. I would live rent-free on the Princess Hotel grounds in furnished employee housing, a two-story apartment building. He informed me of my salary, which I thought was generous, especially considering I was not legally permitted to work in México. We set a day and time for me to meet the parents, sign minimal paperwork, and receive my teacher's guides for the children's textbooks.

My good fortune appeared on the horizon completely out of the blue. I tried to process my unforeseen luck. An overwhelming sense of responsibility transformed into adrenaline as I began to review the teacher's guides. I had so much to learn and review!

Not only was it essential to absorb and retain the academic material, I had to develop a schedule for individual and group instruction during the school day. The lanky, studious Columbian boy was in eighth grade. His curriculum included algebra, which I had always liked, but I certainly needed a refresher to be able to teach it. His studies were advanced for his age and would occupy more of my prep time than the younger children's. I tried to prepare the lessons for each student, enriching the curriculum with examples relevant to their ages. There was no computer and no internet available for my research. They enjoyed it when I shared some of my experiences from around the world when we were in a group. The advantage of my situation was that I had no competing responsibilities and was happy to dedicate all my time and effort to this challenging opportunity.

The Homers often invited me to eat with them at one of the hotel restaurants and a few times in their home. I gratefully accepted and got to know them quite well. I had requested of the parents that I preferred that they and the children called me by my first name.

From the start, it was evident that the six children were *bien educados* (well-raised). Whether we were socializing or in the schoolhouse, I never noticed a lapse of respect for me or their parents. The description in Spanish was much more comprehensive than its literal translation in English, which was well-educated. In addition to formal education, it included being well-mannered, well-behaved, cultured, and treating others with respect.

215

They quietly listened when I spoke and participated with questions and comments in turn. Because they were three sets of siblings, they occasionally forgot about the setting, and sibling rivalry was apparent but not lasting. We all settled easily into our structured daily schedule. Evenings and nights I studied!

Make Mine Milk

During my last couple of weeks living with Liz and Javier, I noticed an uncommon desire for milk. Living on Lemon Street, a half-gallon carton of milk, slipped into a plastic handle for easy pouring, was centered on the nook table during every meal. Since then, my attraction to milk waned considerably. Liz and I made refreshing iced coffee with milk, and Javier loved heated milk with Mexican chocolate and *pan dulce* (slightly sweet bread) for his light evening supper. Christopher had his formula, of course. I started to crave a glass of plain cold milk more frequently.

When I moved to the Princess Hotel employee housing, I went into town on weekends to grocery shop. The list included milk by the half-gallons and peanut butter, which I began eating by the spoonful. The peanut craving remains a mystery to me, but the milk craving was soon explained by the confirmation that I was pregnant.

After more than three years without becoming pregnant, I assumed that I was probably infertile. Of course, Gil had three sons, so I owned the problem. The acceptance of childlessness did not quell my wish to have a baby; it had only been intensified while helping care for Christopher. Always carrying my secret wish, pushed slightly below the surface, I never expressed the longing to anyone. Two of my younger sisters, Sher and Trish (who preferred single-syllable names as adults) each had a baby boy.

I was finally pregnant, although I hadn't considered it a real possibility. Be careful what you wish for, especially if you believe it is impossible. I was excited, but there were high hurdles ahead to jump.

First, I had to tell Gil. He rarely came to the Princess Hotel except to pick me up occasionally. It may have been that the upscale environs made him uncomfortable. His habitat was downtown Acapulco and the Malecón area, among friends he had known for years and family.

I don't remember where we were when I told him, but he was speechless at first. A short laugh, almost of disbelief, was his first response. The hope had evaporated – it seemed so long ago that we considered the possibility of a child. He smiled as he processed the unexpected reality, then began to think aloud about details. Doctor Diego, his cousin, would deliver our baby. I immediately agreed if Eduardo would consent. I felt comfortable with him when we all went to the wedding in La Costa Chica.

When Gil told his Mom and sisters, they were ecstatic. They would have a grandchild and niece or nephew they could watch grow up and spoil. Gil's boys had been taken away by their mother.

Next, I had to let John Homer and the other parents of my students know. I agonized, imagining it would be difficult to explain and convince them it was a surprise to me, not at all due to recent planning. We were barely into the school year, and things were going well. Communication and rapport were smooth with everyone. I would be honest, solicit the parents' comments and advice, and continue our successful path.

I talked with John, who was always accessible to me. I should have known he would make it easy for me. He arranged for a meeting with the parents where I could tell them directly and receive their feedback. I told them I intended to continue as planned, except that my baby was due mid-May. They said they planned to end the year before that anyway due to the heat and vacation plans.

My question for them, which weighed more heavily, was how much they wanted me to tell their children. Unanimously, without conferring, they wanted their children to learn as much as I would teach them. No restrictions. They welcomed the extracurricular opportunity. *Whew*!

*****

I was lucky that the soft waves of nausea that would suddenly wash over me receded quickly, but I asked my doctor if there was

218

anything I could take that would not harm my baby to calm the waves. He prescribed Vitamin B6, which helped a little until the nausea disappeared after a few months.

With some nutritional knowledge, I tried to improve my already healthy diet. I stopped drinking coffee and did not drink anything alcoholic. My daily choices were forming a little body I hoped would be perfect.

I smile when I remember the locals' advice concerning my diet. They knew I loved all kinds of chiles and salsas and was accustomed to adding them to whatever I was eating.

"Va a salir bravo(a) el bebe si no dejas de comer cosas picantes," (The baby will be _____if you don't stop eating hot things), they warned me. The word bravo (or brava when describing a female) had a wide variety of meanings: courageous, brave, feisty, angry, and upset. I continued to eat spicy dishes and condiments during my pregnancy, not giving the advice much credence.

The next hurdle was informing my family. I decided to take a short trip during the holidays, which weren't far off. Even though they may not be together in one place, I could tell most of them in person. I would use the trip to buy books about natural childbirth, a couple of maternity bathing suits, pants, shorts, and fabric to sew maternity dresses.

While visiting family in California, I received a variety of well-intentioned comments and advice. My parents seemed open to the idea that they would have another grandchild, and I don't remember any judgmental comments they voiced, to me anyway. I found it humorous that Mom credited the Shaklee vitamins she gave me when I was there working for four months. She was sure the Vitamin E had revived my fertility.

One sister thought I should have an abortion; another sister later advised me to tell my child that her father was dead. I didn't consider either of those suggestions for a second. There was no doubt that the decision was mine alone. It was momentous, but I remained unwavering.

*****

Back in *La Escuelita*, I used the copious resources I bought in California to supplement the students' curriculum. Skipping the explanation about how sperm meets egg, we followed pictures weekly depicting the size of the embryo as it developed. They were amazed that the first picture was the size of one grain of rice. A few months later, one of the little boys asked me if food fell all over the baby when I ate. He was trying to get a visual, so we talked about the baby's private quarters, looked at drawings, and learned how it got its food. I updated them briefly each week, and they knew they could ask me any questions that occurred to them.

My daily schedule was challenging yet rewarding. All my efforts were focused on the success of my students and the healthy formation of the small life evolving within me.

As I grew out in front, my center of balance changed, and I thought that caused the increasing pain in my lower back. When I had the time, I lay on my back on the hot sand at the beach. The warmth penetrated and soothed me temporarily, but the pain finally became fierce, and I went to town for an urgent, unscheduled doctor appointment. Testing revealed I had a kidney infection for which I was prescribed antibiotics. There was no alternative medication, but the doctor assured me they would not harm my baby. The antibiotics soon took effect, relieving the pain.

For a while, my body seemed to accept its state of pregnancy. Nausea had disappeared, and I guess I developed a happy, glowing look. I enjoyed teaching and interacting with the students; however, most of my out-of-class time was spent studying for the next day's class and getting more rest.

But my body's peace with pregnancy was not for long. I suffered another kidney infection whose symptoms I knew well. I got to the doctor and took more antibiotics. Later, in the third trimester, it would recur a third time, this time accompanied by blood in my urine. At first, I feared I was miscarrying.

"Have you had a history of kidney disease?" the clinic doctor asked after the third occurrence.

"No, not even urinary tract infections," I replied.

"Well, after you have the baby, you must have your kidneys thoroughly examined." Again, I took a course of antibiotics.

Years later, when I was in my 60s and working for the Mono County Health Department, a Hispanic grandmother brought her infant grandson to our office for his vaccinations. She explained to me in Spanish that her daughter-in-law developed kidney problems during her pregnancy, had to be hospitalized, and was now on the list for a kidney transplant.

I asked one of the Health Department nurses about the correlation between pregnancy and kidney disease. She answered that a few women's bodies struggle to handle the additional toll of pregnancy. I told her about my infections during pregnancy. Silently, I wondered if my kidney infections during pregnancy were an effect of the preeclampsia Mom suffered during my gestation. I will never know, but the nurse said it was probably a good idea I did not have another child.

*****

One evening, just after 7:30 pm, I was on the sofa in my apartment studying the kids' lessons for the next day, as usual. With a powerful jerk and the sound of an approaching train, the room lunged one way, then back, and continued its violent thrusts. I grabbed the lamp I was using as it teetered toward me, threatening to fall and shatter. The bulb went out, the hum of appliances shushed, and the darkness surrounded me in eerie silence. The fierce movements finally calmed to a roll. The hallway outside my second-story apartment filled with voices.

"*Salgan! ¡Vamos afuera!*" (Come out! Let's go outside!)

I opened my door quickly, merging with the residents' rapid but orderly flow. We walked as if drunk between the walls of the hallway, trying to keep our balance as the building rolled. Descending the staircase as a river, we took hold of the railing to steady ourselves. We went outside to reach safety away from the buildings. I was seven months pregnant, and my neighbors became very protective, finding a place for me to sit.

Someone had grabbed a bottle of Presidente brandy as they exited and urged me to have a few sips to calm myself.

"*Para el corazón,*" (for your heart) they prescribed.

I told them I hadn't drunk anything alcoholic during my pregnancy, but they insisted that the effects of the shock I was experiencing would be more harmful to the baby than the liquor. The smooth, warm liquid and their concern and kindness calmed me as we sat together outside.

They knew there would be aftershocks and advised that we all stay outside that night and wait to see what damage the dawn would reveal. On the grass, in the balmy tropical air, we talked and rested, slept if we could, until morning. Each aftershock brought new fear, but we were outside where nothing could hurt us.

In the morning, we learned it had been a 6.4 earthquake centered 17 miles away. Some exterior decoration on our buildings and the hotel fell off in the quake, but the damage was minimal. While we experienced strong shaking in Acapulco, Mexico City residents felt only light tremors.

Our electricity did not return for three days, which meant early evening darkness, and the *bomba* that pumped our water was inoperative. There was a reserve tank of water, but we could use it only sparingly. No showers, only birdie baths.

*****

When the parents of my students signaled they would like to end the school year in April, I was relieved to have a few weeks to prepare for the arrival of our daughter. Gil said we could return to the apartment I loved, high above the narrow rocky bay. I was anxious to start a thorough cleaning and convert it into a home again.

A few months earlier, we knew the baby was a girl. I had no idea the student's parents had been buying frilly sundresses, onesies, shorts sets, and an assortment of useful items I would need. When they surprised me with the array, I was overcome by their generosity.

I attempted to thank them, not only for their gifts for my baby but for all the assistance they gave me as I did my best to teach their children. Their trust, confidence, and support were the best gifts! Goodbyes were cheerful and filled with mutual gratitude and best wishes.

The Homers had kept a crib long after they decided their family was complete and offered it to me. They said the paint was chipped, but that was not a problem for me; I would sand and repaint it. I was very grateful they solved the problem of a bed for my baby. I would make a small version of our net *pabellón* to fit over the top of the crib, falling down the side slats and tucking under the mattress to protect her from mosquitoes.

I needed to sew a few diapers as I had done before my brother was born because disposable diapers could be bought in Acapulco, but they were prohibitively expensive. I wouldn't need so many because I hand-washed every day, and the breeze dried everything quickly.

I knew all of this preparation was my responsibility. The reasons for Gil's non-involvement were probably cultural as well as characteristic. He helped me pick up the crib at the Princess when I finished my job there, and I think he would have contributed more if I had asked more of him. However, having become more independent in the last year or so, I avoided asking for help. I would adhere to my timeline and did not want to be only partially prepared if the baby came early.

The tasks were not only necessary but a welcome distraction from the increasing apprehension I felt as the time to give birth neared. Having read numerous books on natural childbirth and practiced breathing techniques to tolerate pain, I had learned all I could short of what the experience would teach me. Reminding myself that every woman in the world must have similar fears before delivering her first child did not eliminate my anxiety, but realizing my commonality with all women somehow soothed me. I also worried about the possible effects of the multiple courses of antibiotics on the baby, even though I had been told they were safe. While the unknown loomed and neared, I kept busy, trying to allow the happy excitement welling up inside me to dominate my thoughts.

It's Almost Time

The day started peacefully with the usual routine. I stood under the tepid water in the shower, amazed at the tightly stretched skin over my enormous belly. Could it expand any more? To conserve water, I turned it off as usual while I spread soft soap bubbles all over my transformed body. I rinsed the bubbles, wet my long hair to wash it too, turned the water off to shampoo, and on again to thoroughly rinse it. I dried, applied soothing lotion to my tightened skin, slipped a comb through my hair, and put on a last-stage maternity dress. It looked more like a tent.

Breakfast was oatmeal because I read it was good for milk production, and I liked it. I poured plenty of milk over it and shaved some *piloncillo* (brown sugar in cone-shaped molds) on top. Dark orange papaya slices completed my meal. After the baby arrived, I would again drink the strong dark coffee I loved and missed during pregnancy.

My size, slight imbalance, and inability to get a full, deep breath had slowed me as I swept and mopped since returning to the apartment, but I got it done. I wanted all my chores caught up because I had no way of knowing when my body would decide it was time for me to finally give birth.

Before I started to wash a few clothes, I felt a sudden strong pinch low inside my belly that lasted several seconds. I noticed the clock. The wash could wait. I spread the middle of the hammock that hung from the ceiling in our bedroom, eased my butt down heavily into the loop, then raised my feet into the hammock and laid my upper body back into the comfortable weave. I sighed and relaxed, wondering if the pinch was the first contraction or just the first in a series of false alarms of the Braxton Hicks nature. I thought about the amazing fact that I would soon meet our little daughter, who already had a name.

We experimented with names from the beginning of my pregnancy. If the baby were a boy, we liked the name Diego. We decided against lengthening the name by adding a middle name because Latino culture ordered names with first, middle (if any), father's last, and mother's last. When we knew we would have a daughter, we considered Andrea and Camila.

Ana said, "How about Lolita?" to be the namesake of Doña Lola. We were both happy with the name. Doña Lola's name was Dolores Rivera de Martinez, and she had more than her share of *dolores* (suffering, pain) being an orphan, having to leave the US, starting over in a dirt-floor dwelling in Acapulco, and I could only guess what else. She accepted me from the start, despite social restrictions that she side-stepped, and her generosity was constant. I wanted our daughter to have her nickname, Lolita.

My body had been commandeered by pregnancy for the last nine months. I bent to its demands for extra sleep, uncharacteristic food cravings, and more frequent bathroom visits as my hormones, weight, and balance changed. Additionally, my kidneys had rebelled painfully as they reacted to forced double duty. But now, my ability to remain in control was slipping. Soon, I would be overtaken with repeated barely bearable contractions for an undetermined length of time, and my water could break without warning, causing an embarrassing flood.

My Braxton Hicks were uncomfortable but short and at long irregular intervals, which made me decide to stay home and rest unless they accelerated or intensified. The hammock was perfect.

During the day, I alerted Dr. Diego's office and called Doña Lola so she could tell Gil when he had a break from the ship. I packed a small bag with hygiene essentials, a couple of shifts for me, diapers, tiny lightweight pajamas, onesies, two tiny dresses, and the carrier basket for Lolita. And I waited, entertaining a variety of thoughts ranging from excitement to fear.

Gil came home in the evening, and we went to a restaurant in town because I hadn't cooked during the day. I nibbled, but the irregular cramping interruptions hijacked my hunger. We decided that if I didn't go into serious labor during the night, Gil would take me to the hospital the next morning.

Birthday and Beyond

Upon arrival, hospital staff determined that I was starting to dilate but not close to ready yet and I had not broken water. They took me to a semi-private room and assured me they would return periodically to check on me.

Although my contractions became more painful and frequent, the dilation was slow to progress. Around one o'clock in the afternoon, the staff decided to induce labor to speed up the process. That was when the torture began in earnest. Intensely gripping, racking contractions became more frequent. Watching the second hand of a large clock on the wall, I breathed as the books taught, trying to mitigate the cramping pain. Unable to distract my attention from anything else between contractions, I forced myself to relax by slow breathing, knowing the next wave of torment would soon begin. As it started to clench, I watched the rhythmic twitching of the clock's hand while trying to maintain outward composure until the wrenching finally eased. I passed the afternoon alone, and dusk was closing in. There had been several disappointing cervix checks.

I got the impression in local culture that pregnancy and birth were solely in women's realm, remaining well-maintained mysteries to men. I saw no evidence that a man at that time would keep his wife company during labor, much less choose to witness the birth of his child. Maybe times have changed since then.

The creeping darkness was especially demoralizing for me. Would this torture go on all night? Was something wrong?

I endured another couple of hours until night blackened the windowpanes of my room. The pain had so debilitated me that I worried I would not have the energy to push when it was time to give birth. My adamant wish to give birth naturally waned rapidly.

The next time a staff member came to check on me, I begged them to do something!

"Just take her out by cesarian surgery," I pleaded.

They gave me the option of an epidural, explaining that it would slow the process of labor but give me a chance to rest and hopefully sleep. That sounded wonderful! I welcomed the needle to my spine and felt like kissing the anesthesiologist when the pain could no longer torment me. I slept peacefully for a few refreshing hours.

When the staff determined it was time to call Dr. Diego, they prepped me and told me they would give me instructions about when and how forcefully to push when it was time to do so. Some of the effects of the epidural probably remained. I was relieved that the birth, which happened at 4:45 am, was not nearly as arduous as the labor.

Lolita let out a healthy screech, and the nurse held her up so I could see her. I knew she was perfect even before they cleaned her.

"¡Es morenita!" (tan or olive-skinned), one of the staff members said excitedly as they took her to be washed. Meanwhile, Dr. Diego performed his magic, suturing me with practiced skill.

Now, it was my turn to take a refreshing shower, wash my hair, and let motherhood become a personal, ecstatic reality. I reclaimed my body; pregnancy and birth were past tense, all was well, and I had a beautiful baby girl! I was completely content.

When the nurse came to ask what I would like to eat, I realized I was ravenously hungry. From the choices she offered, I chose liver and onions. During pregnancy, it became one of my cravings and I made the dish for myself many times, being careful not to overcook it. My usual diet contained lots of seafood, so maybe I lacked the iron and vitamins that liver provides. It never tasted so good as it did that morning in the hospital!

They brought Lolita, tightly wrapped like a burrito, for me to hold. Her *cafe-con-leche* skin, almond-shaped brown eyes, and curved dark lashes made her face exquisite. It was complemented by unmistakable miniatures of her father's eyebrows and earlobes. An ample dark shock of hair stood up rebelliously from her head and made me smile. Neither chubby nor thin, she was just perfect. I appreciated the hospital's practice of giving the mother time to prepare herself and have a bit of time with her baby before they notified visitors.

Around this time, Gil appeared, smiling hugely as he checked out his tiny daughter.

"*Es bien chula. Tiene los ojos almendrados*" (She's very pretty. She has almond-shaped eyes) "*y es morenita*," (and she's dark-skinned) he observed with a constant broad grin.

He put his arms around both of us and kissed me briefly.

"¡*Te quiero*!" (I love you!) I murmured as I kissed him. It was more a reflex, an expression of my overwhelming joy; no thought preceded it. It was the debut of those words in our relationship. Neither of us had ever made that declaration to the other.

"But you know I can't marry you," he responded.

I said nothing. Of course, I knew that. I had known that from the start. Did he assume that was what I wanted? Did he judge my motive to be manipulation?

I used to think we communicated openly, at least until trust was lost. Maybe it devolved even more during my pregnancy while I was teaching at the Escuelita. My independence was evolving, continually increasing.

I could have clearly stated that I did not expect the birth of our daughter to force him to do anything. But this was not the time or place to start that discussion.

*****

As promised, I let nothing diminish my joy on my daughter's birthday. Soon, I was happy to see Gil's sisters, Ana and Irene, and Doña Lola arrive to welcome the new family member.

"¿Préstamela, sí?" (May I hold her?) Doña Lola requested to hold her namesake. Of course, it was an honor to transfer her granddaughter to her arms and ample body. This was the first time I had seen her, despite talking innumerable times by phone. As I imagined, she was unassuming, kind and loving.

"Ya tenemos nuestra, Miss Universo," (Now we have our Miss Universe.) she said, admiring Lolita, who was comfortably dozing, enveloped in the arms of her *abuelita* (grandmother).

In two months, on July 24, 1978, the Miss Universe Pageant would be held in Acapulco at the Teotihuacán Forum. It was the first time México hosted the event, which was televised by CBS, with Bob Barker and Helen O'Connell as presenters. Doña Lola thought her new granddaughter could easily rival any of the international beauties who would soon arrive in Acapulco.

As word spread that Lolita had been born, several visitors came to the hospital to see and hold the new little bundle. They all brought something: outfits, dresses, short sets, tiny booties, bonnets, light blankets, and other more practical gifts.

One lady gave me a *faja* (strip, girdle). It was a long, very wide (12 inches?) ace bandage. I was ignorant of its use, so she explained that it was wrapped snuggly around a woman's waist many times to support her back as her body, bones, and tissue reverted to its normal state. It supported the back while sweeping and mopping. I started wearing it in the hospital and agreed that the reinforcement felt good. Continuing to wear it, I believe, helped me get back into my pre-pregnancy shorts and clothes sooner.

I was grateful to everyone who came to visit us! I did not know most of the visitors, but each of them explained their connection to the Martinez family. The day passed pleasantly as I met people I had never been introduced to. Had social mores changed now that I was the mother of Gil's daughter? Time would tell. I had always been open to people and would continue to be.

"¿Pásamela, sí?" (Pass her to me, OK?) was repeated as each visitor wanted to hold Lolita. Even some hospital employees who had assisted me wanted their turn to hold her. Lolita seemed to enjoy the attention, and I couldn't stop smiling with pride.

Later in the afternoon, Gil returned with some of his friends. The atmosphere was party-like, with abundant humor, laughter, commentary, and congratulations.

"¡Ni manera de negar que es tuya!" (No way to deny that she is yours), one jokingly advised Gil.

"¡Es la estampa! Tiene tus cejas y tus orejas," (She's a stamp. She has your eyebrows and your ears) added another, entering the roast.

"Ya se mescló el ganado," (Now the cattle are mixed up) another friend chimed in.

Their joking had us all laughing. Gil's close friendships were reinforced, and I felt accepted. I was happy they came by to wish us well.

*****

The nurses advised that we stay another night or so to make sure Lolita's navel was kept clean and was healing properly. They also coached me and gave helpful tips for breast-feeding.

I loved that my bed had a small bassinet attached to its railing, where Lolita slept. I changed her diapers and dressed her. It was all so convenient. When she was hungry, I could easily lift her into my bed to nurse her. I liked the hospital's system that let me be her mother from the start, changing her diapers, dressing her, and feeding her whenever she wanted to eat.

Although I should have been physically tired the night of Lolita's birthday, I didn't want to sleep. The euphoria was a powerful stimulant. I watched her sleeping peacefully, nursed her when she made the slightest awakening noises, and was almost incredulous at the miracle of her existence.

At Home

Lolita would soon feel at home in our apartment with the sounds of rumbling rocks and birds. I started to adapt to her rhythms and needs as all other responsibilities took their place after her.

The first day or two were peaceful as patterns in our lives took shape. Then, suddenly, she was fussier, had diarrhea, and could not eat well or digest properly. She cried more painfully as the day progressed.

Caring for siblings and babysitting had not prepared me for what I sensed must be serious. When Gil came home, I was about to call Doña Lola to ask if Irene or Ana could take us to the clinic. He agreed that being so young, she might quickly become dehydrated. We went to the clinic to wait with all the others who needed to be seen by a doctor. The wait seemed interminable, especially with Lolita's crying, her discomfort, and our worrying. When it was finally our turn, we described her symptoms, and the doctor took a stool sample. We waited for the rapid results that would yield a probable cause.

When he returned a while later, his expression told us the diagnosis was not good.

"Tiene una bacteria bastante agresiva, Shigella Flexneri," (She has a very aggresive bacteria, Shigella Flexineri) he told us.

It is highly infectious and multiplies rapidly in the intestinal tract, he explained. We asked him where a newborn could have contracted the bacteria. We will never know, but it was most likely contracted in the hospital, possibly from staff who held her and did not thoroughly sanitize after performing their other duties.

He prescribed an antibiotic to be given orally in small doses several times daily due to her age. He asked that I stop breastfeeding her and give her a soy-based formula until she improved. He emphasized that I must continue to bathe her daily, contrary to the

234

belief of some locals that it should not be done when a baby is ill. Of course, we would bring her back immediately if her condition worsened. We were both worried, but it must have been more intense for Gil as it must have brought back memories of their newborn twin's death.

We purchased the soy formula and started a regimen of ultra cleanliness. The moist, hot tropical weather was an ideal incubator for bacteria, so we constantly cleaned surfaces, our hands, and anything that touched Lolita.

At times when Lolita was uncomfortable or fussy, I lay with her on top of me in the hammock. I connected a light piece of rope to part of the window so I could control our swaying. It proved soothing for both of us. I loved the feel of her warm, soft body on mine while we relaxed and sometimes dozed.

Of course, Doña Lola was concerned about her little namesake and checked in by phone every day. I felt her support and appreciated her calls.

"¿*Cómo está la Miss Universo*?" she began the call. I was relieved when I could tell her Lolita was improving, taking some formula and sleeping better.

It would be another week or so before she beat the nasty bacteria. Her stools slowly firmed to normal, and she didn't cry as much. I continued with the formula until her next appointment. Not being able to breastfeed caused my milk production to reduce considerably, but that was to be expected. I did not have a pump or any way to extract my milk so it would be sterile. When the doctor permitted me to start breastfeeding again, I had to supplement with non-soy formula. It was so good to see her hungry and thriving again!

Once Lolita regained her health, I was able to complete the household chores more thoroughly. Her naps became slightly more predictable, during which I prioritized the tasks I would try to accomplish.

Her sundresses and a bucket of cloth diapers joined the daily wash. I took her down to the washing area in her carrying basket, wearing a protective bonnet and a light blanket, where she would feel the sea air, watch birds, and listen to the rocks while I washed.

*****

Every Sunday, Ana and Irene brought Doña Lola to visit us. I think it was rare for her to leave their house due to mobility problems and possibly other reasons. I was honored and looked forward to their weekly visit.

They all loved holding and playing with Lolita, but an indescribable demeanor of happiness and contentment came over Doña Lola especially. She sang children's rhythms to her, gently bouncing her and mostly just gazing at her little face. Her aunts showed their love in similar ways as they passed her from one to the other.

Gil admired her features, too, and beamed proudly. He must have noticed the joy our daughter gave his mother and sisters.

"¿De dónde sacó estas pestañotas?" (Where did she get those long eyelashes?), he wondered.

"¿A poco no te has fijado en las de Mara?" (Haven't you ever noticed Mara's?) was Ana's typically terse reply. Mine were long and curled but fine and light-colored without mascara. Lolita's were awesome – long, slightly curved, and dark. We joked about Gil's lashes, which were shorter and straight like palapas (palm fronds).

The thoughtful women always brought us something. On one of the first visits, they brought small gold stud earrings for Lolita. I would get her ears pierced as soon as she felt better because they told me it hardly hurt at all when they were so young. She would look even cuter with earrings. A few months later, they gave her tiny gold hoop earrings. They also brought containers of food they had made on Saturday for us. It was delicious and made my life easier, especially at first.

The women gave helpful and practical tips. They advised that I bathe her before putting her to bed for the night to relax and cool her. It worked. She was ready for bed after her bath. I added a sponge bath during the day when the weather was especially hot and humid.

I placed her plastic bathtub on clean beach towels on the kitchen table for her bath routine. I added tepid tap water and some water heated on the stove, carefully testing the temperature inside my wrist. She enjoyed her baths!

*****

During the time after Lolita recovered, Gil slowly distanced himself from us and became even more unpredictable. When he did show up at home, he seemed irritable and did not stay long or offer to help me. Babies are high-maintenance, and I was constantly busy with either Lolita or the general domestic tasks. Maybe he felt neglected. I wished he would verbalize his feelings, but those days of easy, fluent communication had ended.

I could only guess at his inner turmoil after the birth of his daughter. Soon, when he told me he was going to California "to work for a while," I deduced that he thought the time away would help.

In the four years I had known him, he had not gone to California, although Carlota and the boys had visited a couple of times at Christmas. Now, he was going to live with his Californian family and work as a longshoreman "for a while." The words sounded temporary. He was unwilling to share the source of his discontent with me. I could only guess. Did fatherhood frighten him? Did the birth of another child remind him painfully of his neglect of his first family? He gave no clues.

"Cualquier cosa que necesitas, háblale a mi mamá o Ana o Irene," (If you need anything, call my Mom or Ana or Irene.)

He soon left for California, kissing us both.

*****

I felt even more confident in my ability to care for Lolita and myself after Gil left. Lolita was healthy and alert, and she developed her special personality every day. We had found a rhythm in our daily routine, and I enjoyed motherhood.

A bonus was the enhanced relationships with Gil's mother and sisters as weeks and then months passed. Our confidence in each other grew.

"Traémela cuando vas de compras, ¿sí?" (Bring her to me when you go grocery shopping, OK?) Doña Lola pleaded when Lolita's health problems were resolved.

"Claro que sí, gracias." (Sure. Thank you.)

I was grateful for both the assistance and the acceptance.

As is normal for many babies, Lolita began to lose the hair she had at birth. I found clumps of longish strands in her crib. Her aunts and Doña Lola advised me to have her head shaven so that her hair would all grow out evenly. It was another useful tip, but I had to laugh at how cute she looked with her smooth bald head and miniature gold hoop earrings.

Ana asked if I would bring Lolita to her in the mayor's office so her coworkers could meet the new Miss Universo. We visited for a while as she was again passed from arms to arms. They were amazed at the way Lolita adapted to different people and environments.

"Le gustan los brazos" (She likes to be held), Ana explained. I agreed that she loved attention.

On my last visit to California when I was pregnant, I bought a cloth baby carrier that I could use now. Lolita rode face-forward over my chest, loving to be outside, when we walked to Doña Lola's and later to the beach. She became known as *La Bebe Kanguru* (The Baby Kangaroo), and locals always stopped to greet us.

When Lolita was only a few months old, we went to the beach at Caleta, which was lake-like with warm water and almost no waves. I took Lolita's sunsuit off, leaving only her diaper so the water could cool her, and she would get accustomed to it. We sat on the shoreline where the water barely lapped the sand, Lolita propped against my body between my outstretched legs. She showed no fear. We cooled in the water for a short time, then retreated to the shade, where I changed her diaper and redressed her, including her bonnet.

¿Cómo se llama?

Soon after Gil left, I realized we had not gone to *Registro Civil* (Vital Records) to register Lolita's birth. Gil told me hospitals there did not facilitate the creation of a birth certificate as they do in the US.

Now he was gone, but I found out where to go. I would do it myself. I took my passport, tied Lolita to my chest, and we were off to accomplish this important task.

It went badly from the start.

"¿Cómo se llama la niña?" the official asked me.

"Lolita Martinez Harper," I replied simply, using the Hispanic order of parental surnames.

"Lolita no es un nombre," (Lolita is not a name), he countered.

I explained in Spanish that we wanted to name her after her *abuela* (grandmother), Doña Lola Rivera de Martinez. I told him I knew her grandmother's first name was legally Dolores, meaning pain and suffering, and that her name had proved an ill omen in many ways in her life. I did not want my daughter to have that name.

"Lolita no puede ser un nombre. Es un apodo" (Lolita cannot be a name. It is a nickname), he emphasized, pronouncing the words slowly with a rising voice that warned his patience with me was waning.

In his exasperation, he turned to a coworker to say, *"¡Ésta gabacha no entiende!"* (This foreigner does not understand!) And he explained the whole situation to him in Spanish in front of me as if the coworker hadn't heard or understood me.

I stood my ground, and he relented, typing the date, Lolita's birthday, and the fact that she was live born.

He typed my name as the person registering the birth, based on the questions he asked me, as La Sra. Marlys Harper Gehrig (Mom's maiden name).

"¿Y su padre?" (And her father?)

"Gilberto Martinez Rivera," I responded.

"¿Dónde está? "(Where is he?)

"Le urgía salir a California," (He had to leave suddenly for California.)

"Pues entonces, su nombre no puede aparecer en el Acta de Nacimiento" (Well then, his name may not appear on the birth certificate), he stated firmly without a modicum of flexibility.

I told him I didn't know when Gil would return. My truthful answers must have sounded suspect to him as if I was trying to pin Lolita's fatherhood on some unsuspecting man in another country.

He continued plinking on the typewriter, filling in rows of dashes where all of Gil's information should have been. On my side of the form, he entered my name, Marlys Harper Gehrig, my age as 30 years, my address at the apartment, and that I was North American.

He entered a string of dashes in the section for paternal grandparents. It stung that Doña Lola could not be included! He asked and entered my parents' names and the cities in which each of them currently lived.

Two men who waited in line after me were enlisted as witnesses. Following their names, ages, professions, and addresses, the form stated that these witnesses "knew the parents of the child." An additional page bore the Estados Unidos de México seal, an affirmation of the verity of the copy of the original, and the name and signature of the official. I took my copy, and we left.

On Sunday, when Doña Lola, Irene, and Ana came to visit, I explained my experience at the Registro Civil. They were extremely distraught but restrained their condemnation of me. I felt their disappointment acutely, but also that they must have known on whom the fault accurately lay.

"¿Por qué no agaraste a cualquier fulano de tal en la calle para decir que él era Gilberto Martinez Rivera?" (Why didn't you just grab any Joe Blow off the street to say he was Gilberto Martinez Rivera?)

"No se me ocurrió" (It didn't occur to me), I said sadly.

I would never dream of falsifying a vital record, so that remedy was not an option for me.

Deliberations and Decision

Gil talked to me by phone once or twice briefly while he was away. There were no cell phones in the late seventies, and international calls were very expensive then. One time, he said he was calling from the home of another dockworker. I deduced that he had not mentioned Lolita to Carlota.

He asked how we were, and I described Lolita's latest accomplishments, like rolling over, grabbing a toy above her, lifting her upper body with her arms off a flat surface, eating cereal, etc. We could not talk for long, but he seemed happy to hear the update.

After another long interval, he called with bad news. He had injured his foot on the job and had begun a Workman's Compensation claim. He was having the foot treated, but it would be a lengthy process. His mother and sisters received the same news.

Lolita and I enjoyed each day with a variety of activities. Observing her growth, awareness, and expression gave me joy. But I began to think, having plenty of time to mull our situation. As a couple of months passed after the call when Gil told me about his injury, doubts crept into my thoughts. I wondered if Gil had decided to stay in California indefinitely.

By this time, I think Liz, Javier, and Chris had returned to the US to live. I didn't get all the details, but one reason was most likely expanded employment opportunities for them. Also, I know Liz wanted to be near her family, a longing that was only intensified when Chris was born.

When the notion first broke into my consciousness, the possibility of Lolita and I returning to the US was too fraught with emotion to seriously consider it. How could I think of taking Lolita away from her grandmother and aunts? Every time they, especially Doña Lola, were around her, their happiness and love for her were almost palpable. Her birth had revived hope, pride, and purpose in their lives.

It was not all about her grandmother and aunts; I had always loved the absence of pressure to compete and the general peacefulness of our lives in Acapulco. Also, the weather was ideal for me. Forcefully, I tried to distance myself from the thought of us leaving.

Still, I needed to contemplate our future and try to foresee our lives in five or ten years and beyond. Gil would make his own decisions. I had no way to predict, much less control his actions. It would be up to me to decide Lolita's future and mine.

Thoughts recurred, swirled chaotically, and bounced from extreme to extreme. I tried to separate them into pros and cons for Lolita, myself, and the three women who adored her.

I imagined Lolita in a khaki and white school uniform as she joined neighborhood children walking to school. Physically, she would blend perfectly with the other students. Maybe she would stop by her grandmother's house on the way home, have a snack, and chat about school. Her command of Spanish would far surpass mine by the time she reached school age, so classes taught in Spanish would not be a problem. The onus would be on me to cultivate her knowledge and use of English.

Her two foreign surnames would require explanation because the townspeople knew who her parents were, and surnames were arranged in a specific order to reflect ancestry. That was just a random, unimportant issue, but I considered the small stuff, too.

Her grandmother and aunts would dote on her, but I could not imagine her father spending much time with her if he did return to Acapulco.

Selfishly, I pictured myself in a few years. Whether Gil returned to Acapulco or not, I would continue to be *la Señora de Gil y la Mamá de Lolita.* (Gil's wife and Lolita's mother) Of course, I would always be Lolita's mother, but belonging to Gil in people's minds would extremely restrict my future. Was it a sacrifice I should make?

In past years, when Carlota and the boys came at Christmas, I had to retreat to the shadows for the length of their stay. The unspoken mandate was difficult to understand, considering I had taken care of Ari during his stay in Acapulco. A nine-year-old must have related some of his activities to his mother upon his return to California. In any case, I no longer wanted to allow myself or my daughter to be relegated to second place.

Practical considerations weighed in more heavily. I was not permitted to work in México, and my resources would run out. Then what?

Trying to imagine us in Southern California was even more difficult. I would live with my family for a few weeks until I got a job, then Lolita and I would have our own apartment. Dad lived alone in an apartment, and I was sure he would love to have us stay with him until I was employed. A babysitter would be necessary while I worked.

I could retrieve my Datsun from Leta so that I would have transportation. We would both need warmer clothes, and I would need to buy appropriate work attire.

I recoiled from the idea of going back to live there, remembering the overblown importance of appearance in California, especially for women. I had become comfortably accustomed to a more natural look and a valuation less based on appearance.

On the pro side, if we returned to California, we would celebrate holidays and birthdays with family. There, women's birthdays were celebrated just the same as men's.

A song titled *No Soy de Aquí ni Soy de Allá* (I'm Not From Here nor From There), written by Argentinian Facundo Cabral in 1970, came to mind. I first heard the song in Caleta, sung by Gil's friends. It resonated with me as my assimilation and integration increased. It described my current dilemma.

245

Thinking about the ramifications of my choices sometimes became overwhelming, and I had to remind myself to enjoy our life in the present.

My thoughts reached the level of introspection and critique. I realized that I had not planned my life well; I had not focused on personal goals or allowed thoughts about the future to extend very far. Now, motherhood awakened me to the necessity to look ahead. Not everything was within my control, but looking to the future became imperative.

With the polar pulls of stay or leave, I reached a mental state that demanded a decision and action. If I were to decide to leave, I had to research the steps for taking an infant out of México without her father's consent. Lolita didn't even look like me.

I contacted the immigration official who had extended my visa and set up a consultation. I took Lolita, my passport, her inaccurate birth certificate, and some pesos to the appointment.

I explained my predicament in abridged form. He could not undo the birth certificate, but it may have worked in my favor. I was the only parent on it; he had met me previously and believed me. He wrote a short letter that would permit us to travel to the US. I was grateful and relieved.

With that perceived impediment resolved, I made airline reservations. Purposely, I took that step before telling Gil's family. It may have been insurance that I would not be persuaded to stay. I was painfully aware of my vulnerability to that outcome.

I let my family know that my plans were firm. I think they were pleasantly surprised and excited. No one had met Lolita yet, although she was almost six months old. Sher and Trish would meet me at the airport and take me to Dad's apartment.

To say I dreaded telling Doña Lola, Ana, and Irene would be a gross understatement. The task weighed heavily on me as I looked for a good time. The longer I waited, the more dishonest I felt. I resolved to talk with them when they visited on Sunday.

There was no way to ease into the subject. I told them I decided we must go back to the US.

"¡No! ¡No se vayan!" (No! Don't leave!)

"¡Sí va a regresar Gil! Ten paciencia." (Gil will return! Be patient). They each begged repeatedly.

I tried to make my case, starting with my immigration status and my lack of permission to work in México.

"No te preocupes, ni por un minuto. Aquí les cuidamos a ti y a Lolita" (Don't worry for a minute. We will take care of you and Lolita here.), they pleaded.

So far, I had avoided blaming Gil but now told them he had called me only a couple of times in more than four months and that Lolita would be six months old soon. She would not even recognize her father if or when he returned. I did not even have a way to contact him to let him know we were leaving.

They explained that it was difficult to call from Carlota's house.

"Regresará tan pronto que se cura su pie" (He will return just as soon as his foot heals.), they assured me, still trying to persuade me not to go.

"Desgraciadamente, ya hice la decisión. ¡Lo siento muchísimo!" (Unfortunately, I made the decision. I am so sorry!), I said sadly. I told them the day and time of our flight, and they said they would pick us up early to take us to the airport.

Packing would not take long. My things would fit in my large suitcase. I would get a big box for Lolita's clothes, diapers, bottles, and anything else that would fit. Her ample diaper bag would be a carry-on as well as her small carrier. I would leave her crib, bathtub, my snorkeling fins, and any staple foods to be given away.

*****

They came to pick us up at the apartment with plenty of time before the flight. I had our suitcase, box, diaper bag, and Lolita's carrier near the entry.

We were all emotionally fragile. I doubt that any of us slept well the night before. The day's finality hung like a heavy dark cloud, and any one of us could cause it to rain.

Doña Lola picked up Lolita and held her closely to her body, wanting to savor all the seconds.

I think it was Ana who took a tiny white box from her purse and gave it to me, saying it was for Lolita when she was a little older. Lifting the lid, I saw a small gold butterfly on a fine gold chain, resting on a bed of cotton. The simplicity of the design made it elegant. I loved it! I said Lolita would always wear it when she was old enough. It was perfect!

Doña Lola handed me a velvet drawstring bag. I opened it and pulled out an adjustable necklace made of a multitude of small garnet beads. The wine-colored beads tightly spiraled around a core. I liked the necklace, and the gesture of generosity intensified the sensitivity of my emotions.

Irene told me I could have something new made from the beads. She thought they might be worth a small sum. I thanked Doña Lola and said it was beautiful just as she gifted it to me.

It was time to drive to the airport. We loaded our luggage pieces into the car and arrived at the airport with a little excess time. While one of Gil's sisters held Lolita, the other helped me check my suitcase and the box.

The wrenching moment had arrived. Doña Lola had Lolita in her arms while I fought tears as wet cheeks touched, and I hugged Ana and Irene tightly. Doña Lola gently lowered Lolita into her carrier and handed it to one of her daughters. Both of us were crying as we embraced. I told her how much I appreciated her and their support and acceptance.

As we said the final *adiós*, I still had recurring doubts about my decision. Fighting the doubts, I put the diaper bag over my shoulder, picked up Lolita in her carrier, and walked mechanically away from the women toward the departure gate.

We were among the first to board, and the stewardess led us to the bulkhead seats. I settled the diaper bag and Lolita in her carrier with the help of the stewardess, who anticipated our needs and assisted me as I had done numerous times on Pan Am. I wondered if she could tell I had been crying.

I sat in the window seat with Lolita in her carrier at my feet. She was happy to intently watch the flow of people in the aisle as they stowed carry-ons and settled into their seats. I hoped the flight would not be full and that passengers would avoid sitting next to a mother and her baby. I wanted to sort out my emotions but could not tolerate chit-chatting with another passenger today. As the people streamed by, they passed up the bulkhead, fulfilling my wish.

Closer to take off, I brought Lolita up to my lap and held her outside my seat belt. When we taxied, I offered her a bottle to ease the effect of cabin pressurization on her ears. She took it hungrily and relaxed.

As the plane surged diagonally upward, I watched Acapulco diminish with the growing distance from the ground until it almost fit framed in my small window. I had flown back and forth from Acapulco several times during my four years there, but now I wondered if this would be the last time. Again, I fought unsuccessfully to hold back tears.

I pictured the three Martinez women at the airport where I left them. Their grief flowed into mine. It was heavy, but I would carry it with me always. Surely, these three strong, independent women understood that I had to leave.

Lolita had fallen asleep in my arms. I stowed the empty bottle but continued to hold her until she was deeply asleep. Her soft, warm body against mine comforted me.

Life is complex and messy at times. Its tests seldom contain simple true/false questions. There are multiple choices and sometimes more than one correct answer. There is much more gray than black and white.

Lolita's arm flopped out limply as I slowly eased her down into her carrier and arranged the light blanket over her. She had no idea of the emotions that had surrounded her or that we were setting out on a new road.

Reaching into the diaper bag, my hand felt the small white box and I brought it to my lap. I took off the lid, wanting a longer look at the lovely butterfly. While admiring its delicate design, I realized the gift had a message for me.

I found the clasp behind the cotton, opened it, and closed it again under my hair at the back of my neck. Until Lolita was old enough to wear it, I would wear this meaningful symbol every day.

Photos

Grammie (Julia S Gehrig), 15 years, left with friend, 1903

Grammie, 18 years old at High School graduation, 1906

Pops, age 65

Grammie's immediate family in Staunton, Illinois

Pops (Arthur G Gehrig) in work clothes as an engineer on the Panama Canal construction

Ship, Colón, on which Grammie and Pops traveled to honeymoon in Panamá

Mom, 14 years old, 1931

Grammie and Mom

Dad (Charles E Harper) in the Army during WWII

Me, 18 months, 1949

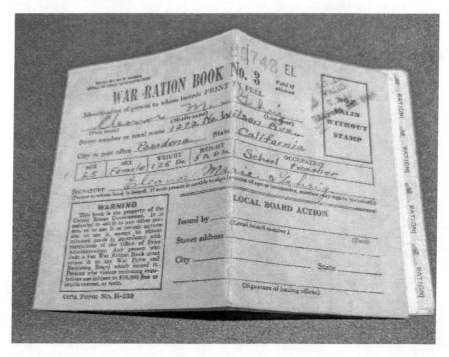

Fuel and Food Ration Coupons during WWII, used 1942 until 1947

Top row: Marlys, Dad, Mom, Sheri
Lower row: Trisha, Tim, and Denise

Manuel and Sara Barrios - My hosts in Guatemala City and
Retaleleu

Me in native Guatemalan *huipil* (blouse) and *corte* (skirt)

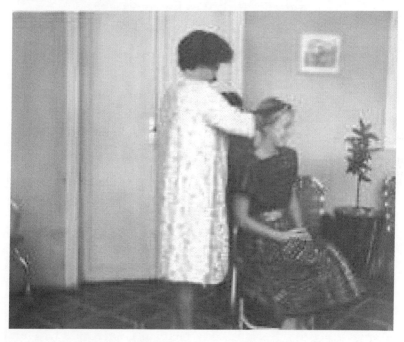

Sara Barrios braiding my hair in native fashion

Merced Church where Señora Betancourt went daily, and we visited on the way to shop

La Escuelita students and I at the Acapulco Princess Hotel.

Pan Am Stewardess Training Graduation, 1970. I am top row, third from right.

Pan Am Graduation, 1970

Lolita and I in 1979, after returning to California

Acknowledgments

My husband, Mike Bangle, was unaccustomed to me disappearing to the office for undetermined lengths of time, but he adapted admirably. It was difficult for him to imagine that I enjoyed piecing together words for hours at a time. He was the first to use the word "book" long before I had the necessary confidence to say it. I was only writing a few of my stories, I told him. His patient support permitted me to document my experiences in this book.

From the first time I apprehensively entered a meeting of the Quail Creek Writers & Poets Club, its members have boosted my confidence. They accepted me despite my lack of writing experience and education. Some members offered to read and critique my first stories. The constant encouragement of the club members has made me believe I could write this book.

Dan Shearer, the general editor of The Green Valley News, accepted *A Brief Break* (that later became a chapter in this book) and designed an artful page for my debut publication in the Veterans Day edition. I am grateful for his encouragement.

Jolyn Young, who was in charge of the *Get Out* section of the Green Valley News, accepted a couple more of my submissions. Her book, *Never Burn Your Moving Boxes*, gave me the courage to write my memoir honestly, without whitewash. She inspired me to continue writing.

My sister, Denise, has been a valuable resource. She is our family historian who leafed out our family tree online, contributing not only names and dates but also documents and details about our forebears. With her help, timelines and sequences were verified when possible. Denise read an in-process partial draft of this book, listened intently during our lengthy phone conversations, and contributed details to my story that were new to me. I wasn't prepared for the emotional toll some of the excavated memories would cause. Her support was and continues to be invaluable.

I'm grateful for the countless opportunities and experiences I've been given, and I look forward to what each day will bring.

About the Author

Marlys Harper is a woman whose journey is a blend of twists and determination. Picking up where this memoir ends, she found herself in Hollister, California, as a bilingual aide at San Benito High School. Daily, she left her infant daughter in the care of a coworker's loving mother. As fate shifted, she navigated various jobs, from waitressing to housekeeping. Dissatisfied with the area's opportunities for her and her daughter, she returned to Southern California, where her bilingual skills opened doors at Van de Kamps Frozen Foods. It was her responsibility to assure quality on the production line and as a Raw Materials Analyst until Pillsbury bought the plant and moved its operations to another state.

Her bilingual skills were again utilized for translation and interpretation at her next career start at the Orange County Department of Education. She contributed to impactful programs like The Outdoor Science School while resuming classes toward her higher education goals.

After almost 20 years at OCDE, she and her husband relocated to the solace of the Eastern Sierras, living in the rural county seat of Bridgeport, California. She was employed for nine years as support staff for the Mono County Health Department. After retiring in 2016, she and her husband eventually settled in Green Valley, Arizona, after a fulfilling journey through diverse roles and locales.

Made in the USA
Columbia, SC
06 October 2024

43214027R00162